ROMANTICISM IN PERSPECTIVE:
TEXTS, CULTURES, HISTORIES

General Editors:
Marilyn Gaull, *Professor of English,*
Temple University/New York University
Stephen Prickett, *Regius Professor of English Language and Literature,*
University of Glasgow

This series aims to offer a fresh assessment of Romanticism by looking at it from a wide variety of perspectives. Both comparative and interdisciplinary, it will bring together cognate themes from architecture, art history, landscape gardening, linguistics, literature, philosophy, politics, science, social and political history and theology to deal with original, contentious or as yet unexplored aspects of Romanticism as a Europe-wide phenomenon.

Titles include:

Malcolm Kelsall
JEFFERSON AND THE ICONOGRAPHY OF ROMANTICISM
Folk, Land, Culture and the Romantic Nation

Mark S. Lussier
ROMANTIC DYNAMICS: The Poetics of Physicality

Andrew McCann
CULTURAL POLITICS IN THE 1790s: Literature, Radicalism
and the Public Sphere

Ashton Nichols
THE REVOLUTIONARY 'I': Wordsworth and the Politics of
Self-Presentation

Jeffrey C. Robinson
RECEPTION AND POETICS IN KEATS: 'My Ended Poet'

Anya Taylor
BACCHUS IN ROMANTIC ENGLAND: Writers and Drink,
1780–1830

Michael Wiley
ROMANTIC GEOGRAPHY: Wordsworth and
Anglo-European Spaces

Eric Wilson
EMERSON'S SUBLIME SCIENCE

John Wyatt
WORDSWORTH'S POEMS OF TRAVEL, 1819–42
'Such Sweet Wayfaring'

Romanticism in Perspective
Series Standing Order ISBN 0–333–71490–3
(*outside North America only*)

You can receive future titles in this series as they are published by placing a
standing order. Please contact your bookseller or, in case of difficulty, write to us at
the address below with your name and address, the title of the series and the ISBN
quoted above.

Customer Services Department, Macmillan Distribution Ltd
Houndmills, Basingstoke, Hampshire RG21 6XS, England

Romanticism on the Road

The Marginal Gains of Wordsworth's Homeless

Toby R. Benis

Assistant Professor
Department of English
Saint Louis University

First published in Great Britain 2000 by
MACMILLAN PRESS LTD
Houndmills, Basingstoke, Hampshire RG21 6XS and London
Companies and representatives throughout the world

A catalogue record for this book is available from the British Library.

ISBN 0–333–71887–9

First published in the United States of America 2000 by
ST. MARTIN'S PRESS, INC.,
Scholarly and Reference Division,
175 Fifth Avenue, New York, N.Y. 10010

ISBN 0–312–22302–1

Library of Congress Cataloging-in-Publication Data
Benis, Toby R., 1963–
Romanticism on the road : the marginal gains of Wordsworth's
homeless / Toby R. Benis.
p.   cm. — (Romanticism in perspective)
Includes bibliographical references (p.   ) and index.
ISBN 0–312–22302–1 (cloth)
1. Wordsworth, William, 1770–1850—Characters—Homeless persons.
2. Wordsworth, William, 1770–1850—Political and social views.
3. Literature and society—England—History—19th century.
4. France—History—Revolution, 1789–1799—Influence.   5. Rogues and
vagabonds in literature.   6. Marginality, Social, in literature.
7. Homeless persons in literature.   8. Homelessness in literature.
9. Tramps in literature.   10. Romanticism—England.   I. Title.
II. Series.
PR5892.H553B46   1999
821'.7—dc21   99–20436
                                                                           CIP

This book is printed on paper suitable for recycling and made from fully managed and
sustained forest sources.

10   9   8   7   6   5   4   3   2   1
09   08   07   06   05   04   03   02   01   00

Printed and bound in Great Britain by
Antony Rowe Ltd, Chippenham, Wiltshire

Contents

Acknowledgments

Unlike the homeless women and men that people this study, I have been fortunate enough to benefit from a great deal of support and advice. Karl Kroeber, who sponsored the dissertation on which this book is based, provided me with encouragement, suggestions, and criticisms that continue to influence my scholarship and my teaching. I also am deeply indebted to Marilyn Gaull, whose dedication to Romanticism and to me helped make this book possible. Steven Marcus, Martin Meisel, Deborah White, and John Tucker all commented on and materially improved versions of the text. My colleague Georgia Johnston has provided invaluable emotional and intellectual support, as well as many meals, during my time at Saint Louis University; she and Raymond Benoit also read parts of the manuscript and offered constructive suggestions. Annette Wheeler Cafarelli spurred my interest in Romanticism in general and Wordsworth in particular at a formative stage in my graduate career. My comrades from Columbia, Christina Biélaszka-Du Vernay and Heidi Brayman Hackel, also get my thanks for their ongoing good humor and kindness. More than anyone else, I owe Michael for his patience as well as his editorial expertise. This book is dedicated to my mother and the memory of my father.

A portion of Chapter 3 originally appeared under the title 'Martha Ray's Face: Life during Wartime in *Lyrical Ballads*' in *Criticism* 39 (1997): 205–27.

Introduction: Homelessness Yesterday and Today – Repression or Relief?

To the contemporary reader, the 200 years separating us from the Romantic period may appear a formidable barrier; like the speaker of Wordsworth's "The Solitary Reaper," perhaps we only indistinctly perceive in its poetry and prose "old, unhappy, far-off things, /And battles long ago" (19–20). To scholars seeking a more profound understanding of the culture of the era, this gap may seem wider still. Typically recipients rather than providers of charity, the homeless nevertheless offer this gift to us: a particular and immediate opportunity to reduce this distance. Unlike the poor who have housing, however inadequate, the homeless in today's cities and towns are unique in their visibility. If the French Revolution or the Napoleonic Wars seem remote, many Americans have become all too familiar with one of the most common occurrences in the tumultuous Romantic era generally and in Wordsworth's poetry in particular – an encounter with the homeless. Then, as now, these encounters engendered the twin responses of pity and fear, of relief and repression. Then, as now, the homeless were perceived both as broken people in need of help – as victims of economic and social forces beyond their control – and as willfully idle, as dangers to life, as threats to the value of homes and property. Their poverty elicits pity, even as their social alienation evokes the frightening specter of disorder and crime.

What follows is a cultural history of vagrancy in the Georgian period as refracted through the early poetry of William Wordsworth, whose interest in, or obsession with, the homeless outdistanced that of any other writer of his generation. At this time, vagrancy's reach as a legal category was enormous: it was as volatile a term as the multitude of activities it was supposed to encompass. In their voluminous study of the old poor laws, Sidney and Beatrice Webb explain that "It was, in fact, the habit of the House of Commons, during several centuries, whenever it took a dislike to any irregular course of life, to enact that those who followed it should be deemed

1

rogues and vagabonds, and thus, as such, subject to all the penalties of the Vagrancy Acts"(352). From the sixteenth through the eighteenth centuries, people liable to be punished under vagrancy law included persons refusing to work for customary wages; bearwards; unlicenced peddlers; gypsies; wandering scholars; players; persons collecting ends of yarn or cloth; persons possessing tools used in burglaries; poachers; hedge-pullers; unlicenced dealers in lottery tickets; and ultimately, anyone on the road without adequate cause. Over the centuries, vagrancy became a catch-all category for anyone besides the rich whom inclination, occupation, or the search for employment kept on the move. The trunkloads of legislation against these activities targeted not only physical mobility; they were also laws against pursuing inappropriate occupations, against diluting the power of class differences, and against holding and spreading unorthodox, dangerous opinions. Since Tudor–Stuart times vagrancy has been identified with sedition and potential insurrection, imparting to homelessness elements of what contemporary historians have come to refer to as social crime. E. J. Hobsbawm defines social criminality as "a conflict of laws, e.g. between an official and an unofficial system, or when acts of lawbreaking have a distinct element of social protest in them, or when they are closely linked with the development of social and political unrest"(5).[1] Vagrancy law was designed to arrest the wanderer on the road but also the more general mobility of mind, the openness to new, unsettling ideas, that he or she embodied. Vagrancy statutes aimed to bring the homeless, lacking a clear station or role, within the realm of law and under control of the crown. The ambiguous, the obscure, was to become transparent and consequently manageable, a goal that acquired new urgency amid the political, social and economic turmoil of the 1790s.

This desire was at odds, however, with the discretionary character of the Georgian legal system. The complex feelings vagrancy generated could lead discretion down unpredictable paths. The poor laws – the main focus among critics of Wordsworth investigating his interest in vagrants – often overlapped with vagrancy law to frustrate clear judicial classifications and guidelines for punishment. And as Wordsworth's poetry suggests, the very scope of the law, with its brutal provisions for a bewildering array of offenses, militated against its enforcement. Georgians confronted with the homeless in their parishes only sporadically responded with the legal rectitude Parliament continually demanded. Instead, parish officials met the marginal figure of the vagrant with alms or threats, even both at once. While literary scholars have displayed an awareness of some of these perceptual complexities, they have not formed the basis of a systematic exploration of the period's writers.[2] In referring to the homeless as marginals, I invoke a concept more specific than a generalized notion of individuals at the edge of a particular social formation. Following Victor Turner, I suggest almost the reverse – that by virtue of the contradictory reactions they generate, the homeless are at the center of a complex social matrix. For Turner, marginals "are simultaneously members (by ascription, optation, self-definition or achievement) of two or more groups whose social definitions and cultural norms are distinct from, and often opposed to, one another" (233). Simultaneously cast by society in the opposing roles of criminal and victim, the homeless further conform to Turner's model in having "no cultural assurance of a final stable resolution of their ambiguity" (233).[3] The unresolved implication of the homeless in conflicting roles – in short, their social and moral polyvalence – subverts the utility of binary thinking. Wordsworth's conviction that the homeless are powerful not because they operate outside of society but because they are inescapably enmeshed in it anticipates Frederic Jameson's dictum that "the only effective liberation from [socio-historical] constraint begins with the recognition that there is nothing that is not social and historical – indeed, that everything is 'in the last analysis' political" (20). We don't have to leave the 1790s to find a formulation of this claim, albeit from the opposite end of the ideological spectrum. Edmund Burke's *Letters on a Regicide Peace* (1796) argues:

> As to the right of men to act any where according to their pleasure, without any moral tie, no such right exists. Men are never in a state of *total* independence from each other. It is not the condition of our nature: nor is it conceivable how any man can pursue a considerable cause or action without its having some effect upon others; or, of course, without producing some degree of responsibility for his conduct.[4]

If we recognize Burke's "nature" as a version of Jameson's "society," we comprehend the affinities between these two very different theorists. This unlikely comparison emblematizes the effort throughout ensuing chapters to imagine the distance between radical and reactionary as bridged by a continuum rather than marked by fracture – an idea unwelcome during the 1790s and still in disfavor today. The representations of homelessness at the heart of this project insist on the pervasiveness of cultural context and eschew a solely psychological or individual pursuit of deliverance.

Wordsworth's interest in vagrant marginality took on particular urgency in a century that ended with revolution abroad, calls for reform in England, and a war that would last more than twenty years. Burke's *Reflections* proclaimed that the home and domestic affections were the kernel of broader commitments to culture and nation: "to be attached to the subdivision, to love the little platoon we belong to in society, is the first principle (the germ as it were) of public affections. It is the first link in the series by which we proceed towards a love to our country and to mankind" (135). From this resting place it followed that the homeless threatened an anarchy that must be contained. The French wars that Burke foresaw would inaugurate new ideas about government and provide the impetus for the birth of the modern British bureaucratic state, with a burgeoning Treasury office, a secret service, and an increasingly professionalized sense of law enforcement. Such developments would lead to gradual but steady modification and, finally, curtailment of asystematic and discretionary codes of eighteenth-century law with its local, decentralized practice. Amid political and economic uncertainty, authorities in both England and France took new measures to police the mobility of the homeless and the ambiguous legal status for which they were a trope. In particular, governments sought to polarize political opinion into loyalist or subversive, patriotic or traitorous. Drawing on the cultural marginality of the homeless, Wordsworth's early representations of vagrancy act as an index of the failings of any cultural agenda seeking to suppress people's inevitable spectrum of feeling and belief. Calling attention to our changeable perceptions of the homeless, Wordsworth points to the limitations of political discourse organized around expedient yet inadequate oppositions.[5] At the same time he indicts the Georgian valorization of the domestic for its complicity in such discourse.

HOMELESSNESS YESTERDAY

Historically, the dominant feature of public response to the homeless was precisely its range, its inability to be definitively characterized as either hostile or sympathetic. On one hand, vagrancy had been a nationally codified crime for centuries, and the laws complemented traditional parish anxieties about the itinerant poor. During the English early modern period, vagrancy was criminalized as landed aristocrats tried to condition poor laborers released from manorial servitude to accept wage-labor discipline.[6] The fear of the masterless man persisted well into the eighteenth century: "The masterless stranger who was poor and ... traveling, and who was not apparently on his way to or from service, was held in deep suspicion, especially if he were far from home" (Taylor, 16–17). By the Georgian period, these fears were often financial as much as anything else; local authorities seeking to keep their poor rates as low as possible were provoked whenever people entered their jurisdiction who appeared incapable of supporting themselves. In the first half of the century, Parliament had refined an elaborate taxonomy of vagrants to cope with varying infractions and repeat offenders. The basis of vagrancy law for most of the eighteenth century, 13 Geo. I c. 24 (1739–40) and its successor, 17 Geo. I, c. 5 (1743–4), divided the homeless into idle and disorderly persons; rogues and vagabonds; and incorrigible rogues. Typically, the first category could apply to even domiciled persons and covered an array of situations: for example, people who lived idly, who did not work regularly, or who threatened to abandon their families. Rogues and vagabonds were those found "wandering abroad, and lodging in barns and other outhouses, not giving a good account of themselves, and ... begging" (13 Geo. I, c. 24; quoted in Ribton-Turner, 200), although a variety of suspect activities are mentioned in the law by name.[7] Incorrigible rogues had a prior arrest for vagrancy, had resisted arrest, or had escaped from a house of correction. The unified goal behind vagrancy legislation into the early nineteenth century was discipline in the form of whipping, incarceration, and/or hard labor, followed by the granting of a vagrant pass. The pass ordered the constable to convey the vagrant in the direction of the parish responsible for relief. At his parish border, the constable was to transfer his charge to the constable of the next parish, and so on, until the vagrant reached the approved destination. The local Justice of the Peace determined vagrants' parish of settlement by examining them, the results of which were summarized in written form.[8]

This system struggled to designate the social valence of the travels of the poor by designating their home, or home parish, and returning them to it. Parliament did its "uttermost" to ensure the laws' enforcement, insisting throughout the eighteenth century on the necessity of physically punishing vagrants, empowering practically any domiciled person to arrest them, and offering a system of rewards for those who did (Webb, 355). However, the practical, local execution of vagrancy law reveals a tangled state of affairs. Vague laws punishing even a settled person leading a disordered life confounded a clear definition of vagrancy, and the line between the pauper deserving of help and the threatening vagabond was incoherently expressed and easily confused.[9] The Elizabethan poor laws had designated the parish as the unit of poor relief, and made ongoing community participation and residence a prerequisite for receiving public help. This system, designed to arrest mobility, could do the opposite, since people needing assistance – or even those who were judged likely to need it in the future – were forced to leave their homes if local officials decided their parish of settlement was elsewhere. This decision could hardly be disinterested when authorities were aiming to keep their poor rates low and rid themselves of undesirables. The law of settlement created a concept of residency subject to negotiation by time, place, and local personalities. Laws governing vagrancy, settlement, and poor relief were "conceived with surveillance uppermost in mind," but their complications made administering this constellation of statutes a central component of the "migraine of local government" (Porter, 127).[10]

As the century progressed, the growing numbers and visibility of the poor caused by the dislocations of industrialization, enclosure, and war meant that poverty itself was seen by legislators less as an inevitable state (for some) than as a social problem. Nevertheless, benign neglect was the response pitiable vagrants frequently evoked on their journeys. No parish officer was likely to encourage the homeless to start life anew in his area. But Parliament's insistence that such people be whipped or jailed often was ignored as being too severe a penalty for having no roof over one's head. The Webbs state that

> … of any continuous endeavour to carry out the intention of Parliament and really suppress idle and irregular modes of living among the lower orders there is no trace. To the ordinary Justice of the Peace – still more to the average parish constable – mere idleness, asking for alms, or travelling about the country on foot

seemed no crime at all; whilst even the other offences penalised by the Vagrancy Act appeared only venial misdemeanours.

(375)

To avoid adhering to burdensome and morally questionable procedure, many constables resorted to bribes and threats rather than arrest to guarantee that the homeless moved on. Alternatively, local officials might grant poor travelers a so-called free pass, asking the parishes such people traversed not to molest them. Lacking any legal province, these documents nevertheless often were honored by authorities and were further evidence of the ways in which individual perceptions undermined national policy. In such situations, the defiance of authority associated with the homeless themselves appeared contagious, a disease contracted by upstart justices of the peace (JPs). In his *History of the Poor Laws* (1764), Richard Burn specifically objects to free passes because through them a low-level official, who might be little better than a "tradesman or handicraftsman," subverts the authority of his social and political superiors. Himself a Westmorland Justice of the Peace, Burn finds such insubordination as dangerous as more dramatic transgressions precisely because the seeming insignificance of the offense exempts it from notice. He explains:

The validity of these passports is no more than this: An act of parliament says, such a person shall be taken up as a rogue and vagabond. A justice of the peace says, Permit him to pass: That is, with a non-obstante to the said act of Parliament. Kings have been sometimes censured for setting themselves above the law; but justices of the peace have been suffered to pass unnoticed.

(117)

The rhetoric of Burn's concluding comparison of renegade JPs to the despotic Stuarts converts the justice of the peace into the vagrant, who "passes" through the system without punishment. The sense that vagrant impropriety was a kind of contagion infecting the low-level officials who routinely dealt with the homeless persisted into the nineteenth century. In 1817 jurist Edward Christian, a master at Hawkshead Grammar School in 1781 and a Professor of Law at St. John's College when Wordsworth was at Cambridge, was still complaining that virtually all vagrancy passes had no legal validity, "and might as well be signed by the Justice's groom or his housemaid" (*Charges*, 152).[11] Like Burn, Christian condemns the JPs' behavior as a violation of fundamental codes of class deference. JPs who did follow the law found that crowds could become angry, even violent, when the poor were whipped, particularly when they suspected the person had been apprehended by officials seeking a reward. By the turn of the century, whipping had become the exception rather than the rule; even the vagrant who was arrested might escape any punishment at all. In this climate, the rewards system itself added to the confusion over who the real criminals actually were. An 1821 Commons Committee reported that in some cases vagrants actually welcomed arrest, since they often went unpunished and would receive free transport to a neighboring parish. To this extent, the system appeared to be subsidizing, rather than condemning, the very kinds of mobility Parliament sought to restrain. In turn, there were cases of constables who had bribed people into committing acts of vagrancy, that they might be arrested; the constable and his prisoners then would split the reward money (Ribton-Turner, 228–34).

The system's flexibility could work against, as well as in favor of, the mobility of the homeless. By the late eighteenth century, a strict adherence to the law's punishments and procedures might indicate a secret grudge or simple caprice as much as a commitment to enforcing parliamentary mandates. A servant who had angered his master, a woman who had taken a secret lover, or any person particularly obnoxious to the local squire might find him or herself apprehended as an idler (Webb, 367).[12] Although the Georgian gentleman abhorred the idea of professional (i.e. French-style) police, motivated officials could be every bit as efficient as their French counterparts. William Olejniczak, analyzing the statistics from France and England in the 1780s, finds the arrest to incarceration ratio for vagrancy in the countries to be comparable.[13] Though formal national enforcement mechanisms did not exist in Britain, there is evidence that neighboring counties consulted each other about policies of arrest and punishment. By the century's end, "vagrancy legislation ... was one of the most typical ways by which ruling authorities and plebians met on a contested, legal terrain. Both sides were continually engaged in testing the boundaries of the permissible" (Olejniczak, "English," 637). Discussing turn-of-the-century vagrancy in metropolitan London, Nicholas Rogers emphasizes that legal discretion was not synonymous with negligence: "JPs were allowed considerable leeway as to how they handled vagrants, and despite the Webbs' claim to the contrary, there is little evidence that they exercised this discretion in a haphazard or incompetent manner" (130). Olejniczak and Rogers offer important correctives to earlier historians including the Webbs in that they present the verdicts of local magistrates as part of a broader system of social control that was reasoned and frequently effective.[14] The view of eighteenth-century law enforcement as desultory is to some extent a legacy of early nineteenth-century police reformers who justified a more bureaucratic approach by recasting legal discretion as outright laziness or ineptitude. The attack against the old system began to make significant headway from the 1780s on, and the changes that resulted from this campaign form the backdrop to the new vagrancy initiatives discussed in this study and to which Wordsworth is responding.

The archives help flesh out how stories of misery and economic instability, as well as other circumstances, could influence the enforcement of vagrancy law. In October 1787, for example, Thomas Alkin was arrested as a rogue and vagabond before a JP in Wordsworth's native Cumberland. There is no evidence that Alkin, who had wandered from his home parish and was picked up for begging, was punished in any of the ways dear to Parliament, such as whipping or imprisonment. He was quietly passed to a neighboring parish, a decision presumably made easier by the information conveyed in his vagrancy examination. According to the JP, Alkin swore that

> ... he was born at Moorhousehill in the Parish of Hesket and County aforesaid – and lived there till the said Parish of Hesket did bind him the said Thomas Alkin out Parish Prentice with one John Sowerby, in the Parish of Skelton till he was of age of twenty one: but – his said Master John Sowerby Fail'd in the world – and he the aforesaid Thos. Alkin only Stay'd, with his said Master about one year and a half, and the said Thomas Alkin has been Traveling about from Place to Place ever since, but has never gained any other settlement but at Skelton. ...
> (PR/3/78: Carlisle PRO, Cumbria)

His parish sponsored Alkin's abortive attempt to become an artisan, implying that from childhood he depended on official charity. When his master's business failed, Alkin fell through the wide open spaces of England's makeshift safety net. He was left destitute and took to the road – a scenario of victimization that Parliament's pronouncements did not take into account. This examination underscores the discrepancy between the official script of vagrancy law, which held the homeless were lazy and deserving of punishment, and the actual dramas of their often hapless lives. The law gives no real guidance to the JP confronting this story, and in the end failure may have appeared as much the state's as Alkin's own.

A more flagrant case of ignoring the rules comes from the records of the Westmorland Quarter Sessions. In 1773, Christopher Wallas, his wife and children were arrested begging in Kendal. Rather than take them to their place of settlement, the constable dumped them on the boundary of a nearer parish "and there left and exposed them" (WQ/SR/376b/5: Kendal PRO). The constable was caught and reprimanded at the Epiphany Sessions, but fined only for the token amount of 1 shilling by JPs well-versed in the daily burdens and pressures of administering the laws. Wallas and his family, meanwhile, never appear to have been punished for their initial offense, and the constable's conduct led the judges to nullify Wallas' vagrancy pass, setting him free with no supervision. The Sessions defended proper procedure, but in the process the vagrants themselves slipped through the snare Parliaments had set to trap them. Ultimately, overseers of the poor, churchwardens and constables struggled to maintain order in their communities without unnecessarily brutalizing people already worn down by circumstances.

HOMELESSNESS TODAY

As I began by noting, 200 years is a long time; of course, there are important differences between the way we view homelessness today and the way the Georgians saw it. At the same time, through those changes certain core problems have remained the same, and I now touch on these to illuminate the origins of this book as well as its broader implications. The current literature on the homeless throws into relief our failure to make many significant advances on the debates of the past two centuries. Although American vagrancy laws were declared unconstitutional in the early 1970s, contemporary fear of vagrants is written clearly in the statutes against sleeping in public places, in neighborhood opposition to locating shelters in residential areas, in laws forbidding panhandling on subways or near banks. Yet at the same time, sociologists writing about homelessness believe that its widespread existence calls into question nothing less than the legitimacy of current political arrangements and laissez-faire economics unqualified by a progressive agenda.[15] These commentators have grappled with the central puzzle of homelessness today, existing as it does not amid the economic desolation of a great depression but alongside the most robust economic expansion since the end of World War II. Some argue that contemporary homelessness is an inevitable byproduct of trends and policies that have enriched many – of the transition from a manufacturing to a service economy, of budget cutting and tax breaks. In these terms, homelessness is a disease drawing strength from the workings of the contemporary market, the cancer of capitalism that can be destroyed only by far-reaching changes to the entire system. Above all, the transience of the homeless continues to force us to confront the mobility of our own perceptions and feelings about the value of government spending, safety nets, and human inability or unwillingness (depending on one's political orientation) to adapt to changing modes of production. Like our Georgian predecessors, we have difficulty confidently labeling the homeless as purely outlaws or scapegoats. One's perceptions of the homeless change from day to day, from encounter to encounter. In the morning, a man's visible sores and haggard appearance may incline us to see him far more as victim than criminal, and to offer him food or money. We will likely avoid the same man at night, if he is clearly drunk and yelling obscenities, as a threat to our safety. And individual police officers, like constables in times past, may have little inclination to enforce disorderly conduct statutes if they perceive homelessness less as a crime than a social problem.[16]

Insofar as vagrant mobility baffles systematic evaluation, the homeless continue to challenge the utility of straightforward data collection and classification. Contemporary studies of the homeless openly acknowledge that numerical estimates are necessarily incomplete; can one ever accurately count the underground homeless population of Manhattan that, as Jennifer Toth's *The Mole People* shows, lives in a maze of train and utility tunnels beneath the city?[17] When researchers do make contact with the homeless, the people themselves can lie about or simply not remember details about their lives. They may not to respond to questions about drug use or previous hospitalizations that sound suspiciously like those of the police. And the disordered nature of homeless life can make it difficult for even the willing respondent to recall relevant details

(Blau, 20). In their study of the Austin, TX, homeless, David Snow and Leon Anderson note that the homeless often do not exchange names, even among themselves; one person may know parts of another's biography, but this history may be peppered with outlandish exploits whose truth is questionable. The anonymity common among the homeless naturally hampers the researchers' ability to ask questions about or even keep track of people they meet on the street (Snow and Anderson, 345n.).[18] An even more fundamental question emerges when commentators try to define what exactly homelessness, or the home, is. Should one include families in welfare hotels? People doubled up in apartments with friends or relatives? Different social scientists treat these groups in different ways, making comparison between studies virtually impossible.[19] Brendan O'Flaherty observes that most social scientists today think of homelessness as a housing condition, but that there is an older tradition, still very much alive, of using the term homeless "as a synonym for 'vagrant' or 'bum'; homelessness then has to do with ties to the community, clothing, alcohol consumption, and occupation (or lack of it), not where you sleep at night. This usage still prevails among the American public" (7). True to the slippery nature of these terms, I generally use "homeless" and "vagrant" interchangeably in my analysis, taking both to signify either those who lack housing or those with vexed relationships to the community – the latter being the sense which the Georgians and many today would recognize. Living on the border of social and scientific categories, the homeless justify a form of inquiry less dependent on the quantitative data traditionally grounding much sociological study. Given this situation, we may learn as much from poetry as from science.

Research posture has reflected these complications. Several recent books about the homeless have openly adopted an anecdotal approach in which statistical findings play only a part or are not considered at all. Elliot Liebow's *Tell Them Who I Am* almost entirely eschews numbers for participant observation research, in which he takes notes on conversations and compiles life histories of women staying in the D.C.-area shelters in which he worked. A respected social scientist, Liebow nevertheless begins by announcing that he does not consider the women he writes about research subjects, and that he regards his book as a collaborative enterprise with them (xvi). Trained as a journalist rather than a sociologist, Toth proceeds in much the same way when describing life in the tunnels beneath

New York City. Snow and Anderson straddle the divide between science and anecdote by positioning themselves as "buddy-researchers," spending months with the homeless they study in addition to compiling quantitative data (24). Margaret Morton's *The Tunnel*, also dealing with the underground homeless, and Steven Vanderstaay's *Street Lives: an Oral History of Homeless Americans*, communicate only the words of the homeless themselves, in Morton's case juxtaposed with haunting photographs of the derelict train tunnels beneath Manhattan.[20]

The unstable valence of the homeless resonates throughout the characterizations and policy recommendations of even the most sympathetic studies. Snow and Anderson's *Down on their Luck* is as humane as any, depicting the homeless as resourceful people who have in many cases been forced into street life. Essential to this aim is showing that the homeless are in many respects like everyone else: "Up close and in context, they are remarkably like most of us in their basic needs, their dreams and desires, their interpersonal strategies…" (314–15). Realizing this will help dispel the myth that the homeless owe their plight to "their own imperfections or moral failings" (9). The authors are well aware of the range of response to the homeless:

> At one end of the scale, the homeless are objects of sympathy who are seen as victims of social forces and bad luck. At the other, they are objects of fear and scorn who are thought to have chosen this way of life and who therefore should be run out of town or at least constrained…
>
> (102)

But though their study clearly concludes that the former response is closer to the truth than the latter, its rhetoric portrays a homeless population situated through a series of negotiations between these extremes. Their findings, for example, show that some of the homeless are indeed thieves, drug dealers, or prostitutes. *Down on their Luck* adumbrates these facts in part by arguing that the homeless do not choose to be criminals: they steal because they rarely can find legitimate employment, and when they do, it does not pay a living wage. Snow and Anderson also explain these and related activities, which they call "shadow work," as an unorthodox manifestation of the work ethic.[21] Engaging in shadow work ultimately testifies to a person's victimization as much as to his or her criminality: "No single strategy can ensure subsistence on the streets, and no matter how strongly one subsistence activity is preferred over another, there is no guarantee from one day to the next that it will still be a viable option" (168). To survive, the homeless must engage in an array of activities, some of which may indeed be illegal. Similarly, the weak social ties among homeless individuals – friendships may form, then dissolve, within a matter of hours – do not result from choice and so don't prove they are different from the domiciled. Instead, we must consider the "survival value of weak ties in resource-depleted contexts" (197). The authors' simultaneous desire to show the homeless as victims of circumstance and as "like us," as people actively engaged in shaping their lives, often leads to a language of almost Wordsworthian paradoxes that, as effectively as anything, points to the elusive nature of attitudes toward homeless life.

> The homeless are not merely pawns in this process, responding lockstep to the structural and organizational constraints they encounter. Rather, they contribute to the production and reproduction of the order of street life by indexing many of their behaviors to such moral codes as "what goes around, comes around," by the social ties they form, and by the sheer necessities of survival. They do not do so because they are all willing players. On the contrary, evidence of resentment and resistence is abundant in the talk, laments, and behavior of many of them.
>
> (314)

On the one hand, the homeless are active agents, creating a unique subculture and surviving in situations difficult to imagine, much less document. At the same time, they are not "willing players," and the passage concludes that it may be only in their talk, rather than their actions, that any meaningful evidence of agency emerges. The historical binary applied to the homeless, that of criminal/victim, has been reconfigured into a new opposition, agent/victim, but its final resolution appears as remote as ever.

The struggle accurately to locate the homeless along such a continuum is also a central preoccupation of Christopher Jencks' *The Homeless*. Jencks considers the role of individual decisions, for example crack use and unwed motherhood, in creating homelessness more than do Snow and Anderson. In a clear attack on their tone, he explicitly argues that the homeless are not like most people, but in many cases require specialized and long-term assistance to stay off the streets. Calling the "down on their luck" approach "myopic," Jencks perceptively notes that debates over the role of luck or character in creating homelessness are in fact "covert arguments about the assignment of blame" (47). Seizing on many of the same ambiguities identified by Snow and Anderson, Jencks goes farther in apportioning blame to the homeless themselves even while he criticizes a sometimes hostile populace and uncaring government: "In trying to explain this situation, we need to replace our instinctive either-or approach to blame with a both-and-approach" (48). Jencks even gives limited support to the controversial notion that shelters actually encourage homelessness. Since homeless families receive the highest priority on waiting lists for subsidized housing, Jencks believes that some housed families in particularly desperate situations will actually choose to move into a shelter for a few months rather than remain in overcrowded housing or with abusive relatives. Jencks concludes by using the vocabulary of *Down on their Luck* to significantly different effect: "… the homeless are not just passive victims. They make choices, like everyone else. The choices open to the homeless are far worse than those open to most Americans, but they are still choices" (104). O'Flaherty agrees, believing that homelessness will only escape its old stigma when we view the homeless in these terms; only accountability for one's actions (in an echo of Burke) across class lines will eliminate the remaining vestiges of class distinction continuing to make homelessness a social crime in the eyes of many (278). Jencks' belief in the existence of choice, coupled with a practical recognition of the political resistance to wide-scale housing reform, leads him to propose a system of vouchers for housing, food, and services for the homeless. His ongoing commitment to seeing the homeless as marginals is underscored when, in closing, he calls for us "to reconcile the claims of compassion and prudence" (122). The victim deserves compassion; the active agent requires vigilance.

Perhaps the most even-handed view of the homeless, tracing its origins almost equally to bad choices and systemic paralysis, comes from Liebow. Like Jencks, he finds that many of the women he interviews have become homeless precisely because they are, in some important sense, unlike the rest of us, even as he argues that this is not necessarily their fault: "Many homeless women have tried to conform but have failed, often for reasons outside themselves, and many are still trying" (16). A family may push a wife, daughter or other relative out on the street because they, not the woman, were "crazy, unreasonable, greedy, violent, or otherwise impossible to live with" (86). Along with Snow and Anderson, Joel Blau (*The Visible Poor*) and others, Liebow denounces stagnant wages and "do-nothing job and housing policies" (228) for their role in what he sees. Yet with characteristic sensitivity, he also understands and documents the fear of violence and criminality homelessness engenders. This explains public opposition to locating shelters in residential neighborhoods (the so-called NIMBY, or Not In My Backyard, response), the fear the homeless themselves have of the thefts and assaults that occur in shelters, and the fear service workers have of the very people they are supposed to help. After speaking of a "brutishness to life in shelters and on the street" (115), Liebow summarizes:

> ... the citizen on the street, the merchant, the householder, and whole communities fear the homeless, and the homeless fear the non-homeless citizens. And, to complete the circle, the homeless are afraid of the homeless. Thus, everyone is afraid of the homeless, including the homeless themselves, and what is so terrible and intractable about this situation is that everyone is right to be afraid.
>
> (116)

THE HOMELESS IN WORDSWORTH

Each of the following chapters reads Wordsworth's early representations of vagrancy through specific political developments and historical changes in the status of the homeless during the period of his poetry's composition. Wordsworth's earliest work grew out of a reaction to the vagrant poor as complex as that of any of his contemporaries. *An Evening Walk* provides an instructive entryway into these complexities, negotiating the speaker's sense of vagrant isolation as aesthetically empowering and yet socially dangerous and ultimately self-destructive. The continuum the poem establishes between a homeless family and respectable society – a continuum on which Wordsworth the man occupies a middle position – gradually gives way to fears of vulnerability, and the speaker concludes by conceding the value of home, albeit in a highly personalized fashion. Tellingly, the poet's awareness of the vagrant's destabilizing power is quickened during his time in France, where the situation of the itinerant poor was perhaps even more problematic than in Britain. In *Descriptive Sketches*, the narrator's wandering perspective endows him with an empowering skepticism about the value and authority of a range of commitments including those to family and nation, the institutions at the core of conservative assaults on the French Revolution.

The text suggests that such affiliations regularly fail to provide the confidence and security they promise, and that when they do, the rewards are tainted by a repressive underside. When the attractive veneer of ideology is pierced in *Descriptive Sketches* – and it always is – both the hardships and enhanced self-awareness of homeless life remain the constant of human experience. Written during Wordsworth's second visit to France (1791–2), *Descriptive Sketches* goes on to critically assess the political ideology and goals of the revolution in progress during its composition. Successive revolutionary regimes did little to clarify the vagrant's social standing as one *sans état*, or without a clearly defined place within the community. For the text's vagrant speaker, being *sans état* offers the opportunity to ironize and even debunk the confident certainties of revolutionaries intent on creating equality by eradicating political opposition.

The Britain that Wordsworth returned to in 1792 was dominated by an increasingly repressive political climate. Michel Foucault reminds us that this was the era of Jeremy Bentham's panopticon; during the war with revolutionary France, the developing Tory governmental bureaucracy employed Benthamesque tactics to regulate the physical wanderings of the homeless as well as the ideological deviations of political reformers. The early Salisbury Plain poems counter both policies by focusing on a homeless couple whose seditious conversation directly criticizes government war efforts. Their power to do so is in keeping with the marginality of vagrancy and of political opposition to the crown. While authorities worked to declare all political discourse either loyalist or treasonous, British juries situated reformist language in the shadows in between by acquitting leading radicals of treason. In "Salisbury Plain," the marginality of homelessness is realized through isolation from the state apparatus of parish officials, spies and informers. Her homelessness also releases the poem's female vagrant from victimization by her family, a victimization consistent with the contention by early feminists that home life necessitates the submersion of women's individuality in gender-based roles hostile to personal inclination. Significantly, the rejection of Pitt's agenda in "Salisbury

Plain" is not accompanied by an endorsement of British radicalism. Amid Britain's political polarization, radicals often shared their opponents' refusal to acknowledge the legitimacy of marginal beliefs and equivocal feelings. The intensifying climate of dispute and repression is reflected in the poem's early revision into "Adventures on Salisbury Plain," composed as the Pitt ministry redoubled its effort to compel public support for the war. The revision's unrepentant homeless thieves and carnivalesque traveling profiteers suggest that no government effort can or should obliterate the marginality such figures represent.

In 1797–8, Wordsworth works to shore up this position in works like "Tintern Abbey," which defines memory as a home whose instability and flexibility allies it with the ambiguity of homelessness. By dwelling in such memories, the wandering narrator can guard against victimization by a hostile society. Sharing these memories with his sister also allows him a meaningful, enduring connection to her that honors their relationship while finally acknowledging the unpredictability of her future perceptions and experiences. Yet much in the first two editions of *Lyrical Ballads* qualifies this hope. Written as invasion fears at last granted the war widespread support, the poems respond to the public's diminished tolerance for anyone not openly supportive of the government. Wordsworth's own persecution as a French spy in Somerset shapes the portraits of community in "The Thorn" and "The Old Cumberland Beggar," where vagrants are subject to persecution and exploitation by their neighbors. The village of "The Thorn" repudiates the confusion engendered by a wandering woman's movements in favor of a familiar narrative about infanticide that all understand. By believing her to be a murderer, her neighbors can devise normalizing stories about her life that bolster community stability at her expense. In the second edition of *Lyrical Ballads* "The Old Cumberland Beggar" documents a similar process, illustrating how the travels of the homeless can be manipulated so as to bind together neighbors divided by social and economic difference. Emphasizing the beggar's stabilizing role in his neighborhood, in "The Old Cumberland Beggar" Wordsworth registers how the wartime climate is squeezing out marginal space – how such people increasingly are perceived purely as threats or allies.

Chapter 4 charts the progress of the homeless through Wordsworth's poems of the spring of 1802 in light of developments in vagrancy law during the Peace of Amiens. To outward appearances, the truce was a much-needed cooling down period not only for a war-weary public but also for political rhetoric. The temporary departure of Pitt from the governing ministry introduced a more tolerant tone into domestic political debates, as well as foreign affairs. But the spring 1802 re-authorization of the Middlesex Justice Bill, originally passed in 1792 as a complement to other repressive legislation, signaled the persistence of elite anxieties about domestic "Jacobinism." Countenancing the ongoing existence of a system of metropolitan police offices staffed by paid professionals, the Middlesex Bill also singled out reputed thieves as being liable to arrest on suspicion alone and punishable as rogues and vagabonds under the 1744 Vagrancy Act. In its separation of crime from a verifiable and discrete act, this provision, Rogers has suggested, is in line with Foucault's definition of delinquency, a legal category enabled by a three-part investigation into the perpetrator's social standing, upbringing, and psychology. In "The Sailor's Mother," "Alice Fell" and "Beggars," Wordsworth responds to the biographical impulse of investigations into delinquency in a variety of ways, insisting through vagrants' stories the difficulties of perceiving motive behind the impulse to wander in addition to complicating the notion of a transparent investigative observer. This latter approach takes center stage in "Resolution and Independence," in which the suspect reputation of poetry as a profession poisons Wordsworth's own belief in the financial and spiritual value of his vocation. This advancing tide of self-doubt and accusation finally is stymied by his encounter with a destitute old man whose comments, in straying from the speaker's obsession with occupation and job security, reassert the power of the homeless to defy the law's stereotypes and evade its mechanisms of enforcement.

Chapter 5 explores how conflicts between delinquency and marginality are played out in the composition of the 1799 and 1805 *Prelude*. The earliest drafts of the 1799 *Prelude* present a portrait of the poet as what we might be tempted to call a juvenile delinquent, but Wordsworth uses images of vagrant poaching to insist on political and moral ambiguity as defining and aesthetically empowering features of homeless life. The 1805 text charts a crucial shift in the representation of homelessness and its ambivalent relation to society and domesticity. When Britain declared war on Napoleonic France in 1803 after the Peace of Amiens collapsed, mixed feelings about the values of British government and culture virtually were impossible to distinguish any longer from treason itself. As a result, the author of the 1805 *Prelude* abandons any sign of ambiguity in his political allegiance. Instead, the poet devises a Wordsworthian history that includes early radical sympathies, but defined as youthful indiscretions now firmly past. This plot was particularly intelligible and acceptable in the context of the times, for it situates the poet's life amid the masterplot of his generation: many, *The Prelude* repeatedly tells us, had been prey to the same "mistake." This political history is accompanied by praise of newfound domestic stability with his extended family and growing distance from the vagrant life to which it is opposed. Insofar as vagrants appear in the later books of the 1805 *Prelude*, they are cleansed of all ambiguous potential. Rather than portray the homeless as the threats to order they commonly were felt to be, Wordsworth describes them as embodiments of virtue and fellow-feeling. This clarified view of vagrant life complements the concluding descriptions of a narrator whose wanderings are managed by placing them in the past and end in his committing himself to his art and country. The poet's new affiliations with his generation and Georgian home life confirm Wordsworth's membership in respectable British society and his suitability to write the nation's great philosophical poem.

This summary suggests how this study revises the findings of other historicist scholars even as its conception and approach is indebted to their pioneering work. Nicholas Roe has pointed out that some radicals in the 1790s embraced the conservative equation of vagrancy with political upheaval. The young Samuel Taylor Coleridge and Robert Southey, for example, identified the walking tour with the government reforms they hoped to instigate (*Politics*, 128–9); whether Wordsworth himself saw wandering in this way, however, is more problematic.[22] Supplementing Roe's findings with new intuitions and formidable research, Kenneth Johnston has now brought to light a man he calls the hidden Wordsworth, whose political and romantic involvements in the 1790s outstrip the imaginings or the evidence of any of the poet's earlier biographers. More detailed responses to some of Johnston's observations appear below; at the moment I venture only a few preliminary comments. Johnston's cheerfully avowed aim in *The Hidden Wordsworth: Poet, Rebel, Lover, Spy* is (as his subtitle shows) to inject some excitement into Wordsworth's youth: "Wordsworthian biography does not need more facts, though these are always welcome, so much as it needs more speculation," he begins, acknowledging that his "'method' often consists of no more than raising questions" (8, 9).

Johnston turns over the unknown months of Wordsworth's life, gaps that have never been explained, and works to fill in these absences. Wordsworth's missing months in the fall of 1793 become a third trip to France to marry Annette Vallon; Wordsworth's unexplained spring in London in 1795 becomes a period of furtive work on a radical journal; and an unaccounted-for month in Germany in 1799, together with some intriguing government records, enables a suggestion that Wordsworth went to Goslar on an errand for the British secret service. The contents of his biography's missing time are recovered by Johnston as periods of feverish mission that the poet later works with almost complete success to erase from the record because their political implications were too explosive to air in the flammable milieu of the Napoleonic Wars.

Johnston's assertions usually have their origin in facts which he interprets with a great deal of intelligence, skill and wit; *The Hidden Wordsworth* thoroughly succeeds in presenting a new, existing protagonist and will become an invaluable sourcebook of details about the poet's youth. Yet the evidence for Johnston's views is often inconclusive and some of his most dramatic claims create thorny contradictions. This difficulty becomes clearest in his theory that Wordsworth, even as he dedicated himself to a career in radical journalism on *The Philanthropist,* may also have been spying on his comrades for the Home Office. Because government correspondence concerning Wordsworth at Alfoxden indicates his name was known to Richard Ford, Bow Street magistrate and espionage liaison, Johnston surmises that Wordsworth also may have been employed by the secret service while in Somerset – while he was entertaining figures like John Thelwall (533). An entry in the secret service account books in 1799 for payment of almost £100 to a "Mr Wordsworth" among other operatives working out of Hamburg leads Johnston to conjecture that the poet may have been paid for his time in Germany as a courier or in some other low-level capacity (616–18). These discoveries compel a renewed and indispensable awareness of the web of informants, government agents, and other operatives comprising the hidden army that won Pitt's war against domestic reform as surely as Wellington would defeat Bonaparte. That Wordsworth crossed paths with such people is indisputable, given the government surveillance of his activities in Somerset; what is less clear is William Wordsworth's role, if any, in the kind of activities *The Hidden Wordsworth* describes with such vision and daring. As Johnston himself tells it, Wordsworth in

Germany did not appear to have the sense of purpose we would expect in a man on a secret government mission: William and Dorothy "had not really thought what they were going to do when they arrived [in Hamburg], and they were quite unprepared for the expense. Wordsworth's main motive in coming to Germany with Coleridge was just that: to go wherever Coleridge went" (627). This kind of Wordsworthian dithering, however, generally takes a back seat to depictions of intrigue and passion worthy of Byron, the model Johnston aims to set his subject alongside (5). He begins by avowing a healthy skepticism for *The Prelude* (10–11), yet his investigations are guided by one of its dominant narrative strands: that Wordsworth awoke from political indifference while in France, that he held some very radical opinions in the early 1790s, that the collapse of the revolution's promise sent him into a deep depression, and that he recovered from his despair by writing poetry for profit that either turned away from political issues or embraced the party line.[23] Where Johnston reads *The Prelude* against the grain, he assumes that it, like other evidence, is a sedated version of much more sensational events. I advocate as far-reaching a re-evaluation of Wordsworth's autobiography, or one perhaps even more radical, that sees its political plot almost purely as a cultural construct whose surface narrative testifies to political pressures even as its inconsistent details hint at a more sophisticated reality. Wordsworth's 29 July 1802 letter to an enthusiastic young Thomas DeQuincey can serve as a preliminary cue to the ways in which self-fashioning can obscure biographical verisimilitude. Wordsworth writes, "How many things are there in a mans [*sic*] character of which his writings however miscellaneous or voluminous will give no idea" (*Early Years*, 401). Wordsworth's most "voluminous" poem is the one we must read with precisely this injunction in mind.

Though the poems explored in this study span the years Johnston takes as his focus, a different kind of hidden Wordsworth emerges from these pages. Johnston worries after divulging his spy scoop that leftist critics will seize on his theory as the ultimate evidence of Wordsworth's apostasy; in conceding this possibility, he adds "Any imaginative work will have a political coloration, ultimately, in one direction or another, and none will ever be politically correct except from a perspective that shares those politics" (*Hidden*, 669). It is precisely this assumption that I believe Wordsworth's early verse sought to interrogate, developing representations of homelessness into an index of his attitudes toward a variety of public and private commitments. The puzzle of many of these poems, as incarnated through tropes of vagrancy, is precisely a refusal to fall "ultimately, in one direction or another," a refusal that suggests a writer less a Byronic hero than a cautious, ambivalent, and even confused human being. Karl Kroeber has remarked that Wordsworth "was not a political creature, born into political times when political commitments began to be enforced upon every man" ("Presence," 5). During Wordsworth's era, every Briton became immersed in a national climate pressing people to choose: radicalism or reaction, revolution or repression. Wordsworth hesitated before these two equally unattractive alternatives and gave voice to his diffidence through his portraits of the homeless.[24] His ultimate capitulation to the choices of his time testifies to their immense organizing power within his culture, a power with which our view of his commitments continues to be complicit.

1

Unsettling Powers in the Early Landscapes

Calling them "juvenile productions, inflated and obscure," in a letter of 1801 Wordsworth nevertheless offers Anne Taylor *An Evening Walk* and *Descriptive Sketches* as examples of his independent thinking, referring specifically to their "new images, and vigorous lines" (*Early Years*, 327–8). Wordsworth's choice of texts emphasizes his belief that their artistic characteristics have an intellectual as well as ideological basis. In choosing productions for publication that would in effect introduce him to the public in 1793, Wordsworth fixed on poems that from their inception acknowledge and interrogate law, culture and literature's assumptions about wandering and respectability. Both poems depart from conventional topographical writing by introducing speakers who identify with traditionally ornamental homeless people, even as that identification arouses anxiety and physical danger. The 1793 version of *An Evening Walk* explores similarities between poet and vagrant only, in the end, to prefer a life of directed wandering to the aimless rambles of the text's opening lines. More than an exploration of a place, *An Evening Walk* presents the Lake District through the eyes of an observer familiar with the terrain yet estranged from the people and settings he describes. In its tentative exploration of the possibilities of the topographical genre and the rewards and perils of a vagrant aesthetic, the poem is an instructive baseline against which to measure Wordsworth's subsequent compositions. *Descriptive Sketches* is the most immediate indication of deviation from the cautious conclusions advanced in the earlier poem. An unlikely affront, *Descriptive Sketches* is also a topographical poem but this bolder effort invokes cultural guideposts, including the family, religion, and political ideology, only to disregard openly the certainties affirmed by such markers. For they always, in the end, fail to lead to their promised destination, in large part because they rely on convictions that inconstant humanity can never accept

24

unequivocally. Whether we admit it or not, the author of *Descriptive Sketches* declares, we are all homeless in our hearts. This truth eventually is thrust before our notice with special force by the twin figures of the vagabond and the mercenary. These figures compel us to acknowledge the volatility of human feelings and allegiances, a volatility revealing that apparent opposites such as homelessness and domesticity, guilt and innocence, traitor and patriot are divided by permeable membranes, not watertight compartments. The instability of human perception and cultural institutions designed to regulate it have an unsettling impact on the poet's views even of the revolution he witnessed while composing this poem in France during 1792. Written when conventional wisdom dictates that Wordsworth's radical fervor was most intense, *Descriptive Sketches'* critiques, particularly of old verities like Catholicism, are consistent in some respects with the revolutionary project. But the text's representatives of homelessness ultimately become the backdrop for a qualified, even ironic, depiction of the program and promise of revolutionary ideology.

PAINFUL PROSPECTS DURING *AN EVENING WALK*

Lines sketching a female vagrant were the germ of *An Evening Walk*, begun at Cambridge in the fall of 1788 and largely complete by the following summer (Reed, *Early*, 89). The text's pathetic vagrant mother is no threat to any government, and although critics usually refer to her as "the female beggar," she does not beg – one of the vagrants' activities that local officials found most obnoxious. Her physical mobility is strangely at odds with her mental state: her thoughts do not wander but tread the same fruitless path repeatedly. Mother and child cannot escape the memory of the absent father, "Asleep on Bunker's charnel hill afar" (254).[1] In the speaker's eyes she is constant to a fault, calling to a husband she knows cannot respond: "For hope's deserted well why wistful look? / Chok'd is the pathway, and the pitcher broke" (255–6). Likewise, her son asks if his father sees the moon shining overhead "in that country, where he dwells afar" (265). The speaker reproaches such curiosity as idle hope: "all light is mute amid the gloom, / The interlunar cavern of the tomb" (267–8). We may admire the family's devotion, but we are directed to its ultimately delusive, even destructive, nature. In context, this portrait seems

even more exceptional. While such women were stock subjects for
late eighteenth-century magazine poets, in 1788 the public con-
ceived of vagrants in very different terms. The demobilization of
soldiers after the end of the American war produced spiraling crime
and one of the few historical moments when many local officials
actually enforced vagrancy laws. According to the Webbs, 1787 saw
"an epidemic" of whipping as punishment for vagabondage (374).
Parliament also passed laws expanding the scope of the vagrancy
acts, one of which offered justices of the peace reluctant to author-
ize whipping the alternative of gaoling vagabonds. In this light, the
vagrancy Wordsworth offers us wears an unconventional face; the
scars of war are present, but the widow, not the returning veteran,
is the focus.

At the outset the poem itself occupies a peculiar position. The
most convention-bound of Wordsworth's poems, *An Evening Walk*
announces its debts to a locodescriptive tradition through countless
quotations from and allusions to earlier eighteenth-century land-
scape poetry. In his posture, however, the text's speaker upsets
generic expectations in troubling ways. In his distant views of labor-
ers returning home from a day's work, Wordsworth's speaker
appears to respect picturesque protocols that "affirm the spectator's
superiority over the vagrants, idlers and gypsies who are allowed to
remain as humble spectacles" (Harrison, 64). Yet the speaker
announces he is something of a gypsy himself: "Far from my
dearest friend, 'tis mine to rove" (1). He identifies not with
landowners but with the vagrant mother he imagines. He uses the
same term, "wilder," to describe both her wanderings in a storm (285)
and his own night-time disorientation (376); his own melancholy –
"Still the cold cheek its shuddering tear retains" (388) – appears as a
reflection of the freezing mother's "flooded cheek" (296). Like the
homeless mother, the speaker feels displaced and craves the
company of a missing companion. At the poem's end he is home-
ward bound (434), but not to the home he really desires – that can
only be imagined, a few lines earlier, as a "distant scene" (414) to be
shared in the future with his absent friend. Just as the apparent
opposites of night and day are linked by intervening changes in
light and shadow and the rhythms of human activity, in *An Evening
Walk* extremes initially appear to even out: vagrant and gentleman,
woman and man, are not clearly divisible but are part of a contin-
uum whose individual components may vex attempts to assign dis-
tinct affiliations to one or the other.[2] This perspective assumes a

metaphysical dimension in the poem's 1794 revisions: that most treasured distinction, between the movements of life and the stasis of death, itself is negotiated by subtle connections. The playing schoolboys the speaker observes cannot imagine their own deaths, or their connection to the decaying bodies in a nearby churchyard. The fact remains that "their warm light motion [is] allied / To the dull earth that [crumbles] at their side" (45–6).[3]

Economically and emotionally, the young Wordsworth was certainly familiar with the marginality he confers on his speaker. Johnston's biography assiduously describes the social and political conflicts framing the poet's childhood. The Wordsworths' outwardly grand Cockermouth residence actually was owned by John Wordsworth, Sr's employer, James Lowther, and so both was and was not the father's house. Wordsworth's services to the immensely powerful and widely feared Lowther included fixing elections, bribing officials, and threatening the recalcitrant. Wordsworth's job as Lowther's legal agent placed himself and his family in a kind of political and social no man's land, "associating young Wordsworth with the dominant social power in his home region, while alienating him from its popular base" and consequently determining the poet's "wandering life during the formative years of his manhood" (Johnston, *Hidden*, 23). The affiliations of the Wordsworth children were further complicated by the longstanding connection among their mother's relatives with some of Lowther's most powerful political adversaries, the Howards. Wordsworth's future was openly plunged into crisis when, on his father's death, Lowther refused to pay money due to his agent's estate, effectively cheating the Wordsworth children out of their patrimony. Raised by relatives who openly viewed him as a financial burden, as a boy and young man Wordsworth experienced first-hand the dissatisfaction with home communicated by the speaker of *An Evening Walk* (Gill, *Wordsworth*, 35–6). He went on to attend Cambridge alongside Britain's elite, but his position as a sizar reflected his ongoing financial dependency.[4] He resisted academic discipline and his guardian's plans for his future as a curate, even as he chastised himself for lacking direction. By the fall of 1791, Wordsworth's letters to his college friend William Mathews fully display his ambivalence, condemning his behavior and irresolution in spite of, or perhaps because of, finding them vaguely satisfying: "I am doomed to be an idler thro[oughout] my whole life. I have read nothing this age, nor indeed did I ever. Yet with all this I am tolerable happy; do you think this ought to be a matter of congratulation to me or no? For my own part I think certainly not" (*Early Years*, 62). Wordsworth's rejection of established literary models – "I have read nothing" – is in keeping with his poem's complex relation to the topographical tradition. The poem's extensive quotations and heroic couplets parade a debt to convention, but it jettisons locodescriptive poetry's typically careful management of digression and deployment of didactic milestones.[5] In the poem's opening lines, the landscape itself is displaced by a description of the speaker's dejection, which endows objects with a significance all out of proportion to their actual import: "While, Memory at my side, I wander here, / Starts at the simplest sight th' unbidden tear" (43–4). The speaker's melancholy instigates his unfettered digressions like that of the homeless mother, as well as his own physical wanderings.

Wordsworth's nuanced but significant aesthetic innovations become clear by examining William Cowper's popular *The Task*, published three years before *An Evening Walk* was begun.[6] Firmly planted in the topographical tradition, Cowper's narrator is a member of the landed gentry, a position his afternoon excursions only enforce. Like Wordsworth's speaker, his current walks recall childhood rambles when as "a truant boy I passed my bounds / T' enjoy a ramble on the banks of Thames" (ll. 14–15).[7] But Cowper's adult unselfconsciously encases these tendencies within a world of affluent domesticity. As he revisits the walks of his youth, he is accompanied by the "dear companion" Wordsworth longs for but pointedly lacks (l. 14). Throughout, Cowper casts himself as a squire who delights in describing and maintaining his estate. Unlike Wordsworth's speaker, he goes far to distinguish the sloth of gypsies – this "vagabond and useless tribe" (l. 77) – from his own industry in supervising his lubbard laborers and inspecting his lands. Playing on the common theme of the gentleman living in rural retirement, Cowper argues that such landlords are superior both to indolent aristocrats who float from country to town and to the homeless gypsies who are "self-banish'd from society" (1. 78). Cowper carefully distances his gentrified speaker from the lackadaisical vices that some peers and the homeless share, managing the implications of his narrator's wanderings as carefully as he modulates representation of labor. *An Evening Walk* is distinguished by its willingness to acknowledge and explore social confusions *The Task* ignores. In this respect, Wordsworth's poem stretches picturesque convention until its status as a compromise category, tempering freedom with supervision and desire with its arrest, is given full force.[8]

By May of 1792, Wordsworth's letters show he had begun to think of ways in which he might recast his idleness into a career that would sustain him. A typical example of his rhetoric from this period demonstrates that a literary life is appealing partly because he manages to express it in terms that reinforce an element of vagrant marginality. Writing again to Mathews, this time from Blois, Wordsworth encourages his schoolfellow and himself about the career possibilities of writing for money, a goal that will terminate two years later in the ill-fated *Philanthropist* project.

> … [our talents] if properly made use of will enable you to get your bread unshackled by the necessity of professing a particular system of opinions. You still have the hope that we may be connected in some method of obtaining an independence. I assure you I wish it as much as yourself. Nothing but resolution is necessary. The field of letters is very extensive, and it is astonishing if we cannot find some little corner, which with a little tillage will produce us enough for the necessities, nay even the comforts, of life.
>
> (*Early Years*, 76).

Mathews was depressed by the prospect of life as a schoolteacher; like Wordsworth, he had literary ambitions that seemed an attractive but impractical alternative to professional drudgery. This letter justifies this impression by contending that "The field of letters" can provide the undetermined space essential for authentic intention, passion and productivity. Wordsworth also reassures himself and his correspondent that a literary life freed from intellectual or political dogma can be respectable and profitable. The language describing these aspects of writing for money problematizes the author's image of it as nonconformist or vagrant. The goal of an "unshackled" existence, unchained to a particular ideological terrain, undergoes qualification with the introduction of tillage and fields. If a successful literary career is like agriculture, then adhering to one space, intellectual or physical, may be necessary after all. Somehow, the letter claims, intellectual hunting and gathering – the life of the professional writer – can produce fruits like those derived from the planning and toil of a farming life.

As it progresses the letter continues to argue for a cultural position where competing, even contradictory, notions about independence and commitment coexist. Wordsworth says he plans to take orders in the coming year, and denies his contention in an earlier letter that a curacy would be stultifying. Perhaps a reflection of his need for money to marry Annette Vallon,[9] Wordsworth's thinking here moves to make the cleric's job of living in one place and professing one belief now compatible with intellectual independence and other professional ambitions. Finally, Wordsworth encourages Mathews to get a sense of the British literary market: "Would it not be possible for you to form an acquaintance with some of the publishing booksellers of London, from whom you might get some hints of what sorts of works would be the most likely to answer?" (76). In effect, Wordsworth concedes an awareness that the marketplace may enact its own kind of tyranny, necessitating the espousal of particular systems of opinion after all. Writing becomes a vehicle both for capitulation and independent thought.[10] Throughout, the letter tries rhetorically to accommodate opposites such as freedom and commitment, or independent writing and doctrinaire sermonizing. It conveys Wordsworth's hope during the early 1790s for a free-thinking life, unchained by the ideas and expectations of others, even as it characterizes this life through social conventions such as property ownership and land cultivation.[11]

Recent studies exploring Wordsworth as a literary professional have seized on this text precisely for its contradictory rhetoric: Mark Schoenfield notes that it demonstrates how the poet's "radicalism was even at its inception constrained within Wordsworth's ability to imagine the project as economically viable" (77). Thomas Pfau similarly analyzes the tensions here between the pull of the marketplace and the respectable materiality of landed wealth: "the agrarian metaphor ultimately collapses under its speculative weight," since in the new realm of a professional imaginary, "notions of a natural, material harvest no longer apply" (108). For Pfau, Wordsworth's correspondence during the early 1790s is less interesting for its ambiguous political content than for its dedication to the broader goal of literary professionalization *per se*. This argument helpfully redirects discussion of young Wordsworth's politics away from unresolved, and perhaps unresolvable, arguments about the precise nature of his beliefs at any given point in time. Its utility for describing Wordsworth's situation in the early and mid-1790s is qualified by the fact that these are precisely the years when he became a writer who did not publish. His silence would only be broken by the 1798 *Lyrical Ballads* that would be published anonymously and with the much-needed confidence inspired by Coleridge's literary achievements. After the initial foray with his landscape poems, Wordsworth deferred a second excursion into the professional marketplace by not publishing "Salisbury Plain," by not pursuing *The Philanthropist*, by not publishing *The Borderers* after its theatrical rejection, and by engaging in what Johnston openly terms legacy hunting with regard to Raisley Calvert. Ultimately, the poet of the early 1790s frustrates confident assessments of his commitments, whether we find it more productive to speak of Wordsworth's dedication to the emergence of middle-class professionalism or of his investments in various political ideologies. Pfau discovers Wordsworth's nascent professionalism in the claim that nothing but "the *appearance* of producing a decent harvest" is necessary, the transmutation from manual labor to metaphor registering the shift toward commodified professional identity (*Early Years*, 76; emphasis added). The tenacity with which Wordsworth clings to the metaphor, if not the reality, of the field of letters, however, argues for its stubborn retention as a polyvalent terrain where motion and stasis, acceptance and iconoclasm contest the same ground. Complications in the ideological tenor of *Descriptive Sketches* will imply that insofar as the young Wordsworth is writing for money, he positions himself less as a career man of letters than as a vagrant warrior, or mercenary.

The 1793 *Evening Walk* postpones the full impact of such contradictions by jumping to a set piece that naturalizes and valorizes key elements of Georgian domesticity through what David Simpson recently has described as localism, an attachment to place that shared the home's "strong association with the feminine" (*Academic Postmodern*, 143). The trials of the homeless mother and children immediately follow a description of a family of swans whose version of home life protects them from physical threats and hostile observers. The pains of losing such an existence, graphically depicted in the homeless mother's fate, goes far toward accounting for the speaker's final subtle but significant shift in tone toward wandering life. The swan's retreat is stationary and secluded, residing in a "secret bay" (196) and their "home" (227) in a tuft of grass hears "not the trip of harmless milkmaid's feet" (226), much less the sounds of the hunt, "The hound, the horse's tread, and mellow horn ..." (234). These qualities are complemented by the presence of a selfless female who maintains the family. While the almost Satanic male "swells his lifted chest, and backward flings / His brindling neck" (201–2), the female caring for the offspring follows behind with the less obvious charm of "tender Cares and mild domestic loves" (207). The male – like the poem's imaginary troops parading with heraldic banners and the cock on the farm flaunting his plumage – is intent on personal appearance and spectacle. The female swan, by contrast, is a caretaker of the home and children largely because she "in a mother's care, her beauty's pride / Forgets" (213–14). Self-forgetfulness is part of what allows her to shelter the ducklings when they are weary by having them "mount her back, and rest / Close by her mantling wings' embraces prest" (218). The mother's body through the shelter it imparts replicates the advantages of a physical home. In the description of the cock on the farm, the reader knows nothing of the "sister-wives" beyond the fact that they exist. They are so unobtrusive that they cease to be a subject for narration. These characteristics are commensurate with late eighteenth-century views of domesticity that cast the bourgeois woman as a homemaker who oversaw details of family life rather than delegating such tasks to servants. Georgian middle-class families prized their homes as protection not just from the weather but also from the public gaze; the home became "an isolated world into which only the well-screened visitor was permitted; the world was kept at bay, and the privacy of the family, and of the individual, was disturbed as little as possible" (Rybczynski, 107–8).[12]

The homeless mother's appeals to such a life are lamented as futile by the speaker of *An Evening Walk*, yet the alternative is ultimately horrific. Deprived of a home, her family is killed by a storm in which her failure to fulfill the socially defined maternal role kills her children. The beggar's children cannot rest in her arms for long, for she soon must "Shake her numb arm that slumbers with its weight" (251). While her children totter along the road, she fruitlessly daydreams about her lost husband. In moments of repose, particularly at night as the family rests by the roadside, she can be the attentive parent, pointing to shooting stars and showing off glowworms to her children. The storm scene shows that the return of physical exhaustion and pain overwhelm her obligation to think of her children:

> Oh! When the bitter showers her path assail,
> And roars between the hills the torrent gale,
> – No more her breath can thaw their fingers cold,

Their frozen arms her neck no more can fold;
Scarce heard, their chattering lips her shoulder chill,
And her cold back their colder bosoms thrill;
All blind she wilders o'er the lightless heath,
Led by Fear's wet cold hand, and dogg'd by Death;
Death, as she turns her neck the kiss to seek,
Breaks off the dreadful kiss with angry shriek.
Snatch'd from her shoulder with despairing moan,
She clasps them at that dim-seen roofless stone.

(279–90)

Her own mental and physical torments cause her to spiritually abandon her family. She seeks to end her suffering, resigning herself to a kind of suicide. Interestingly, Wordsworth figures this as an infidelity to her dead-soldier's memory – she seeks Death's kiss. Like her soldier, though, this second lover abandons her as well, and she returns to the awareness of her and her children's circumstances, though she knows her efforts to save them must fail.

On the surface, the vagrant's death scene appears a study in gratuitous, graphic detail (Jacobus, *Tradition*, 136). The drawn-out manner of her death becomes more purposeful, however, if we see the episode in relation to the speaker's final efforts to identify himself, after his early portrait of himself as a rambler, with something akin to Cowperian domesticity. The imaginary drama of the homeless mother enables the speaker, to some extent, to purge those aspects of his wanderings that are troublingly open-ended.[13] The similarities between speaker and mother – the fact that one is in fact the imaginative creation of the other – enable the poet to substitute the fate of one for the fate of both. Within the structure of the text, the deaths of the mother and children seem to absorb some of the most worrisome doubts the speaker articulates over the propriety and success of his art and prospects. Her death's intensity burns out the deeper conflicts between his position as poetic loiterer and society's approbation of settled life. Because the homeless suffer, the speaker may not have to. René Girard's comments about the uses of the scapegoat as a "sacrificable" victim are instructive here (4). Girard's anthropological model assumes the existence of a larger community, which both experiences pressures toward violence and devises formal procedures for unleashing them on selected individuals. The homeless had traditionally been one of the most

convenient scapegoats for projecting fears about the breakdown of
social order, and this desire would only intensify in the chaotic
1790s (as well as the 1990s). *An Evening Walk* replicates some of
these tensions by distilling them into a kind of psychomachia
within the speaker, who straddles the line between vagrant disloca-
tion and respectability. The homeless mother's death conveys a
sense of release, for with her dies half of the speaker's conflicted
subjectivity.

   The best argument for this theory lies in the striking change after
the imagined beggar's demise in the speaker's view of his own des-
tination. At the beginning of the poem, he makes no mention of a
destination or ideas of a home, creating a sense of vulnerability as
well as possibility. At the end of the text, after the episode of the
homeless mother, a vision of future repose emerges out of nowhere.
It is as if the beggar's death has contributed to some process that
enables the narrator to finally imagine what she has irrevocably
forfeited, a home.

> – E'ven now [Hope] decks for me a distant scene,
> (For dark and broad the gulph of time between)
> Gilding that cottage with her fondest ray,
> (Sole bourn, sole wish, sole object of my way;
> How fair its lawns and silvery woods appear!
> How sweet its streamlet murmurs in mine ear!)
> Where we, my friend, to golden days shall rise,
> 'Till our small share of hardly-paining sighs
> (For sighs will ever trouble human breath)
> Creep hushed into the tranquil breast of Death.

> (413–22).

Like the episode of the mother and children, this home itself is
imaginary, but it serves the crucial role of an objective, a goal that
the speaker now claims is the organizing, "sole" aim of his wander-
ings. The provisional status of this aim, dreamed but not yet
achieved, allows the speaker to have it both ways. He acquires the
respectability associated with such a hope, yet in the meantime pos-
sesses the intervening freedom of movement and impulse that have
proven aesthetically fruitful. And in sharp counterpoint to the
mother's shrieks before death, the narrator now imagines a future
of "hardly-paining sighs" after which he will be enveloped by a

Death whose comforts recall the behavior of the mother swan. In the wake of the mother's suffering, death itself has been domesticated. The sadistic lover who toyed with her prayers has been converted into a maternal entity that wipes away all griefs and constitutes the soul's final home.

MARAUDERS AND MERCENARIES IN WORDSWORTH'S EUROPE

In *Descriptive Sketches*, Wordsworth from the first announces the wanderer's peculiar cultural position and claims that unusual powers of discernment result from it. The dedication to Robert Jones, the poet's companion during his 1790 continental tour, defines the text's mission of locating in the vagrant a capacity to mediate between independence and community. Wordsworth writes,

> In inscribing this little work to you I consult my heart. You know well how great is the difference between two companions lolling in a post chaise, and two travelers plodding slowly along the road, side by side, each with his little sack of necessaries upon his shoulders. How much more of heart between the two latter!
>
> (2)[14]

Wordsworth and Jones are presented as frugal travelers – all that they have can be carried, and all that they need, they have – rather than identified as friends. But they have a "much more" sincere and profound emotional connection than the carriage occupants, though we might expect the "companions" to be the genuine friends here. The vagrant's double role as comrade and autonomous traveler makes him the best audience for the poem that follows. On the other hand, the connection between the two men means, for a relieved Wordsworth, that at least one reader "will approach the conclusion of these pages with regret," and the author anticipates that his friend "will meet with few images without recollecting the spot where we observed them together" (32). At the same time, the wanderer's distance from others means he relies on his own judgment and experiences. He is unencumbered by other people's limitations, even those of his fellow traveler: "what ever is feeble in my design, or spiritless in my colouring, will be amply supplied by your own memory" (32). As a gentleman vagrant, Jones represents a conflation of scarcity and abundance – he may only carry his little bag of necessaries, yet he has the psychic capital necessary to give the poem its fullest reading.[15]

The prosperous French who travel by post-chaise, following a predetermined route, lack both the wanderer's awareness and his feeling. Almost comically semi-comatose ("Lolling"), they are detached from each other and the landscape they traverse; their enclosed method of travel implies a more far-reaching isolation within a class ideology aimed at preserving economic and social privilege. In this, they resemble the reactionaries Wordsworth's letters accuse of being unable to value or even apprehend the new social and political configurations taking shape in France during the writing of *Descriptive Sketches*:

> It will be impossible to make any material alteration in the [French] constitution, impossible to reinstate the clergy in its antient guilty splendor, impossible to give an existence to the noblesse similar to that it before enjoyed, impossible to add much to the authority of the king: Yet there are in France some [? Millions] – I speak without exaggeration – who expect that this will take place.
>
> (*Early Years*, 78)

In their resistance to the progress, literally the unpredictable movement, of the revolution, aristocrats can expect merely the reversal of the events of change. They only pass through history, rather than experience it, and this narrow perspective prevents their imagining another trajectory for the future that departs from established patterns. Their calcified understandings overlook what the wanderer can discern – the existence of alternative possibilities, other points of view. It is precisely the refusal to cross the lines of rank and acknowledge other political agendas – a refusal shared by revolutionaries and royalists alike – that attracts Wordsworth's notice on his arrival in Orléans. In a letter to his brother Richard, he ties this polarization to economic standing: "almost all the people of any opulen[ce are] aristocrates and all the other democrates. I had imagined that there were some people of wealth and circumstance favorers of the revolution, but here there is not one to be found" (70).

The source of this polarization is predictable enough; the privileged and their inferiors cling to their respective beliefs because they promise personal advantage. The roving speaker of *Descriptive*

Sketches frequently sympathizes with the human weakness and desperation that make such promises so seductive. Yet like the fellow traveler in the dedication, the speaker's performance of vagrant marginality underwrites a critical appraisal of such thinking. Probing the solace of ideological investments, the speaker indicates how the broad outlines of such constructions fall short of articulating the shifting valence of people's actual perceptions and beliefs, much less delivering the consolation that devotees expect from their convictions. While the poem considers the idea of the home as one ideology among many, it can serve as a trope for all of them. Like the Georgian home, ideology organizes intellectual and spiritual energy, offering adherents a screen against outside dangers by defining and structuring representation.[16] Where the poem allows these comforts to exist at all, Wordsworth equates them with a death-like inflexibility. More frequently, *Descriptive Sketches* dramatizes how comfort necessarily collapses when material circumstances and internal contradictions belie some of culture's most cherished assumptions and convictions. The text presents a kind of psychic homelessness as an honest, even inevitable, alternative to delusion in a world littered with the ruins of ideology's false homes. The plight of the Grison gypsy demonstrates the obvious cruelties of actual life on the road, but the poem explicitly develops the gypsy life as a trope for a larger, inescapable human condition.

> – The mind condemn'd, without reprieve, to go
> O'er life's long deserts with its charge of woe,
> With sad congratulation joins the train,
> Where beasts and men together o'er the plain
> Move on, – a mighty caravan of pain;
> Hope, strength and courage, social suffering brings,
> Freshening the waste of sand with shades and springs.

> (192–8)

Everyone shares the gypsy's guilt as one of the "condemned," but these lines present vagrancy not as a crime in itself but as a metaphysical result of an earlier, unnamed offense – perhaps the simple, universal tragedy of existing in a flawed world. Companionship can ameliorate our spiritual suffering and create opportunities for rest, but human response remains a stubbornly complex and idiosyncratic affair, resisting reduction to a fixed location on an ideological map.

The wandering trail of the vagrant, rather than the insubstantial fantasies of any creed, stand as the inescapable sign of mortal existence.

It is significant that the destabilizing aura of homelessness begins truly to flower in Wordsworth's writings while he is in France. The wanderer's problematic cultural position was grossly magnified by that country's late eighteenth-century political and social milieux. Lacking any state-sponsored system of relief, the French poor traditionally had relied on themselves for survival even more than their English counterparts. To cope with circumstances, the poor developed a repertoire for survival that Olwen Hufton calls an economy of makeshifts, combining annual migrations for work, begging, petty theft, and occasional help from local clerics or overextended charity hospitals.[17] A career patched together in this way might well involved periods of vagrancy. The indigent survived because they ignored many of the social strictures and values of respectable French society. Hufton summarizes that the poor generally endured by virtue of "their aggressive independence and their desire to be left alone to live out their lives without the intrusion from higher authority..." (367).

Higher authorities continually tried to supervise that independence and restrain the wanderings that were its manifestation. Traveling migrant workers as well as homeless wanderers legally were grouped with debauched individuals considered *sans état*, without a social station, or *sans aveu*, without the certification of good character customarily issued by parish priests. Throughout the eighteenth century, royal declarations targeted vagabonds, the supposedly willfully idle who lived by rural begging and extortion, for punishments ranging from whipping to life in the galleys. The move in the 1760s to create rehabilitation-oriented *dépôts de mendicité* gave such repression an enlightenment face: the *dépôts* sought to instill what Thomas Adams calls "a panoptic sense of regularity and discipline ... conveyed throughout the establishment by the actions of trained civil servants" (180). Efforts by the crown and its revolutionary successors to manage the vagrancy problem failed because the transient aspects of many French people's lives continued to perplex the law's narrow definitions. While all begging technically was illegal under the ancien regime, the maréchaussée – the mounted royal constabulary – particularly was ordered to detain the beggar who was homeless. Yet the likelihood of a poor person's begging while traveling to or from seasonal work, for example, undermined systematic application of the law's distinction between migrant workers and so-called professional beggars or vagrants. Attempting conclusively to define homelessness, the crown decreed in 1767 that even a domiciled person could be called a vagabond if found wandering more than a mile from home. At this point, begging ceased to be a prerequisite for police action, and an array of suspect qualities – a questionable appearance, clothing from another region, even physical deformities – could justify arrest or interrogation. This meant that the term" ... vagabond acquired a much broader meaning and both police and judges applied their own criterion" (Hufton, 227–8). The definition of a vagabond changed from year to year and province to province, and magistrates generally were circumspect in applying the law's more stringent criteria.[18] As in England, a contradictory matrix of "fear, disgust and compassion" structured the French public's feelings toward the itinerant poor and impaired efforts to enforce edicts against vagrancy (Olejniczak, "Elite," 138).

The political turmoil of the 1780s and 1790s only intensified this confusion over who the real vagrants were, what they were capable of, and how they should be treated. The public's conflicting views of the homeless made them ciphers onto which collective fears of the most contradictory nature could be projected. Perhaps the clearest expression of this phenomenon was the Great Fear of 1789, when French farmers and peasants became convinced that bands of vagabonds were storming the countryside, cutting down unripe crops and burning down homes whose residents refused to pay extortion money. The panicked association of vagrancy with brigandage reflected beliefs solidified over decades: Georges Lefebvre explains in his classic study of the Fear that in the summer of 1789 these apprehensions were refracted so that destructive vagabonds were transformed into signs of the aristocracy fighting to wrest control from the newborn National Assembly. Townspeople and small landowners believed the bands of vagrants (who appear to have been largely mythical) were "an instrument of civil war, used by the privileged classes to crush the Third Estate" (Lefebvre, 23). Aristocrats, in turn, held that the rumors of vagabond bands were being concocted by the peasants themselves, who sought an excuse to arm themselves and slaughter their masters.[19] The ballooning rumors about groups of homeless marauders also drew energy from the longstanding ambivalence of farmers who had often begged themselves to survive bad years but who still distrusted the unknown itinerant. Insofar as the Fear poignantly revealed poor people's fear of themselves, it argues for the timelessness of Elliot Liebow's parallel observation about homelessness in America quoted in my introduction. George Rudé notes this complex mix of anxieties would revive with special urgency at crisis points during the revolution: in the summer of 1790; after Louise XVI's flight to Varennes in June 1791; and before the September massacres in 1792 (xiii). Anxieties about the homeless peaked in conjunction with larger flash points over the course of political and social change.

At the conclusion of its research, the National Assembly's Comité de Mendicité failed to address, much less resolve, the confusion about vagrancy that the law's protocols only exacerbated. The Comité did recommend the establishment of a national system of relief, but it clung to the old attempt of segregating professional vagrants from the deserving poor. The Comité's January 1791 report to the Assembly could only recommend as punishment for the incorrigible vagabond transportation to an overseas prison colony – a proposal left over from the ancien regime.[20] The Comité's condemnations of professional vagrants would echo throughout the coming years. The penal code appended to the Constitution in September 1791 authorized the continued arrest and incarceration of itinerant beggars in *maisons de correction*. Explaining the appeal of such laws, William Olejniczak emphasizes their continuity with both pre-revolutionary and Napoleonic statutes: the persistent hostility of those in power to the so-called incorrigible vagrant was "the core element" in the way the successive governments viewed the poor ("Elite," 144). Translating that hostility into consistent and enforceable government policy, however, would remain an elusive goal. As the revolution progressed, even the treatment of the supposedly deserving poor became enmeshed in larger debates about the province and excesses of revolutionary authority. After the Terror, the Convention held back from implementing the Comité's proposal for national poor relief. The idea of a national system of *bienfaisance* had come to be identified with the same policies of centralized power that enabled bloodletting in 1793 and 1794. Commentators found it significant that Bertrand Barère, Jacobin minister of the Terror, also had sat on the Comité de Mendicité (Adams, 256).

In his ambiguous relation to society, the vagrant speaker of *Descriptive Sketches* is as hard to pin down as France's itinerant beggars. Even more than in *An Evening Walk*, this solitary wanderer driven by a painful past subtly mediates between opposites: a love of the open road coexists with an appreciation of village and domestic life. The natural world, whose "lost" flowers exude their "idle" scents for him (19), mirrors and legitimizes his own lack of direction. Nevertheless, he is mesmerized by the forms of community, finding that a country dance of village maidens binds his "charmed soul in powerless trance" (98). When he chooses to make his presence known, he is accepted by strangers, even taken into a family's home for an evening and treated as "a brother at the cottage meal" (38).[21] But the pull of *liberté* is ultimately stronger than the desire for *fraternité*, and the speaker's detached, tentative connection with family and home life never becomes stronger than this. Although socially superior to "the passing poor," he shares his own roadside meals with them and avoids sustained engagement with the villages through which he passes (32). The speaker's uncertain relation to settled society, despite his economic security, draws energy from an important fact about the perceptions of revolutionary authorities: Wordsworth's foreign gentleman vagrant might seem as *sans état*, and as dangerous, as much poorer travelers. The experiences of agriculturalist and political moderate Arthur Young during a visit to France in the summer of 1789 – roughly the time of the Great Fear – provide a revealing example. Gathering material for his new book, Young found that his movements and his note-taking excited acute suspicion in the passport officers of the revolutionary government. Young's journals are replete with anecdotes of harassment and close escapes as at village after village he is accused of being a spy, not for the British government but (like the vagabonds of the Great Fear) for the extremely unpopular Marie Antoinette and the king's brother Artois. The language he uses to describe his tormentors' attitudes reflects that of the vagrancy laws; he knows that he is in trouble at one village when he overhears someone in a crowd surrounding him "say that I ought to be secured till somebody would give an account of me" (156). In another vignette, on 19 August 1789 Young records that he was roused from his sleep by a group of armed militia men who

> entered my chamber, surrounded my bed, and demanded my passport. A dialogue ensued, too long to minute; I was forced first to give them my passport, and, that not satisfying them, my papers [including letters of recommendation]. They told me that I was undoubtedly a conspirator with the Queen, the Count d'Artois, and the Count d'Antraigues (who has property here),

who had employed me as an *arpenteur*, to measure their fields, in order to double their taxes. My papers being in English saved me. They had taken it into their heads that I was not an Englishman – only a pretended one; for they speak such a jargon themselves, that their ears were not good enough to discover by my language that I was an undoubted foreigner.

(187)

Young's account underscores how revolutionary panic was fueled by pre-existing regionalism; speaking patois themselves, the guards do not even recognize the glaringly English accent behind Young's standard French. Being an alien – being English – "saves" Young because ironically the militia most fears its own countrymen. But as this anecdote shows, even what it means to be "English" (or French) is negotiable at this juncture, subject to interpretation that a passport does nothing to guide. Now, no one is "an undoubted foreigner," or an undoubted *anything*. In an atmosphere where nothing is taken at face value, the unrecognized appearance of the man on the move is the most menacing face at all.

In *Descriptive Sketches*, Wordsworth clarifies the political value, as well as the dangers, of a vagrant life. As the dedication intimates, the speaker can plumb the reductive deficiencies characteristic of cultural and political institutions and that also enable the paranoia Young struggles against. This insight comes to the fore early on when the speaker's travels take him along a perilous cliff-side path, where he imagines a cautious traveler seeking, and failing, to find reassurance in his Catholic faith.

> By cells whose image, trembling as he prays,
> Awe-struck, the kneeling peasant scarce surveys;
> Loose-hanging rocks the Day's bless'd eye that hide,
> And crosses rear'd to death on every side,
> Which with cold kiss Devotion planted near,
> And bending, water'd with the human tear ...

(254–9)

The poem's many footnotes indicating a point off the text's path are formal emblems of the vagrant's power to scrutinize established belief. Here, the frightened peasant tries to derive comfort from the contemplation of the small niches placed along the roadside housing holy images. But the cells, which a note states are "very common in Catholic countries," cannot erase the threat of overhanging rocks which might, at any moment, fall on the terrified peasant (2). A second note reinforces this possibility, explaining that the "Crosses [are] commemorative of the deaths of travelers by the fall of snow and other accidents very common along this dreadful road" (2). Though he wants to believe, the tokens of Catholicism cannot assuage the peasant's panic because they are ironic reminders of faith's failure. Others who knelt at the shrine have been blessed not with safe passage but with a fatal blow seemingly from heaven itself. The most the church can offer these victims is an impotent talisman, a cross along the path marking another instance of the church's own inadequacies to future travelers. The promise of resurrection remains suspended, and we are left certain only of an equation between Catholic dogma and the final motionlessness of mortality. Even the faithful who with the "cold kiss [of] Devotion" (257) plant the crosses seem corpse-like and sterile.

Similarly, before being thrust from their home by revolutionary troops, the monks of the desecrated Chartreuse live a sedentary life characterized by "death-like peace" (57). Like the millions of French aristocrats in Wordsworth's letter who cannot imagine political evolution, the monks at last are startled by the movements and actions of the soldiers, by the progress of history. After the occupation of the monastery, the exiled monks resemble apparitions who frighten others and are shocked by the vital sexuality they encounter in people: "Strong terror checks the female peasant's sighs, / And start th'astonish'd shades at female eyes" (64–5). Their isolation from female contact has transformed the members of the religious order into desexualized specters not at home in the world of the living. Yet if the downfall of that deceptive "Power whose frown severe / Tam'd sober Reason till she crouch'd in fear" should probably not be mourned, the poem does convey nostalgia – in this term's Greek root, literally a longing for home – for the lost religious order. An old fisherman weeps when he hears of the monastery's desecration, and the speaker himself sighs for the fate of the monks and admits he is "more pleased" by sights like Lake Como (80). Although he ultimately cannot countenance the deadening faith of the Chartreuse, its security nevertheless appeals to him. His ambivalence becomes explicit in a later description of ill pilgrims under the "delusion" that holy springs will cure them (689). The narrator does not share the pilgrim's faith that they have reached a place where pain ceases, but he "half wishes" he did (679). It is important to see these meditations about organized religion as something more than a naive reflection of British or the revolutionaries' hostility to the Church's wealth and power. The multifaceted response of the poem's vagrant narrator is not reducible to condemnation: he understands the lure of the Catholic faith even as he recognizes its flaws, an equivocation in keeping with the wanderer's ambivalent relation to a variety of cultural markers.[22]

If ideology functions as a kind of home, the home as a repository of its own ideology is scrutinized relentlessly in *Descriptive Sketches*. In isolated moments, family life seems to offer the intimacy, privacy and security that defined the happy home for the Georgian middle class and characterized the secure family of swans in *An Evening Walk*.[23] Home and the domestic affections, however, frequently are unstable and continually are under siege, imperiled by structural weaknesses within and attacks without. Wordsworth's own ambivalence about family life during these years amply is suggested by his desertion of Annette Vallon and his natural daughter Caroline. This episode represents evidence of a choice on Wordsworth's part to continue a life of improvised, gentlemanly vagrancy rather than marry his mistress and establish a home with her and their child. Despite his attachment to Vallon, Wordsworth put returning to London and publishing his work ahead of a full domestic commitment. In his examination of Wordsworth's early adulthood, Roe has contended that the poet came to see his return to England in 1792 as a betrayal of two great passions, Annette Vallon and the revolution itself (*Radical Years*, 41). Contemporary evidence that Wordsworth saw his acts in this way, however, has remained scant on the ground. Fred Randel has argued the reverse, that Wordsworth deserted his mistress to find "free space from an institution, in this case the *de facto* family which he had established in France rather than a church, state, or ideological camp" (389). The murkiness of Wordsworth's intentions in 1792 is borne out by his biographers' disagreements. Vallon's urgent letters to her lover in 1793 show Mary Moorman a woman "who not only loves but knows herself beloved" (181), a position Kenneth Johnston builds on by arguing that Wordsworth returned to France in the fall of 1793 to marry her. The best evidence for a return of some sort comes from the poet himself, who late in life told Carlyle he had seen Gorsas executed in October. Johnston argues that the "come-hither rhetoric" of Vallon's letters coupled with reports of the deteriorating political situation led Wordsworth to make for France (*Hidden*, 368). Johnston explains Wordsworth's apparent failure to arrive at Blois,[24] in spite of his ability to travel through Paris, to the heavy fighting along the Loire between republicans and counter-revolutionaries; he concludes that when we consider in Paris in 1820 both of Wordsworth's families met amicably, "William Wordsworth and Annette Vallon have few equals for constancy as lovers in the French Revolution ..." (296). Wordsworth's claim about Gorsas is of course powerful supporting evidence, but it remains impossible to tie such a trip to an intention to marry which, in any event, wasn't realized. Wordsworth's later behavior is also shaky evidence for his motivations in the early 1790s; on one hand, he assumed responsibility for Vallon and his daughter as soon as the 1802 peace enabled travel to France; on the other hand, this was a period in his life when Wordsworth's proposal to Mary Hutchinson argues that he had finally resolved to commit to the idea of marriage and starting a legitimate family, probably making evading responsibility for his *other* family seem increasingly unconscionable. As for Wordsworth's feelings in 1792–3, we are finally left only with Vallon's own letters, in which Stephen Gill for one senses desperation and a fear of abandonment, and the fact that Wordsworth did not marry her in 1792 when he resided in Orléans and Blois. Gill concludes that "Wordsworth did not marry Annette when he could have done, and, although she clearly expected that he would marry her in due course, the idea of doing so does not seem to have determined his behavior for very long" (*Wordsworth*, 65).

Once back in England, Wordsworth would write the radical pamphlet "A Letter to a Bishop of Llandaff," but his desire to affirm republican principles outright fell short of committing to publication of the tract.[25] The early biographer of Wordsworth's youth Émile Legouis perceives a connection between Wordsworth's abandonment of his French mistress and this reluctance to publicly assume a radical stance. Legouis attributes both these behaviors to what he calls Wordsworth's "cautious nature," adding cryptically that "his courage was of the passive rather than of the active kind" (34, 35). The unpublished letter to Llandaff explains that intermediate violence to liberty (or individuals) is sometimes necessary and justified in securing long-term freedom: "a time of revolution is not the season of true Liberty ... Alas! the obstinacy and perversion of men is such that she is too often obliged to borrow the very arms of despotism to overthrow him, and in order to reign in peace must establish herself by violence" (*Prose*, 1: 33). The poet's hesitation in marrying Vallon registers as a sacrifice for a similar end, and in this sense echoes the function of the homeless mother who dies in *An Evening Walk*. In 1794 revisions to this text, composed after Wordsworth's return to Britain and the beginning of the French wars, the homeless mother retains her position as a substitute for the speaker, who in the end still dreams of a home. But the revisions emphasize that the home is only a dream, to be shared with the childless "sister-wife" to whom the work is recommended. While it was important to have such an ambition, deferring that dream allowed for intervening possibilities of action and thought. Home meant self-forgetfulness and enclosure from the outside world, but it also meant obligation and sorrow.

Wordsworth's early doubts in his writings and behavior about embracing Cowper-style localism and domestic attachment will receive a more explicit rationale through 1794 changes to *An Evening Walk*. In the revised opening, the speaker's thoughts "that rise in mortal minds from mortal change" inspire a revealing interpretation of a scene of Grasmere schoolboys playing near the churchyard:

> What tribes of youth their gambols there have wrought
> Nor, in their freaks and wild mirth, ever thought
> How near their warm light motion was allied
> To the dull earth that [crumbled] at their side.
> Even now of that gay train who there pursue
> Their noisy sports with rapture ever new,
> There are to whom the buoyant heart proclaims
> Death has no power o'er their particular frames,
> As the light Spirits, the perpetual glee
> [ ] once proclaimed to me.

(43–52)

The freedom of the childhood perspective enables both spiritual vitality and physical movement. The relation between the boys' "freaks" and their "wild mirth" is reciprocal: movements generate high spirits and vice versa. In the original poem, the alternative to this activity was vaguely alluded to as the sundial's inexorable progress. In 1794, that metonymy is given full expression: the antithesis to "warm light motion" is the churchyard populated with dead bodies. The ideals of Georgian domesticity are implicated in this equation, for self is totally forgotten and safety is complete only when body and soul are beyond harm in the tomb. No amount of motion will deny that this is every human's eventual end; whether they recognize it or not, the boys' motions *are* allied with the bodily decay that goes on beneath their feet. At the same time, youthful energy, ambition, and movement dilate spaces constituting the continuum between living being and crumbling corpse. Like the behavior of the Georgian itinerant poor, the children's gambols occur outside of prescribed life patterns and structures of gain and responsibility.[26]

Descriptive Sketches casts light on these revisions, and Wordsworth's behavior concerning his mistress, when we consider that the text's Swiss landscapes are replete with images like that of the man who "hangs his small wood-hut upon the steeps," where "A zig-zag path from the domestic skiff / Thread[s] the painful cragg" of the cliff (294, 297–8). The isolation of one such place is so complete that its residents "never know / The face of traveller passing to and fro" (299–300), and "Their watch-dog ne'er his angry bark forgoes, / Touch'd by the beggar's moan of human woes …" (303–4). Guarded by a dog, this home seems to offer privacy and security against the vagabond rampages so feared by the French: no hungry or ill-tempered wanderer will disrupt this domestic peace. But its very isolation endangers the stability of this home and threatens its inhabitants' safety. The sketch's final image is of an anxious maid waiting up at night for her lover's return to their retreat at the top of a dangerous cliff face.

Throughout these later scenes, the maintenance of the domestic sphere requires acts that may lead to its destruction. The poem is filled with families who are either dismembered or about to be so. The reader never knows if the waiting maiden's love returns safely or not. The chamois chaser's dangerous trade takes him among the mountains, where his death will leave another family mutilated. A more positive, early scene, featuring a old man singing to his grandchildren before their cottage, again emphasizes the home's privacy, but the grandfather appears to have no wife, and the children, no mothers. Among the text's families, the particular absence of wives and mothers, an echo of Wordsworth's own childhood, is as ominous as it is unexplained; the only mother actually present in the poem is the Grison gypsy, who faces the elements with a babe in her arms but no husband in sight.

Perhaps the most pathetic evocation of the family's fragility comes from the mouth of an older father who describes how every "little cottage of domestic Joy" inevitably disintegrates (601). Even the most content family discovers the existence of a necessity that leads full-grown children to abandon their homes and rips apart the connections between parent and offspring. The loving parent is left alone, with only broken, "bleeding ties" reminding him of the lost, loved child (611).

> "For ever, fast as they of strength become
> To pay the filial debt, for food to roam,
> The father, forc'd by Powers that only deign
> That solitary Man disturb their reign,
> From his bare nest amid the storms of heaven
> Drives, eagle-like, his sons as he was driven,
> His last dread pleasure! Watches to the plain –
> And never, eagle-like, beholds again."

> (614–21)

The family, the primary transmitter of knowledge about survival, is an inherently contradictory entity: the affections it is predicated upon are disrupted when, the knowledge of survival passed on, one's children leave home. Of necessity, the son grows up and learns to fend for himself, and the parent's role in life is to fit the child for self-sufficiency. The culmination of this training, however, cripples the parent, since the love motivating the family's instruction defies attenuation. The son's departure from home sunders connections between parent and child, leaving the father in solitary grief. The home's promise of privacy, so often recalled by the sequestered settings for Swiss cottages in *Descriptive Sketches*, becomes only the privacy of the hermit, unknown and unattended. The absence of a wife for the dying man accentuates his isolation and the family's powerlessness over forces, like development and death, that dissolve it. In lines that follow, the speaker cements a connection between the home's self-destructive nature and homeless wandering. After leaving his home and family, the child will become a kind of professional vagrant: the young Swiss mercenary, an "exile" from his family and country, walks along the Seine (624). Mourning his departure through "bleeding Thoughts" and "the mortal tear" (627, 629), the child increasingly resembles his aged father:

"Strong poison not a form of steel can brave / Bows his young hairs with sorrow to the grave" (630–1). The result of the home and family's supposed stability is, ironically, chaos. The sorrowful young man, serving with other Swiss mercenaries in France, opens up a much larger frame for this pattern of estrangement than the individual home or family. This poem, so short on secure homes, is also populated with national exiles, including the speaker traversing the continent and the Grison gypsy. Lacking not only a home but a homeland, gypsies and their origins were being re-evaluated during the late eighteenth century. The traditional view that they came from Egypt was challenged in 1783 by German research maintaining that they actually had emigrated from India. By the early 1800s, representations of gypsies might draw on a grab bag of "exotic" Asian, and even British, characteristics (Garside, 154–62). The indeterminate origins and affiliation of gypsies are one manifestation of the vagrant's unsettling power; as the longtime exile's point of origin recedes into the past it can become unrecognizable, and the notion of a homeland ceases to provide a secure sense of identity or a consistent point of reference.

In *Descriptive Sketches*, this instability originates with the advent of human society itself. Discussing the myth of a prelapsarian Swiss golden age, in which "rock-honey flow'd" and "plants were wholesome, now of deadly taste" (477, 479), Wordsworth draws on Rousseau to argue for the fundamental contingency of the earliest culture.[27]

> Once Man was entirely free, alone and wild,
> Was bless'd as free – for he was Nature's child.
> He all superior but his God disdain'd,
> Walk'd none restraining, and by none restrain'd,
> Confess'd no law but what his reason taught,
> Did all he wish'd, and wish'd but what he ought.

(520–5)

The first man was a wanderer whose unrestrained movements enacted the irrelevance of social hierarchies and their laws, a view consonant with the historical belief, in both Britain and France, that vagrants threatened social and political order. Wordsworth's fascination with Switzerland owes a great deal to his perception of its vagrant origins, which transmitted a love of independence that gave centuries' worth of Swiss warriors the power to resist the imperial pretensions of their neighbors.

The end of this golden age marked the inauguration of institutions like the family, which restricted freedom and conferred responsibility. Wordsworth returns to the fragility of these institutions when he describes a peasant returning home after witnessing a mountain-top vision of glorious moments in Swiss military history. The sun sets and as the peasant descends to his cottage, his vision narrows to focus on "That hut which from the hills his eyes employs / So oft, the central point of all his joys" (570–1). No longer a representative of free-marching race, he is now a conscientious domestic provider. His obligations to and affections for his home and its occupants circumscribe his physical movements and structure his attention; out among the hills, his eyes always come back to the ground that is his. Fraught with gaps and burdens, though, this refuge reminds us that love of family and home can barely succeed in holding at bay the volatility that the vagrant's existence thrusts before our notice. In the peasant's hut, his father is "helpless as the babe he rocks," a condition that forces the peasant "Oft [to] descend to nurse the brother pair" (575–6). When the icy climate traps them in the hut, the peasant provider only "hears Winter, calling all his Terrors round" (580). The vignette shows how even participants in home life are "Condemn'd, in mists and tempests ever rife, / To pant slow up the endless Alp of life" (592–3). In the end, the peasant's settled life is described with the lexicon of the Grison gypsy. The precariousness of home life is reinforced by more familial dismemberment: the peasant's incapable old father, like the bitter, dying swain, lacks his wife. The infant he rocks seems to have no mother, and therefore the peasant, no spouse.

The mercenary is *Descriptive Sketches'* most potent emblem of the contingency of national loyalties and local affections. His services for sale to the highest bidder, the mercenary appears to have forfeited the obligations entailed and protections afforded by sustained involvement in community and nation; like the vagrant, he is *sans état*. If the Great Fear was "a rural revolt against the unknown itinerant" (Hufton, 208), the paranoia drew on an implied connection between the vagrant and the mercenary – peasants saw the marauders as hirelings of an aristocracy seeking to bring political upstarts to their knees. As the 1790s progressed, Swiss mercenaries would come to know the revolution's potential for amplifying the problematic valence of the vagrant soldier, as well as the vagrant. The fate of 600 luckless Swiss guards massacred in the Tuileries in August 1792 gruesomely illustrated how the mercenary could become the magnet for hysteria over counter-revolution.[28] Louis XVI's continued employment of foreigners, rather than countrymen, to guard his own person tainted him with the mercenary's pose of disinterestedness. The king's use of Swiss bodyguards divulged a fear of his own people, a fear that implied he might be his nation's enemy as much as its guardian. The geopolitical accompaniment to the mercenary's detachment, the famed Swiss neutrality, also become a casualty of France's drive to consolidate its borders and prepare for attack. The Swiss federation's attempts during 1792 to remain uninvolved in France's increasingly hostile relations with its continental neighbors gradually crumbled.[29] Geneva's government fell in 1792 to a revolution engineered by French operatives; in 1792–3 France seized a large part of the Bishopric of Basel. In 1798, the old confederation would be dissolved as French leaders created a "Helvetic republic" loyal to France (Thürer, 83–5). Switzerland's assertion of neutrality was denied and its position reshaped into a political and military alignment that reduced it to a more legible cipher on the map of European power politics.

In offering Swiss mercenaries as the modern-day descendants of early Swiss patriots, Wordsworth ventures a definition of patriotism informed by contradiction and ambivalence. The footnotes to *Descriptive Sketches* remind us that the glorious medieval struggles for Swiss freedom were part of a bygone past. By the late eighteenth century, several cantons were as oppressive as their despotic European neighbors, and many of Rousseau's countrymen followed him to France where the political climate was more tolerant of democratic discussion.[30] The mercenary, heir to the old legacy of martial prowess, has been reduced to fighting for someone else's interests. The text draws attention to the erratic, idiosyncratic nature of Swiss loyalty that results from this situation, loyalty that led panicking revolutionaries to see their mortal enemies in the Louvre's foreign guards. In a note on the condition of the mercenaries, Wordsworth explains that "the effect of the famous air called in French Ranz des Vaches upon the Swiss troops removed from their native country is well known, as also the injunction of not playing it on pain of death, before the regiments of that nation, in the service of France and Holland" (100). Hearing a native song, a trope with obvious implications for poetry, can undermine the mercenary's tenuous loyalty to his foreign employer, placing the pull of homeland in a competition with the power of money. The despair that descends when the Swiss hear this melody may not testify to the energy or ambition necessary to engineer the counter-revolution feared by the Parisian crowd. On the other hand, the Swiss malaise also hardly seems consonant with a vigorous or consistent defense of revolutionary policy and principles.[31] The Swiss have achieved fame as unparalleled soldiers for hire, yet this fame paradoxically has its roots in battles for the freedom of the Swiss people, and the Swiss alone. The Swiss are effective mercenaries only as long as they can construe the distance between mercenary and patriot as a continuum rather than an opposition – only as long as they can downplay the conflicts between two essentially different political identities. By calling attention to the strains of this construct, Wordsworth draws out the tragedy of modern Swiss life. The category of the mercenary, like that of the vagabond, becomes a cultural battleground of contested meanings and loyalties.

Also in the background behind the Swiss mercenaries sketched in Wordsworth's poem was the British practice of employing continental mercenaries throughout the eighteenth century. The Whig abhorrence of a standing army meant that at any given moment, the British army was far too small to successfully prosecute the wars necessary to attain Georgian policy objectives. The British had used large numbers of mercenaries in the War of the Spanish Succession and the Seven Years War, but this practice drew national and international publicity during the unsuccessful attempt to retain the American colonies. The internal nature of the dispute made it particularly difficult to cloak mercenary treaties as mutually advantageous foreign policy alliances, a tactic that had sugared the pill for all concerned on previous occasions. Finally the British turned to the Germans, particularly the Hessians, who alone promised to supply 12 000 men on terms that, as the protracted debate in the Lords showed, took full advantage of British desperation (Mockler, 105–29). While the Hessians appear to have performed well in what combat they saw, many went reluctantly: some soldiers had been kidnapped by recruiters, and even among poor volunteers lured by the pay, the pain of separation from family, community, and nation was evident. In a parallel to Wordsworth's image of the Swiss by the Seine, one eyewitness reported "numerous teenage soldiers weeping as they marched off to war" (Ingrao, 143), and as the British defeat in the colonies became certain, desertions mounted into the thousands. It was the potential for this kind of unstable loyalty, coupled with the modern state's desire to assert growing control over citizens through required military service, that would signal the gradual end of widespread mercenary armies in Europe in the nineteenth century.[32]

Ultimately, figures like the mercenary and the homeless wanderer unsettle the authority not only of royalty but of revolutionaries as well. Blazing with a hope that emanates revolutionary sympathy in the eyes of many editors and critics of Wordsworth,[33] the text's ending lines predict "a lovely birth" from the "innocuous flames" that will be the republican impulse as it sweeps throughout Europe (782). Monarchs who claim to stem the rising tide of liberty's leveling waves will be "swept in their anger from th' affrighted shore … to rise no more" (808–9). Political apocalypse will have metaphysical dimensions: the earth will begin anew when "Nature, as in her prime, her virgin reign / Begins" (784–5). But in writing and publishing for money in the literary marketplace,[34] the mercenary poet's own political allegiance proves nearly as enigmatic as that of the Swiss warrior. For all its emphasis on radical change and development, this "revolutionary" faith appears literally only to bring us full circle, recalling the attitudes of the recalcitrant French aristocracy in Wordsworth's letters. The text offers up less a progression than an impossible return to a previous point in history. The viability of this view seems nominal in light of the peculiarly "pulseless hand" of Wordsworth's "unbreathing Justice" (786–7). Justice may be beyond the emotions that cloud human judgment, or she may simply be as lifeless as the Catholic monks earlier likened to ghosts. Insofar as revolutionary government will succeed, it seems no more flexible than the despotism it supplants.

The poem's final lines are the best evidence of this reading. In considering the portion of the text, commentators have emphasized the revolutionary confidence to the exclusion of the lines that cap it.

> To night, my friend, within this humble cot
> Be the dead load of mortal ills forgot,
> Renewing, when the rosy summits glow
> At morn, our various journey, sad and slow.

(810–13)

This concluding moment unexpectedly places the revolutionary creed just enunciated on the level of a beautiful, comforting, but insubstantial fantasy. Just as eighteenth-century alpine lovers are "Heedless how Pliny, musing here, survey'd / Old Roman boats and figures thro' the shade," current dreams of revolutionary triumph extending across Europe may pass away unremembered by distant generations (116–17). The Revolution's incompatible promises of reform and return to a time without taint must yield to the fact that the type of human history and experience is the unpredictable course of the gypsy's caravan, from which no one escapes except through the ephemeral dreams of sleep or the passing imaginings of consciousness.

The concomitant beginnings of the French Terror and the British government's increasingly virulent conservatism would underscore the striking similarities in outlook and method in two opposed regimes. In both countries, governments came to refuse the public's range of political beliefs by trying to coerce an unquestioning loyalty that could not be won voluntarily. *Descriptive Sketches* anticipates these efforts and in its representations of vagrancy foresees their failure. The 1793–4 revisions to *An Evening Walk* further assert the significance of wandering life through renewed assessment of the price of political conviction, an assessment that will occupy Wordsworth's poetry for much of the 1790s. In these revisions, Wordsworth returns to homelessness as a mode of existence because it is preferable to the sacrifices that, ancients and moderns agree, alone can ensure political stability. Through an allusion to Horace's ode to the Bandusian Spring (*Odes*, III, 13), Wordsworth explains why such sacrifices are considered necessary: only an animal sacrifice, Horace states, can preserve the spring's status as a peaceful resting place for travelers. The spilled blood of a goat appeases the gods and safeguards the spring from divine vengeance:

> To-morrow shall a kid be thine,
> …
> For he shall pour his crimson blood
> To stain, bright Spring, thy gelid flood,
> Nor e'er shall seek the wanton herd again.
> Thee Sirius smites not from his raging star;
> Thy tempting gloom a cool repose
> To many a vagrant herd bestows
> And to faint oxen weary of the share.[35]

In connecting the spring's status as a place of rest to sacrifice, Horace's ode reflects the trajectory of the Roman state during his lifetime. The civil war ignited by Julius Caesar's assassination ended when Octavian emerged as the victor over his former partner and chief rival for power, Mark Antony. Romans paid for the prosperous peace that followed when Octavian – now Augustus – used the forms of republicanism to consolidate his own hold on power. Although Horace himself had started out as an officer in Brutus' army, after his commander's defeat he became an eloquent and vocal apologist for Augustan absolutism. Horace in the end was a political pragmatist who used his talents to support "the regime that ended political freedom in Rome and transformed it from an open to a closed society" (Mulroy, 14). The Bandusian ode essentially justifies the brutal means by which rulers like Augustus come to power. In return for the republic's demise, he provided political stability and economic prosperity.

The ethic of sacrifice became crucial both to French regimes invoking Roman models and to their reactionary British enemies. Revisions in 1794 to *An Evening Walk* do not explicitly address the political implications of such maneuvering, but the Horatian allusion grounds a refusal to accept any stability paid for by violence and tyranny. Rejecting Horace's sacrifice, Wordsworth favors the vagrant's unstable cultural position instead of the overbearing conviction characterizing radicals and conservatives alike. He incorporates the language of Horace into his own description of a secluded Lakeland stream:

> And if thy rocky footway not allows
> To vagrant herds the sweets of cool repose,
> May never man thy peaceful glooms explore
> Without a virtuous wish unfelt before.

> (139–42)

These lines imply an awareness that by not, in the poem, offering a blood sacrifice, the speaker has forfeited the wooded retreat as a place of repose. The poet's reward in observing the stream becomes moral goodness predicated on the cost of refusing peace. The stream and its confines are still available, but only to the exploring wanderer. Similarly, at the end of *Descriptive Sketches*, the refusal of the certainties afforded by sacrifice leaves us with the flexibility, as well as the trauma, of a homeless existence. The wanderer's power to diagnose, and in some measure evade, collective illusion and the stagnation of political tyranny explains Wordsworth's decision to employ homeless protagonists when he comes to engage England's own political climate in the Salisbury Plain poems.

2

Salisbury Plain and the Recuperation of Freedom

When Wordsworth returned to Britain in 1792, the marginality embodied by the homeless had come under unique and extreme pressure. Throughout the volatile 1790s, the crown would work to polarize all political discourse into the categories of radical or conservative – traitorous or loyalist. The Pitt ministry struggled to define virtually all government opposition as sedition or treason. Yet the government's many critics advocated various shadings of change, ranging from parliamentary reform to revolution, that strained against the authorities' simplifying agenda, and in key trials English juries defended the right to disagree with aspects of government policy or structure. Representations of the homeless in Wordsworth's "Salisbury Plain" explore the polyvalent social and legal status, not only of vagrancy itself, but also of the varieties of political expression under attack during the poem's composition. The female vagrant's history underscores the injustice of laws labeling her a criminal vagabond by casting her as a victim of powerful political and economic forces. The vagrant and her male companion also indirectly defend an embattled political middle ground, criticizing a conservative government that would lump all reform with revolution. Ultimately the poem views radical and reactionary rhetoric alike with subtle skepticism, implying that these two agendas can be equally restrictive and dogmatic.[1] The female vagrant's homelessness further enables her to evade another kind of tyranny, identified through Burke with the Tory political program: the destructive submersion of individual identity in inflexible, gender-based roles that Wordsworth associates with domestic life.

By the mid-1790s, the crown had enacted new laws and was developing a more sophisticated spying network to silence its critics. Wordsworth's revised poem – "Adventures on Salisbury Plain" – acknowledges the increasingly oppressive political climate by burdening its male character, now a sailor, with responsibility for a murder and the load of crippling guilt. By internalizing traditional legal prohibitions, the sailor cannot offer the female vagrant the companionship so comforting to her in the original "Salisbury Plain." The female vagrant herself now feels guilt over her wandering life and rejects the society offered by a band of homeless burglars. Where "Salisbury Plain" documents the tenuous but significant development of community even among the homeless, "Adventures" shows how fear of the state undermines the capability to form emotional ties. The vagrant thieves' communal presence in this revision is a lone indication that representations of homelessness still potentially blur legal distinctions enabling polarization in British political discourse.

A PASSING GRADE: VAGRANT EXAMINATION IN "SALISBURY PLAIN"

As Wordsworth composed "Salisbury Plain," the British government was moving to make such polarization the organizing feature of political life.[2] By the mid-1790s, the aristocracy's anxieties extended beyond the well-documented paranoia over political organizing among tradesmen: economic woes gave the ruling classes reason to fear more than the corresponding societies wielding their copies of Paine. The working and itinerant poor already had suffered from inflation and bad harvests early in the decade. Misery only intensified when the long war with France began in January 1793. Traditionally, wars had spurred the economy and decreased crime, but for the first time in the century, war aggravated the economic crisis. Severe recessions in 1793 and 1794 meant higher bread prices and still more inflation; the crime rate soared.[3] Conflict with revolutionary France brought trade disruption and heavy taxes in addition to political agitation and anti-war protests, creating intense friction within British society and creating an "apocalyptic" atmosphere (Wells, "English Society," 189).

The crown combated its diverse challengers by broadening the categories of political crime, lumping together and simplifying the often disparate motives behind trade unionism, food riots, anti-war protests and organizing for reform. This response reflected Pitt's hostility to any position not readily intelligible through a political prism neatly separating the blended complexity of people's views into radicalism and conservatism. Throughout the war, the quest for such a prism would distract Pitt's ministry, which employed an army of spies and informers to identify seditionaries and lobbied for the power to imprison them indefinitely. As early as 1791, Edmund Burke told a weeping Charles James Fox on the floor of the Commons that his continued praise of the French experiment meant their friendship was over; occurring during Wordsworth's first visit to London, the dramatic Burke/Fox split "signaled that men of good will could no longer agree to disagree on the significance of the French Revolution, but would have to take stands that broke old patterns of proper behavior…" (Johnston, *Hidden*, 255). Increasingly during the 1790s, every kind of expression was to be classified as either loyalist or traitorous, leaving little maneuvering room for critics of the government. This explains why "the government consistently but mistakenly confounded … reformist ambitions with revolutionary plots" (Roe, *Radical Years*, 32), beginning with the Royal Proclamation Against Seditious Writings, issued in May 1792 and reiterated in December.[4] As a result, in 1793 there were more prosecutions for seditious words and libel, at least 41, than in any other year in the 1790s. Stepped-up surveillance of reforming organizations led to further restrictions. News from royal spies, who had been infiltrating the London Corresponding Society since 1792, was by 23 May 1794 sufficiently damning for Pitt to suspend Habeas Corpus. For the prime minister, the most provocative information, reported by Parliament's Committee on Secrecy, was the reformers' plan to hold a "convention." The Committee's very decision to use this term demonstrates how easily calls for expanding the franchise could be represented as something far more extreme: Clive Emsley observes that the word "'convention' was guaranteed to provoke ministerialists and loyalists, for while there were precedents for such discussion in England, they were … never popular with Parliament: only a year before, moreover, the National Convention in France had executed a king" ("Repression", 808).

The most prominent and immediate casualties of this paranoia were Thomas Hardy of the London Corresponding Society, John Horne Tooke of the Society of Constitutional Information, and lecturer John Thelwall, all of whom were arrested in early May. But although the suspension of Habeas Corpus gave authorities more time to marshal evidence before charging these men, the crown as yet failed to convince juries that all reformers really aimed for insurrection. The Attorney-General began Hardy's trial with a nine-hour speech in which he argued that the planned convention would have led to the usurpation of sovereignty by reform societies, followed by the king's resistance and possible death. This line of thinking proved too circuitous for jurors, who failed to see how supporting more broad-based popular sovereignty would necessitate laying hands on George III. After closely followed trials, Hardy, Horne Tooke, and Thelwall were acquitted, and others arrested but never charged were released in the fall.[5]

The government's assault on the ideological deviations of reformers was part of a wider attack on unsanctioned mobility that percolated down into the vexed domain of the vagrancy acts. In an era when the circulation of people as well as ideas was of unusually great concern, the crown moved to eliminate irregularities in the enforcement of the law. Traditionally associated with insurrection, unsupervised vagrant subjects were as dangerous as seditious, wandering minds.[6] As with treason, in the 1790s the aristocracy struggled to resolve ambiguous perceptions of the homeless into a consistent, clear government policy. This view explains why in the very busy year of 1792, the year of the Royal Proclamation Against Seditious Writings, the government found time to tighten procedures governing repression of vagrancy. Citing "misconduct and negligence of the constables," Parliament made its last determined effort to have vagrants physically punished (quoted in Ribton-Turner, 212). New legislation allowed justices of the peace to order a master of the house of correction, rather than a potentially unreliable constable, to deal with homeless offenders.[7] In reassigning tasks from the amateur constable to the paid master, this legislation anticipates the aim of modern professional policing to standardize the discretionary judgments of its decentralized predecessors (Foucault, *Power/Knowledge*, 41). If the JP punished by imprisonment rather than whipping, the vagrant had to be incarcerated for at least seven days, and no one was to receive any reward until punishment had been administered (Webb, 381–2). This was the first time a minimum sentence for vagrancy had ever been specified by Parliament, and the act as a whole aimed "to bring the discretionary powers of the magistrates themselves under stricter statutory control" (Rogers, 143). This legislation was accompanied by the other laws designed to restrict mobility, in particular the Middlesex Justice Bill (1792), which broadened the reach of professional police in London and justified arrest as a vagrant based on suspicion rather than proof of an illegal act, and the Alien Act (1793), which authorized surveillance of émigrés and other suspect persons.[8]

At this time, Wordsworth would have had personal reasons for being conscious of a relation between dispossession and surveillance by the ruling classes. The Wordsworth children's protracted lawsuit against Sir James Lowther for their father's estate had as yet yielded little besides an increase in the family's fear of him: the Wordsworths believed he was spying on them. On 23 May 1794, Richard Wordsworth wrote his brother William concerning the case against the earl. After registering his dismay at the court costs of the seemingly endless affair, Richard concludes: "I have always avoided writing and speaking upon this subject, because His Lordship has so many Spies in every part of the country" (*Early Years*, 121). Believing he and his siblings were being observed, Richard concludes by advising William to burn the letter when he had finished reading it. Though they could sue for their inheritance, the Wordsworth children had little defense against Lowther's sizeable retinue of informants. Wordsworth did not follow his brother's advice, obviously. But Richard Wordsworth's fears recall the political repressions of the mid-1790s and the aristocracy's longstanding suspicion of the itinerant poor. According to Richard, Sir James felt the ungrateful children of his dead employee required as much surveillance as any pauper who might make a spurious claim on the parish poor rate. In addition, Lowther's political influence had been instrumental in Pitt's ascent to the prime ministry in the 1780s. Lowther chose 24 May 1784, the same day he was rewarded by Pitt for his support through elevation to the earldom of Lonsdale, as the day when the legal agent who replaced John Wordsworth would demand from the Wordsworths the keys to the Cockermouth mansion of the poet's early childhood. The conjunction of these two events effectively conflated the poet's orphanhood and homelessness with the consolidation of Pitt's political power. Wordsworth had other connections to Pitt that were not hostile, though by the early 1790s they probably seemed almost equally oppressive. Pressure for Wordsworth to follow the track to curate in his studies at Cambridge came from, among others, two uncles closely linked to the conservatives: William Cookson had been a preceptor to George III's sons, and electioneer Jack Robinson by the 1780s "was the king's chief go-between in his relations with Parliament, and had already demonstrated his usefulness to Pitt" (Johnston, *Hidden*, 113). The weight of his family's expectations about his career was

profoundly intertwined with its investment in the ruling conserva-
tive political establishment.

As William and Dorothy Wordsworth were working on the fair
copy of "Salisbury Plain" at Windy Brow, the Tories were attempt-
ing to consolidate control over wayward vagrants as well as upstart
reformers. These two sequences of action intersect in the poem's
defense of free speech and association. The importance of such
rights amid economic turmoil and legal repression emerges as a
vagrant tells her story to a traveler while the two people walk the
road. Like the juries who acquitted leading reformers, parish
officials soon disregarded the new vagrancy decrees as they had
done in the past (Webb, 382). The public's stubborn ambivalence
toward the homeless and the reform movement suggests why
"Salisbury Plain" offers a vagrant woman as the everyperson of a
decade when constitutional freedoms increasingly were restricted.
The female vagrant affirms the existence and power of marginal
social states by interrogating the basis of laws outlining the bound-
aries of sedition as well as vagrancy. Her situation, both pathetic
and empowering, grounds a critique of a corrupt ruling class while
undermining Parliament's assumption that homelessness, and the
physical and psychic mobility associated with it, clearly are degen-
erate states. Instead, "Salisbury Plain" offers the female vagrant's
marginal condition as a way to recoup the freedoms being eroded
under Pitt, and by the extension criticizes the desire for determined
oversight that some radical philosophy and government initiatives
shared. In this context, it is instructive to bear in mind the form of
the vagrancy pass. Like the parish document, the opening and
closing stanzas of "Salisbury Plain" use principles and general
orders as framing devices for a consideration of the vagrant at hand.
The final stanza, complete with its commands to the "Heros of
Truth" to drag their opponents before the presence of authority,
even recalls past specifications as to the constable's actions.[9]
However, the center of "Salisbury Plain," what we figuratively
might call the examination of this woman, challenges the
definitions of vagrancy law and the government delineating them.

At the outset, the poem's conversation between a man and a
homeless woman appears to conform to the government's examina-
tion format. That rubric would have a socially elevated, usually
male, interrogator – a justice of the peace or a man of feeling – ques-
tion a vagrant as to her or his origins and prospects. But the woman
has not been arrested, and the man is not a representative of

authority after all. He appears to be another homeless person, who "had withered young in sorrow's deadly blight" (405). He does not begin by questioning the female vagrant; rather, he startles her out of sleep in an isolated spital in which he also has sought shelter. He then offers her solace:

> …when that shape with eyes in sleep half-drowned
> By the moon's sullen lamp she scare discerned,
> Cold stony horror all her senses bound.
> But he to her low words of cheering sound
> Addressed. With joy she heard such greeting kind
> And much they conversed of that desert ground,
> Which seemed to those of other worlds consigned
> Whose voices still they heard as paused the hollow wind.
>
>   (155–62)

The class-based hierarchy underlying the vagrant examination is replaced with kind words that banish the woman's disabling fear. Her "Cold stony horror" results from the gothic story she associates with the shelter, in which a traveler's horse unearths the head of a newly murdered body. This vignette tells of hidden crimes coming to light. The more immediate crime for the hiding vagrant, however, is the fact of her homelessness, and the "cold stony horror" she feels upon awakening reflects the physical and mental paralysis the vagrancy and sedition laws are designed to induce. In the ensuing encounter, paralysis is supplanted by the joy of animated human contact. Intimacy rapidly develops, in part because the backdrop of ruins and ghostly voices emphasizes how much, as living beings, the main characters have in common. The course of the human exchange comes to be guided only by individual desires and needs. The unrestricted nature of their conversation becomes pronounced as the woman describes provincial landowning tyranny, the macabre willingness of military recruiters to capitalize on lower-class deprivation, and the indifference of local authorities to her plight. Such criticisms could have qualified as sedition by the crown during the poem's composition.[10] But her words are hard to judge because the woman is also a victim, whose wrenching situation results from the very political events and economic changes on which she comments. The physical and psychic mobility of the protagonists makes it possible for them to articulate these blunt words.

The relentless "horizontality" of Wordsworth's plain has led Geoffrey Hartman to call it "a no-place," or an "omphalos, a strait between worlds" (120–3). As they pause in their wanderings at a ruined shelter in an endless, unpopulated waste, the political spies and parish overseers who would police this moment are far away.[11]

This moment of fellowship, unsupervised by social superiors, defies eighteenth-century literary protocol as well as the laws. Mary Jacobus has detailed how Wordsworth's work "constitutes an assault on [the] lack of engagement" displayed by magazine poets writing about the itinerant poor (*Tradition*, 185). Even compassionate portraits of the homeless usually show them as isolated figures viewed by a speaker of higher standing. Typical in this regard is Thomas Moss' "The Beggar" (1769). A popular poem much anthologized in the eighteenth century, "The Beggar" is the monologue of a vagrant appealing to a middle-class spectator for money. Standing at the spectator's door, the man explains how his request for aid has been denied at the big house: "A pampered menial forced me from the door / To seek a shelter in a humbler shed" (15–16). He then pleads for a night's shelter against the bitter winter wind, like the woman of "Salisbury Plain" vaguely attributing his troubles to an "oppression" that has killed his livestock, destroyed his crops, and forced him from his home (31). These events have hastened the disintegration of his family; his daughter has been seduced, abandoned, and is herself a vagrant, and his wife died of grief as the family declined. Moss's description is sympathetic, leaving little doubt of the authenticity of the man's claims and the depth of his need. His homeless pauper, however, remains cut off from any society except that of the people he begs from. A related stance emerges in Christopher Smart's "Pray Remember the Poor" (*Hymns for the Amusement of Children*, 1771), which uses the act of giving charity to validate the middle class's generosity. The little boy who gives a penny to a poor criminal in prison is praised by his parents for his kindness, reducing the recipient of alms to an object testifying to another's moral worth. As William Blake remarks in "The Human Abstract" (*Songs of Experience*, 1794), this attitude perversely implies that some people must be kept miserable so that other's attempts to alleviate suffering can verify their goodness: "Pity would be no more, / If we did not make somebody poor" (1–2).[12]

Robert Southey's poems about the poor during the 1790s, among the most radical of their time, are powerful condemnations of war and its impact on the poor. They, too, show the needy alone, in life and death, struggling unsuccessfully to make the wealthy realize what are essentially paternal obligations. In Southey's 1797 *Poems*, "The Widow" is a vagrant woman straggling along a roadside on a snowy night. A rich person's chariot passes by but those inside it do not heed her pleas that "I had a home once – I had a husband – / Pity me, strangers" (15–16)! The poem concludes with a nameless traveler finding the woman's body the next morning amid the drifts. This subject surfaces again in "The Soldier's Wife," in which a homeless woman walking with her children strongly resembles the homeless mother of *An Evening Walk*. The speaker of "The Pauper's Funeral" describes how even the deaths of poor people fail to draw attention to their plight. Southey's "Botany Bay Eclogues," a collection set in the penal colony, are unusual in showing the poor talking among themselves of the horrors of military service and life during wartime. These conversations, however, differ from Wordsworth's "Salisbury Plain" in that they occur only in a prison context. Southey and other authors seem incapable of imagining the itinerant poor as independent agents experiencing a brief sense of community among themselves.

Wordsworth's male traveler offers the female vagrant comfort a second time when she recalls how sickness and fighting destroyed her family in America. The traveler calls her to look at the sunrise, "far other scene" from the "weary night so ruinous" they have both witnessed (334–5). While she gazes on the dawn, "her comrade to her pensive chear / Tempered sweet words of hope ... " (341–2). What is striking in both instances where the traveler offers comfort is the untold quality of his speech. Not only are the aloof questions or imposing pronouncements of an interrogating JP or the treason trials denied to us. These utterances are supplanted by words that remain part of a a private exchange between two people, beyond the transcriptive and regulating functions of official or even aesthetic documents like Wordsworth's poem. In the poem's early revisions, the woman finds that no language can fully articulate the depth and complexity of her experience: "She wept; – because she had no more to say / Of that perpetual weight which on her spirit lay" (ASP, 557–8).[13] The privacy of her exchange with the traveling man is made possible by the status of its participants – like the ghostly voices indistinctly understood, their status as vagrant speakers literally makes it difficult to pin them down. The conflicting responses the text engenders frees this moment of interaction from binding restrictions or expectations. In this space, the speakers are free to move, feel and talk as they like. We only gain access to the man's speech through his intentions and the emotional effects his words produce in his companion.

In this conversation, the examination mode of presenting the homeless used in the vagrant pass is supplanted by a form of storytelling.[14] Both examination and storytelling convey information, perhaps even the same information. Examination grows out of an ethic of detached surveillance; storytelling assumes an environment of engaged exchange. Examination implies an unequal distribution of power and a set of norms which the respondent may have accepted, but has not helped to create. The voluntary act of storytelling depends on a shared sense of emotional potential and involves personal motives. Both storytelling and examination assume the listener has an interest; however, examination asks certain questions and seeks certain answers. Thus, royal decrees defined a vagrant as someone "not giving a good account of himself." There is no right answer to this woman's story; it is just things as they are. Her narrative accommodates a wide range of content and responses. Examination, geared to support a specific ideology, occurs in a courtroom or an official's home. Storytelling occurs when ideology collides with conflicting social realities, for example on the open road or in a temporary shelter.

The encounter of "Salisbury Plain" is important, then, because it briefly creates a healing, communal feeling between two figures. The female vagrant's need to tell her story is expressed in such term: "Gently the Woman gan her wounds unbind" (203). We may not know the traveler's words of cheer, but we perceive his feeling at the narrative's conclusion: "human sufferings and that tale of woe / Had dimmed the traveler's eye with Pity's tear…" (399–402). The final stanzas documenting their arrival at a cottage strongly imply that, after a meal, the two will separate; they remain at the end a "friendless hope-forsaken pair" (415). Such separation, while painful, is an unavoidable counterpart to their moment of intimacy. Like the homeless today, for Wordsworth's vagrants their fundamental anonymity makes the exchange possible. As the treason and sedition trials of the 1790s illustrated, prolonged knowledge and association establish the grounds for surveillance, accusation, and imprisonment.[15]

The irrelevant tyranny of a national imperative that privileges physical stability or limits expression is reinforced by the woman's final question in "Salisbury Plain":

Three years a wanderer round my native coast,
My eyes have watched yon sun declining tend
Down to the land where hope to me was lost:
And now across this waste my steps I bend:
Oh! Tell me wither, for no earthly friend
Have I, no house in prospect but the tomb.

(388–93)

Her ignorance even of where she is going, an ignorance her male companion may share, emphasizes the futility of a legal structure designed around where she is settled. Chance moments of conversation and provisional identification with another individual are, for the purposes of the poem, a character's settlement. These ephemeral moments of unpremeditated interchange are the only kind of "homes" the homeless or perhaps anyone can be sure of, regardless of what the social framework dictates. Such encounters also may be the only type of exchange permitting a spectrum of views and destinations.

BOUND AND DETERMINED: THE CAPTIVITY OF THE DOMESTIC

The prehistoric validation for this sort of encounter occupies the poem's opening stanzas; a savage, "naked and unhouzed" and with only a "fenceless bed" (1, 9), gathers strength from his isolating condition and the general lack of developed society. The perspective offered here has important affinities with the ideas of Godwin, as well as Rousseau; throughout "Salisbury Plain," the poet implies that society has gone rotten.[16] A comparison with such contemporary thinkers, however, misses how truly radical Wordsworth's position is. Godwin and Rousseau both offer systems of change and reform that would remold society from within. While one cannot return to the original state of nature, one can proceed by establishing a new social contract or work for reforms that will in time render the state superfluous. Wordsworth, in contrast, implies that any systematic reform predicated on existing extended, organized communities is doomed. The opening stanzas, repeatedly emphasizing that the fortunate savage was "without home" (6), conclude that any dealings with "the deep / Of social life" inevitably lead to misery and oppression (32–3). As in *Descriptive Sketches*, ideology, even a democratic ideology of change, has few prospects. Only in individual moments of human contact, which are now best epitomized by associations among vagrants, can even a splintered sense of personal freedom and fulfillment reside.

The most damaging overtly confronted ideologies in "Salisbury Plain" concern the family and the home. The fact that the female vagrant's mother died giving birth to her daughter hints at how the family cannibalizes its members. The daughter's fruitless enslavement to a domestic ideal and her powerlessness within the conventional family structure combine to imprison her. From the beginning of her narrative, it is clear that she is tortured by memories of her lost childhood home. Her account obsessively details the physical comforts and activities that defined that environment. She watched her father shepherd the family flocks; she had a garden and hens; she owned a spinning wheel and cooked the meals. Although the loss occurred years ago, her attachment to this life and place remains an undiminished source of agony, as her refrain, "Can I forget" (235, 244, 262), demonstrates. The crippling obsession of her memories suggests that her view is somehow skewed. Other evidence reveals that her attachments are pathetic rather than admirable. For example, although she cannot see it, her own fixation mirrors that of the very landowner she loathes, a point that becomes clearer in the early revisions of "Salisbury Plain." The original poem is vague as to what causes the loss of her father's land and fishing rights – it is simply "Oppression" (57). In the revised poem, the owner of a nearby "mansion proud" conspires to ruin her father (ASP, 300).

> ... cottage after cottage owned [the mansion's] sway
> No joy to see a neighboring house, or stray
> Through pastures not his own, the master took;
> My Father dared his greedy wish gainsay;
> He loved his old hereditary nook,
> And ill could I the thought of such sad parting brook.

> (ASP, 301–6)

There are obvious, important differences between the attitude of the mansion owner and that of the female vagrant and her father.[17] The latter live content to be part of a community of equals; the mansion owner desires only to dominate his neighbors, if he must have neighbors at all. The master is a newly rich upstart. The woman's family has lived in her home for generations.

Yet these differences do not define all that is at stake here. The situation may well be unjust or tragic. But the rigidity of the woman and her father in meeting this crisis, the stubborn attachment to their "hereditary nook," only makes things worse. As the fate of other cottagers shows, it is a battle the family cannot win, at least not on the terms it has chosen to fight. In the face of a fierce desire to acquire land, the father can only counter with an equally dogmatic determination not to sell. When the revisions inform us that the father refuses "proffered gold" for his estate, it is hard not to question the wisdom of his decision (ASP, 307). A more elastic, accommodating view, such as that elsewhere identified with vagrancy itself, ironically might have spared his family the pain of actual homeless poverty. Searching for a new home for her family, the female vagrant marries a youthful lover who has been forced by his own father to "a distant town" to ply a trade (280). She and her husband have three children before, once again, an attachment to domestic ideals creates a fatal inflexibility in the face of hardship. War creates unemployment, and the family falls on hard times. Yet, striving to be the model provider, her spouse "could not beg" (304). He prefers instead to try to eke out a living by fighting the American colonists, despite the strenuous objections of his wife – "my prayers and tears were vain" (304). As a result, every family member except the female vagrant perishes in one year.

Her story implies that women suffer most in family structures that ignore dependents' personal inclinations. In Georgian society, a complex network of parents, relatives and neighbors all defined acceptable community behavior. But within the family, husbands were, of course, the ultimate authority. Even the rise of the so-called companionate marriage, growing out of the seventeenth century's rejection of patriarchal government, did little to improve women's standing. In the end, "successful marriage depended on the docility and adaptability of the woman, as it had always done in the past …" (Stone, 249). Only the wealthiest married women could expect any legal acknowledgment: before the law, wives and their children were the property of their husbands.[18] Burke went on to make the patriarchal family the linchpin in his crusade against revolution: "To be attached to the subdivision, to love the little platoon we belong to in society, is the first principle (the germ as it were) of public affections. It is the first link in the series by which we proceed towards a love to our country and to mankind" (135). This position explains the vilification of figures like Mary Wollstonecraft, whose unnatural interest in female rights and parliamentary reform confirmed Burke's connection of female subservience with the political status quo.[19]

In more theoretical terms, Judith Lowder Newton has pointed out the paradox of women's newly realized place as managers of the eighteenth-century domestic sphere. In the late eighteenth and nineteenth centuries, conduct manuals increasingly differentiated women's "influence" from men's "power" or "ability." The rise of "influence" as a doctrine was caught up with the emergence of a more flexible social structure. As the effects of industrialization spread, middle-class men increasingly worked out of the home at publicly visible, salaried jobs. Tracts on female behavior from the 1790s on refer to female perceptions that men enjoyed greater "economic and social mobility" than ever before (Newton, 15). Meanwhile, the womanly roles of wife and mother, limited by new conceptions of the home as an isolated, private place, seemed to be static or shrinking in both scope and utility.[20] The doctrine of influence was a kind of compensation, an ideological bone thrown to middle-class women "by assuring them that they *did* have work, power, and status after all" (19). Influence was power, in a way; it granted women some decision-making authority over household management, childhood education, and spiritual matters. In her own narrative, the female vagrant is very proprietorial about her childhood garden and home. She also has a degree of control over the management of her adult household, particularly concerning the care of her children.

Newton maintains that women could only gain access to this new influence by renouncing other, overt types of assertion.

The valorization of women's influence … aimed at devaluing actions and capacities which we can only call other forms of power, and, in this way, the peddling of women's influence, in a sort of ideological marketplace, functioned to sustained unequal power relations between middle-class women and middle-class men. Having influence, in fact having the ability to persuade others to do or to be something that was in *their* [women's] own interest, was made contingent upon the renunciation of such self-advancing forms of power as control or self-definition.

(4)

In Wordsworth's poem, the female vagrant's husband possesses artisan skills that give him the option to marry, father children and support his wife's father until death. Even unemployed, the husband still can choose (albeit desperately) in a way a woman cannot: he can enlist. Yet as Newton argues and "Salisbury Plain" bears out, social and economic mobility do not make for democratic domesticity. So the very unit, the home, that male social mobility is supposed to support financially is doomed by the family's monologism. The female vagrant can try to dissuade her husband from enlisting, but her suggestions, although they might have preserved her family, carry no real weight. She at best has influence over, not a vote in, her husband's decisions, and even that is diluted. Accommodating the ideas of only one member, the home produces only vagrants. Her homeless life is undeniably one of deprivation and hardship. Yet in this state the woman, at last, has the mobility – she can express opinions and act more freely than she ever could in the domestic sphere. Her interactions with the traveler are candid and uncensored; she tells frankly of her disagreements with her husband, and with government policy. Now she is beyond the power of a spouse whose decisions may be fatal for them both.

Wordsworth's familiarity with female feelings of uselessness were considerable. Lacking either influence or power, his sister in her early letters felt restricted by and burdensome to the various relatives she was passed off to after her parents' deaths. In her Grasmere journals, Dorothy Wordsworth explicitly will identify women in motion, the female vagrant or the traveling lass, with escape from the confinement of the home and the stasis of the tomb (Woolsey, 31, 37). Wordsworth briefly delivered his sister for a few months in 1794, when they lodged together at Windy Brow and she helped him copy out "Salisbury Plain." Her happiness when Wordsworth asked her to join him at Racedown in 1795 would be immense, in large part because she felt she would have some control at last. Writing to her childhood friend Jane Pollard, Dorothy Wordsworth discusses her new life near Bristol; she writes of the child she will be expected to care for, the servant she plans to hire, and the strict economy she and William must exercise. From her own standpoint, the greatest benefit

in such a situation is that I shall be *doing something*, it is a painful idea that one's existence is of very little use which *I* really have always been obliged to feel; above all it is painful when one is

living upon the bounty of one's friends, a resource of which mis-
fortune may deprive one and then how irksome and difficult is it
to find out any other means of support, the mind is then unfitted,
perhaps, for any new exertions, and continues always in a state of
dependence, perhaps attended with poverty.

(Early Years 150)

Dorothy Wordsworth longs for the ability to make some of her own
decisions, a power she feels atrophies in stifling domestic circum-
stances; in her case, a brother's invitation was the answer to a prayer.
His poem, however, shows how even a clear set of responsibilities
toward a loved one can work to a woman's, or a nation's, ruin.

SUBVERTING SUBVERTERS: GODWIN AND THE CRITICAL LEGACY

The closing stanzas of "Salisbury Plain" reiterate and expand on the
costs of living at "Oppression's portal" (436). Basic social inequalities
lead to starvation for the poor, a corrupt legal system, and imperial
ambitions that devastate foreign lands. This conclusion, rich in the
rhetoric of Godwinesque perfectibility, appears to accord with some
extremely radical critiques of monarchy, war, and property.[21] Yet
the presentation of these ideas seems insincere if we consider
affinities between such a position and the very government policies
criticized earlier in the text. Although William Godwin condemned
current government practices, he shared with his opponents a total-
izing view of history that stands against the local, provisional
moments of involvement the homeless experience in "Salisbury
Plain." Pitt's desire to reign in social disruption finds a strange
counterpart in Godwin's own insistence on the inevitable triumph
of a uniform truth, do what anyone would to stop it.

   In the first edition of his monumental *Enquiry Concerning Political
Justice* (1793) – the only version we are certain Wordsworth read –
Godwin insists that only unimpeded, individual judgment and con-
tentious, rational conversation will advance people and societies.
Indeed, Godwin's lengthy critique of monarchy and oligarchy stems
from the cloistered aspect of these methods of governance. Despite
his contempt for princes, he even condemns regicide because it
"delights in obscurity. It shrinks from the penetrating eye of
wisdom. It avoids all question, and hesitates and trembles before the

questioner" (1: 303 + 3: 163).[22] The philosopher also implicitly links marriage and domestic life, which the first edition of *Political Justice* roundly denounces, with the closed decision-making of monarchy – an open refutation of Burke's view that patriarchal prerogatives were the best grounding for society and government. One typical digression in this regard is an appendix entitled "Of the Mode of Excluding Visitors." Godwin vehemently condemns the popular excuse of avoiding a visitor by having a servant deny one is home when, in fact, one is. He reasons that this desire to selectively cordon off the domestic space destroys sincerity, one of our most important qualities, and makes us and our servants more prone to deceive and manipulate others. Only uninhibited commerce with other people supports a moral outlook: "Can we even understand virtue and vice half so well as we otherwise should, if we be unacquainted with the feelings of our neighbours respecting them" (3: 168)?

However, these views clash with Godwin's equally continual reification of an abstract truth. If truth is unchanging and sure to triumph, conversation comes to seem superfluous at best, and a waste of time at worst. That truth will eventually attain unstoppable domination is assumed throughout: "Knowledge cannot be extirpated. Its progress is silent, but infallible; and he is the most useful soldier in this war, who accumulates in an unperishable form the greatest mass of truth" (3: 299). The envisioned conflict between truth and its opponents echoes the binary thinking that increasingly led the Pitt ministry, as well as the French Jacobins, to view all critics as traitors. This position becomes even clearer when Godwin adds that we are moral beings only insofar as we recognize the inevitability of truth's triumph: "All morality depends upon the assumption of something evident and true [and] will grow…in proportion as these indications are more clear and unequivocal" (1: 304 + 3: 163). In this scenario, rational, sincere human judgment seems almost irrelevant. Assertions that "truth is in all its branches harmonious and consistent," and that it is "at all times and in all places the same" (3: 246, 274) leave little room for individual interpretation of ideas or situations. Such a rubric is in keeping with that fact that Godwin's citizen, at times no more than a collection of Hartlian predetermined responses, seems to have little ability to think for him or herself.

In other words, the trouble with a position like Godwin's is that the methods and even the substance of his truth end up sounding a great deal like those of his opponents.[23] Godwin's description of the individual's obligation to be a moral judge could serve as a summary of the duties of a government prosecutor or spy. According to the philosopher, each citizen "carries about with him a diploma, constituting him inquisitor general of the moral conduct of his neighbours, with a duty annexed to recall them to virtue ..." (3:257). This agenda is taken to its logical conclusion in the final stanza of "Salisbury Plain":

> Heros of Truth pursue your march, uptear
> Th' Oppressor's dungeon from its deepest base;
> High o'er the towers of Pride undaunted rear
> Resistless in your might the herculean mace
> Of Reason; let foul Error's monster race
> Dragged from their dens start at the light with pain
> And die; pursue your toils, till not a trace
> Be left on earth of Superstition's reign ...

> (541–8)

The goal is that of the radicals, the clearing away of gross inequalities that make contemporary life so painful. The metaphors, however, subscribe to the means of the conservative opposition. The poem's central encounter indicates that kind cheering words, not violence, even rhetorical violence, are the best way to effect reformation. Earlier stanzas in the concluding section ask, "Say, rulers of the nations, from the sword, / Can ought but murder, pain and tears proceed? / Oh, what can war but endless war still breed?" (507–9). Yet war is quite clearly what the last stanza describes, and the tactics employed uncomfortably resemble those of the white terror, or the actions of wicker-burning druids presented early on as the ancestors of contemporary zealots. The opposition's goal ultimately does not seem to be the independent exercise of private judgment after all, but the blunt destruction of all disagreement. Accordingly, the image of fanatical heroes of truth gives way to a portrait of both kinds of extremists as idolaters of predetermined historical process.

> Oh that a slave who on his naked knees
> Weeps tears of fear at Superstition's nod,
> Should rise a monster Tyrant and o'er seas
> And mountains stretch so far his cruel rod ...

> (460–4)

"Salisbury Plain" ironizes and ultimately rejects both conservative and radical perspectives and the coercive tactics they share. The question "... reason's ray, / What does it more than while the tempests rise ... reveal with still-born glimpse the terrors of our way?" (429–32) is not merely rhetorical. Like the conclusion of *Descriptive Sketches*, this question underscores the need to reassess our understanding of Wordsworth's commitment to radical ideas, even at supposedly the most radical point in the poet's life.[24] The suffering highlighted by political writers is a reality in the Salisbury Plain poems. Yet these works imply that a solution cannot reside in an absolutist stance that, whether in the service of Pitt or the radical movement, leads to ideological warfare hostile to the marginality embodied by the wandering poor. Vagrant encounters afford space for a spectrum of belief and expression that neither Tories nor radicals allow. The elusive, cheering words of private utterance brought forth by an encounter between the homeless may be the only basis for improvement we can depend upon, when "life is like this desert broad, / Where all the happiest find is but a shed / And a green spot 'mid wastes interminably spread" (421–3).[25]

The biographical investigations of Roe and Johnston have emphasized Wordsworth's familiarity with prominent English radicals as well as Jacobin leaders like Brissot, for whom Charlotte Smith gave Wordsworth a letter of introduction on his way to France in 1790. In the accounts of both critics, the facts of familiarity and friendships have a way of slipping into conjecture about ardent political devotion. Companionship, however, may lead to neither agreement nor action. Investigating the London political scene, Roe's *Wordsworth and Coleridge: The Radical Years* argues for the poet's active involvement in dissenting and pro-revolutionary circles before his second visit to France. After his 1791–2 residence abroad, Wordsworth returned to Britain expecting a British revolution and eager to help bring it about (*Radical Years*, 20–37, 64). Yet Wordsworth's friendships, family connections and even his own actions point in contradictory directions; if he anticipated British revolution in late 1792, he apparently intended to supervise it from the curacy he hoped to receive from his conservative uncles when he returned from France. Even the particulars of his radical associations, such as we know them, provide ambiguous evidence. Consider an event Roe and Johnston cite in adducing the poet's commitment to radicalism: Wordsworth's presence at a gathering at William Frend's home on 27 February 1795. Because Frend's older guests were authors, Johnston states that "a gathering such as this inevitably turned its conversation to writing for publication, and Wordsworth's ready-formed plans and opinions for his *Philanthropist* would have been eagerly seized upon for their flattering congruence with Godwin's rationalist ideology" (*Hidden*, 438). This kind of speculation, assisted by the helpful "inevitably" and "would have been," underpins Johnston's belief that Wordsworth's 1794 plans to publish a radical journal with William Mathews called *The Philanthropist*, a project his letters indicate he abandoned, were realized in 1795, since a journal by this name did in fact run from March until December. Quarrels over the editorial slant of the paper, Johnston hypothesizes, led to Wordworth's hasty departure from the project and from London in mid-August. Frend's gathering, in this account, becomes a planning session for Wordsworth's journal.

A survey of the guests at Frend's home indicates how half-baked Wordsworth's verifiable radical efforts were, for all his associations. By this time, he had written a few politically inflammatory letters to close friends, knew some leading reformers, and had penned but apparently made no attempt to publish one radical pamphlet. His companions on 27 February were of another stripe; in addition to *Political Justice*, Godwin had recently written *Cursory Strictures*, a tract against the government's criteria for treason. The pamphlet was credited with helping Thomas Holcroft, an organizer for the Society for Constitutional Information, and others arrested in 1794 beat the treason charge they had just faced down (Albert Goodwin, 340–2). Holcroft was Frend's guest as well. Frend himself had been dismissed from his fellowship at Cambridge after publishing the reformist *Peace and Union* in 1793. Even George Dyer, whom Roe dubs "unobtrusive," had published three pamphlets declaring his sympathy for and involvement with reformers.[26] Perhaps Wordsworth made no ascertainable effort to publish his radical "Letter to Llandaff," or publicly express the sentiments present in his letters to Mathews, or become an active organizer, because of his youth, his uncertain prospects, a fear of arrest, or difficulty in finding a publisher. These would all have been understandable obstacles. Yet they had not stopped others. Frend's guests also included James Losh and John Tweddell who, like Wordsworth, were four years out of Cambridge; Tweddell had published in defense of France's revolution as had Losh, who currently was soliciting contributions to pay for the successful courtroom defense of Holcroft and the others (Johnston, *Hidden*, 436). Also undeterred from a more public role were other young radicals absent from Frend's gathering, such as Samuel Taylor Coleridge. By these standards, Wordsworth wasn't simply unobtrusive; he was invisible.

Johnston provides a detailed analysis of the actual *Philanthropist's* rhetoric in arguing that it followed Wordsworth's planned format and that some of its compositions are consistent with his writing style. He concludes by acknowledging the problems with his theory: one could easily argue the ideas in *The Philanthropist* were "simply" 'in the air,' and that Wordsworth no more need be connected ... than any other young liberal intellectual" (460). The assumptions behind *The Hidden Wordsworth*'s methodology, however, finally make its conclusion extremely difficult to refute: while the tone of the journal's poetry and prose

> does not sound much like Wordsworth's style, however close it may be to his literary and political concerns ... the difficulty of proving Wordsworth's authorship, or partial authorship, of these and other parts of *The Philanthropist* is part and parcel of the hypothesis which makes his involvement in the enterprise plausible. (446–7)

In other words, the very fact that we have no hard evidence (because Wordsworth later covered the whole escapade up) ends up being more proof of his involvement. Johnston adds, somewhat mysteriously in light of what has preceded, that "Proving [Wordsworth's involvement] requires that we abandon the convenient fiction of single, or even unitary, authorship," since "Wordsworth was certainly not a consistent sum of political opinion" (447). While this final comment finds ample support in Wordsworth's correspondence, actions and poetry, we should remind ourselves what really "proving" his involvement would entail: signed letters or journal contributions or remarks on his work by friends or relatives. One article in the published *Philanthropist* was signed "W." but Johnston has discovered that this was a code initial for a radical contributor from Norwich.

In the end, we can only with certainty say that the poet's known political credentials appear flimsy even when compared with those of men of similar age and circumstances, and that there is no evidence that his admiration for the men at Frend's gathering translated into firm and consistent action in defense of the British radical agenda. Johnston's own account demonstrates how personal cordiality need not guarantee ideological agreement; even after editorial conflicts supposedly led Wordsworth to quit *The Philanthropist* and leave town, he dined with Godwin four times during a 1796 visit to London: "... his disapproval of the philosopher's style and thought did not affect his personal esteem for him" (490). A November 1794 letter to William Mathews in which Wordsworth states his (apparent) withdrawal from *The Philanthropist* project typifies the inconsistencies in the writings from this period that we know to be Wordsworth's.[27] Despite his animosity toward the government, he backs away from starting his own radical journal; in a statement that sums up Wordsworth's radical "commitments," he tells Mathews that "The more nearly we approached the time fixed for action, the more strongly was I persuaded that we should decline the field" (*Early Years*, 134). The poet still considers being a journalist, but his principles are all over the map and less important than the money.

> You say a newspaper would be glad of me; do you think you could ensure me employment in that way on terms similar to your own? I mean also in an opposition paper, for really I cannot in conscience and in principle, abet in the smallest degree the measures pursued by the present ministry. They are already so deeply advanced in iniquity that like Macbeth they cannot retreat. When I express myself in this manner I am far from reprobating those whose sentiments ... differ from my own; I know that many good men were persuaded of the expediency of the present war, and I know also that many persons ... may think it their duty to support the acting ministry from an idea of thereby supporting the government. ...
>
> (135)

In a previous letter, Wordsworth had condemned the British constitution itself (123). Yet he now feels it necessary to specify that he could really only bring himself to work at an opposition paper. The idea of government support, and government supporters, seems by turns despicable – Pitt is compared to Macbeth – and understandable.[28]

The debate over the young Wordsworth's political sympathies is part of a much larger argument, which remains unresolved, over the real character of Britain during the 1790s. Historians continue to disagree about who the radicals were, how radical they were, and how systematic and meaningful the government's opposition to its critics was. E. P. Thompson, Albert Goodwin and Roger Wells, among others, have argued for the revolutionary aims of many reformers, aims they maintain were stifled by overwhelming government repression. Clive Emsley, Ian Christie, and David Eastwood respond that the political crisis has been exaggerated, that the decentralized government was incapable of orchestrating a widespread crackdown against anyone, and that reformers in many cases self-destructed. These debates are not only about interpreting historical evidence, though they are certainly that; such disagreements also reflect the diverse political agendas of participants seeking to assign blame or take credit for (depending on one's perspective) the fact that there would be no revolution in Britain, and that the cause of reform would have to wait for another thirty years. The polarized nomenclature of the 1790s continues to haunt such arguments about the political opinions of those who lived through it, even when their opinions problematize such divisions. In *The Politics of Nature* Roe has persisted in his investigation of Wordsworth's own loyalties by reaffirming the poet's radical connections and sympathies. With this approach, Roe works to recast what he acknowledges might seem Wordsworth's "apparently uncommitted career as a political radical who wrote outspoken pamphlets and poems but did not publish them" (115). Like the radicals whose history he documents, Roe sees this as a moral question; the Wordsworth he seeks to bury is made "shiftless" by his ambivalence (115). But in the end, the "shiftless" Wordsworth (like the "lazy" homeless on the streets today) refuses to die, continuing to defy the expectations of his time and our own.

CORRECTED VISION: DISCIPLINE AND CRIME IN THE REVISIONS

"Salisbury Plain" was revised into a new poem, "Adventures on Salisbury Plain," during the fall of 1795, shortly after William and Dorothy Wordsworth had moved to Racedown.[29] Summing up these revisions, Gill finds in them a shift "from social and political phenomena to the more complex phenomena of human motives and behavior" ("Preface," *Salisbury Plain Poems*, 12). Roe, Johnston, and John Rieder have represented this shift as a retreat from political engagement. From this perspective, Wordsworth's departure from London in 1795 is tantamount to a reversal of his radical sympathies. But rather than retreat from politics, "Adventures on

Salisbury Plain" suggests how Britain's political polarization contin-
ues to pressure the space embodied by the homeless. In the revi-
sions, experiences and ideas no longer freely circulate between the
female vagrant and her companion, for their exchange is now
tainted by concealment and uneasiness. This secrecy stems from a
crucial change in the narrative: the nameless traveler is now a
vagrant sailor oppressed with guilt over his violent criminal past.
For the sailor and the female vagrant, persecution is difficult to
avoid because they have internalized official dogma about behavior
and punishment. In other words, the vagrant's polyvalent social
status is beginning to yield to a legal atmosphere that relentlessly
and pervasively resolves ambiguity. The focus of the revised poem
is not the possibility of expression, but the sense of responsibility
and guilt that can inhibit communication. Composed as the govern-
ment renewed its battle against the opposition, in "Adventures on
Salisbury Plain" there are few places left to hide.

The timing of Wordsworth's declaration that "Salisbury Plain" has
been so revised "that it may be looked on almost as another work"
(*Early Years*, 159) supports the contention that the new poem con-
cerns changes in British politics. Dated 20 November 1795,
Wordsworth's letter implies he wrote "Adventures" as the goals of
governmental surveillance were becoming ever clearer. In the after-
math of the landmark treason trials of 1794, many reformers believed
the worst was over.[30] Yet in January 1795, Parliament, still fearful of
insurrection, failed to muster enough votes to repeal the suspension
of Habeas Corpus. These fears were confirmed when the king's coach
was attacked in October by demonstrators protesting bread prices
and the French war.[31] Claiming George III barely had escaped assas-
sination, Pitt supported bills essentially outlawing talk of reform or
criticism of the established government. On 4 November, a royal
proclamation authorized magistrates to suppress all anti-government
assemblies; the Treasonable Practices Bill, introduced 6 November,
extended treason to "inciting hatred of the king, his heirs, his govern-
ment or the constitution, either by speech or writing" (Emsley,
"Repression," 811–12). The Seditious Meetings Bill, introduced 10
November, outlawed meetings of more than 50 people and gave
magistrates wide-ranging powers over all public gatherings. Made
law on 18 December, both bills were debated during the very weeks
that Wordsworth was revising "Salisbury Plain."

In "Adventures on Salisbury Plain," the crushing atmosphere
engendered by the new laws crucially informs the portrait of the

sailor. Cheated of his pay after discharge from impressed service, he subsequently robs and murders an innocent man. The legal status of veterans during this period again illustrates conflicting perceptions of vagrants. Military men who were returning home after discharge – or who said they were – generally could beg without being arrested as vagabonds (Taylor, 76). In other words, the law won't help the sailor recoup his prize money, but it will allow him to beg. Wordsworth adds another series of conflicts by making his military vagrant a murderer, but a murderer driven to his crime by official corruption. The sailor's pronounced marginality as both a criminal (vagrant and murderer) and a victim (impressed husband and cheated sailor) does not, however, empower him. Like the reformers who found that political change was suddenly criminal, Wordsworth's character feels not marginal but determinate – more guilty than innocent, more criminal than victim. As a result, the comfort he provides to the female vagrant becomes secondary to his overpowering sense of guilt and fear of discovery. As in "Salisbury Plain," he is still able to coax the female vagrant out of her disabling fear when he first wakes her. His own psychic paralysis, despite his physical mobility, is registered in a series of incapacitating fits, the first of which occurs when he sees a body hanging in chains along the roadside:

> It was a spectacle which none might view
> In spot so savage but with shuddering pain
> Nor only did for him at once renew
> All he had feared from man, but rouzed a train
> Of the mind's phantoms, horrible as vain.
> The stones, as if to sweep him from the day,
> Roll'd at his back along the living plain;
> He fell and without sense or motion lay,
> And when the trance was gone, feebly pursued his way.

(118–26)

In some respects, this reaction seems an almost textbook case of the intended response to such forms of punishment. The English Murder Act of 1752 had made hanging in chains an optional additional punishment for those convicted of particularly horrible crimes. The sentence was designed to increase the death penalty's deterrent value, since the hope of resurrection depended upon preserving the body whole.

These sorts of legal spectacles are important because they draw large crowds.[32] The assembled public verifies and validates the legal violence that is being inflicted by royal agents. In light of this information, the sailor's response before a deserted gibbet, long after the execution, is atypical. Overwhelmed by a sense of the evil he has done, it almost appears that he proceeds to punish himself. The parade of imaginary horrors he is subjected to are of his own creation; they are "vain" or without substance (122). Because of his fear, his responses in this situation are constrained by a very specific grid of possibilities. This scene draws attention to the resemblance between the world of "Adventures" and innovative disciplinary schemes like Jeremy Bentham's *Panopticon: On the Inspection House* (1791). The genius of Bentham's prison, overseen by a central tower, was that inmates always would behave as if they were being observed. The scheme arranges "things [so] that the surveillance is permanent in its effects, even if it is discontinuous in its action … the inmates should be caught up in a power situation of which they are themselves the bearer" (Foucault, *D & P*, 201). Britain, of course, had long prided itself on the Protestant independence of its culture, that would brook no despotic network of spies, bureaucrats, or secret courts (unlike Catholic France).[33] However, Bentham's design was not an eccentric oddity completely divorced from the realities of its day. Despite current disagreements among historians over the crown's true repressive capabilities, Britons during the 1790s did perceive a growing government role in their lives, a perception that was not unfounded. Developments in poor law administration, such as the emergence of statistical record-keeping, the expansion of the tax code and revenue collection, and the authorization of stipendiary magistrates in London's environs imply how the French wars and their hardships facilitated the gestation of an apparatus aimed at controlling social unrest.[34] In introductory comments to *Caleb Williams* penned in late October 1795, Godwin maintains that in recent months "Terror was the order of the day" (4). While its successes are in dispute, Pitt's domestic legislation did attempt to exterminate reformist annoyances like the corresponding societies, which were eventually banned by name in 1799. As a publication of 1791, Bentham's plan also offered an alternative to the bloody official response to the most recent crime wave, which had occurred in the 1780s. Despite its apparent distance from the English mainstream, Bentham's plan was very much a work of its time.

The power matrix within which Wordsworth's sailor operates palpably resembles the texture of life in the panopticon. When he collapses on the barren plain, no one is watching him or knows of his guilt. The representation of penal authority he encounters is a shadow of its most effective incarnation, devoid as it is of fellow witnesses or government emissaries. Like Bentham's prisoner, ever conscious of the faceless (and perhaps empty) inspection tower before him, the sailor is paralyzed with anxiety by the sight of the body and scaffold. He has become his own best policing agent. His body assumes the stiffness of the death he struggled to avoid, and his imagination enacts retribution upon his mind for his crime. The sailor eventually regains consciousness and mobility, continuing on but only "feebly" (126). A character whose wanderings in "Salisbury Plain" provided a window onto a world unbridled by official restriction is now governed by involuntary responses to authority. His mental and physical mobility are arrested. As Foucault remarks, nineteenth-century disciplinary modes would focus precisely on the vagabond's or nomad's ambiguities: "discipline fixes; it arrests or regulates movements; it clears up confusion; it dissipates compact groupings of individuals wandering about the country in unpredictable ways; it establishes calculated distribution" (Foucault, *D & P*, 219).

It becomes evident as the poem progresses that the series of responses we first witness at the gibbet are permanently embedded in the sailor's consciousness. An appropriate stimulus will always trigger the behavior. The female vagrant fortuitously refrains from repeating to him the legend about the buried head of the murdered man, "for surely once again / The fit had made his bones with horror quake: / She knew not what a hell such spot had power to wake" (250–2). Hearing such a story would reawaken the man's guilt and fear of discovery; in the tale, the head was buried but the crime eventually came to light. Later, after the female vagrant relates her husband's role in the American war, she pauses, and "Once more a horrid trance his limbs did lock … he was stretch'd upon the wither'd fern, / Nor to her friendly summons answer could return" (401, 404–5). We are not told what part of her story led to his response, but the following lines seem a likely stimulus:

"Oh! dreadful price of being to resign
All that is dear *in* being! better far
In Want's most lonely cave till death to pine,

> Unseen, unheard, unwatched by any star;
> Or in the streets and walks where proud men are,
> Better our dying bodies to obtrude,
> Than dog-like, wading at the heels of war,
> Protract a curst existence, with the brood
> That lap (their very nourishment!) their brother's blood."

(379–87)

The female vagrant unwittingly implies that wartime service has left her listener a monster. This insight gives the sailor a new, devastating perspective on his culpability. His wife maintains much later in the poem that she denied murder charges against his name because he had always been a kind man. The female vagrant's words offer an index for evaluating how war has changed the sailor, even before he murders. He serves one voluntary tour of duty in the navy and is then impressed for more service. Being cheated of his pay is more than he can bear; his dreams of his family's reunion and a life of comfort have sustained him. He has believed that when he lays his prize money, "this bloody prize of victory," in his wife's lap, she will forget the years of deprivation and loneliness she has endured (88). The female vagrant's tale is a reminder of what the sailor had forgotten: a "brother's blood" can never really be sound "nourishment."

The ultimate proof of war's effects is, of course, the murder itself. The sailor has now come to believe that a brother's blood is nourishment not only on the battlefield. He kills partly to gain a new bloody prize for his family. Yet as we approach the moment of the murder, another image eclipses that of the despairing husband and father. By striking out at the nearest victim, he becomes a warrior taking revenge against the "Slaves of Office" who cheated him (91). The furious calculation with which he acts indicates that domestic worries are not foremost in his mind:

> In sight of his own house, in such a mood
> That from his view his children might have run,
> He met a traveler, robb'd him, shed his blood;
> And when the miserable work was done
> He fled, a vagrant since, the murderer's fate to shun.

(95–9)

His behavior immediately after the act reinforces the image of a warrior turned criminal. He has become the figure loathed by the Parisian crowd during the September massacres – the mercenary whose loyalty to society depends on his pay. After he murders an innocent man, there is no sense of remorse or concern for his family. He runs because he does not want to be hanged. His trance-like attacks, mingling the fear of discovery with guilt, only come about later. His response to the female vagrant's words insinuates that he now feels guilty, not only about the murder, but also about the callous attitude that led him to commit it. He killed as much for the official affront to himself as for his family's welfare.

This sailor's crime and his end were common enough in the time in which "Adventures on Salisbury Plain" is set. Wordsworth's focus on veterans of the American war was logical for someone wishing to consider the relation between the government repression and criminal activity in subsequent decades. The early 1780s combined a massive troop demobilization with a severe trade depression and unemployment, since the lost colonies had been a major British export market. From 1783 to 1786, the crime rate soared, largely due to angry, impoverished soldiers who turned their martial skills to illegal ends. Unable to transport offenders to America, authorities increased the hanging rate to its highest since the 1720s, hoping that sheer terror would deter men from violence and theft (Beattie, 224). In a manner consistent with Wordsworth's sailor's rage over not being paid, the American veteran was notable for a lack of deference toward his betters, perhaps because of class mingling brought on by military service. Rather than striking out randomly, however, some men systematically pursued their grievances. In April 1783, approximately 700 sailors gathered at the Admiralty to demand payment for their service. "They then proceeded to unrig any outward bound ships manned by foreigners or landsmen. It was intolerable to the sailors that pinch-penny masters should be able to avoid coming to them to fill their ships' crews" (McLynn, 331).

Wordsworth's deviations from this history are revealing. The sailor of "Adventures" has his moment of indeferent rage. Afterwards, he almost ceases to be a figure from the 1780s. His reactions and his isolation make it seem as if a veteran from the previous decade suddenly finds himself in the 1790s, when suspended rights and the use of spies are ever more common.[35] This sense that an upstart veteran of the American war has been transplanted to the next decade explains both his initial behavior and his subsequent crippling guilt. The poem's plotting underscores the scope of Pitt's restrictions by setting them against the most recent period of near-anarchy in England. Civil demonstrations and riots were the signature crimes of the 1790s, but such offenses take on a diminished significance when compared with the extended crime spree and the moral panic characteristic of the mid-1780s.[36] Yet in the imaginary contest that Wordsworth stages between a vagrant sailor of the 1780s and the atmosphere created by the measures of the 1790s, official repression easily carries the day. The vagrant sailor's weakness before the scaffold becomes even more pronounced when we consider that rioting by sailors in the 1740s, following the demobilization after the War of Jenkin's Ear, led to fundamental changes in the disposal of corpses of those hung at Tyburn. Previously subject to seizure by surgical colleges seeking dissection subjects, most bodies after the 1749 riots were handed over directly to the deceased's family. The scaffold spurred these sailors to action rather than left them dumb.[37]

The sailor's situation affects his relations with others as well as his interior life. In "Salisbury Plain," the male traveler's moment of sympathetic contact with the female vagrant illustrates how homeless life can provide opportunities for unimpeded interchange. In "Adventures," his reaction to her story is the first indication that this possibility has been revised. Their ensuing conversation is reduced to a monologue, and the encounter as a whole is characterized by self-absorption and miscommunication. Not only does she unwittingly accuse him of moral depravity; he is incapable now of comforting her. In "Salisbury Plain," she pauses in despair while telling her tale and he calls her to look at the dawn and offers sympathy. Now, she pauses and he lies paralyzed. The genuine exchange of sentiment – the mobility of experience itself – that might diminish the weight on her spirit has been precluded. The sailor can do nothing to help her: "he sate and spake not, ere her weeping ceased" (563). Rather than him calling her to the dawn, she rises and sees it alone.

The female vagrant's subsequent efforts to draw him out only "In his heart ... anguish threw" (571). Continuing their journey together, they are really very much apart. She tries to make conversation, but he remains silent and in pain: "deep into his vitals had she sent / Anguish that rankled like a fiery dart" (588–9). The woman's story has not created a bond between them but has reinforced in the man an obsession with his own fate: "On themes indifferent often she begun / To hold discourse, but nothing could beguile / His thoughts, still cleaving to the murder'd man" (595–7). Her story creates in him a heightened awareness of his guilt and vulnerability that is a reduced version of his response to the scaffold. Just as the fear of the gibbet impedes his physical movements, her comments paralyze his thoughts. His own fears prevent him from disclosing any of his own story, while his memory of her tale distances him from others. For example, the sailor now fears the greeting of the mail coachman, while earlier he confidently had hailed the post boy. The final sign of their inability to communicate surfaces when the sailor's mysterious silence is misinterpreted by the female vagrant. She believes he mourns not for himself but for her.

Only once, and briefly, in this poem are understandings like those of "Salisbury Plain" recreated. As the female vagrant and the sailor walk along, they come upon a homeless husband and wife fighting over a blow he has dealt their son. As in *Political Justice*, the family, like the state that is modeled on it, creates discord and misery. The father and the paternalistic government that stands behind him are doubles. Both deal out blows to those who challenge authority, be they children who assume a father's place at the table or sailors who take revenge for a denied salary. The sailor resembles the father insofar as both "in monster mood" strike an innocent (617). The child and the sailor share the experience of weakness before a figure of power. But the child knows no guilt, whereas the state drives its citizens to acts of violence which are a source of torment. In this instant of self-knowledge, the sailor understands his relation both to the father and child.

> Within himself he said, "What hearts have we!
> The blessing this the father gives his child!
> Yet happy thou, poor boy! compared with me,
> Suffering yet not doing ill, fate far more mild."

> (649–52)

This flash of despair provides the backdrop for the sailor's one moment of triumph in "Adventures on Salisbury Plain." His fleeting apotheosis stems from his ability to assume a marginal mindset. His sense of guilt is balanced by the insight acquired through suffering, and this enables him to deliver a lesson, even though the irate husband "With bitter insult and revilings sad, / Calling him vagabond, and knave, and mad," predicts the sailor will end up on the gallows (634–5). The vagrant sailor almost breaks down at this uncanny guess as to his guilt, but still manages to set aside his fear of discovery and offer some wisdom.

> "Tis a bad world, and hard is the world's law;
> Each prowls to strip his brother of his fleece;
> Much need have ye that time more closely draw
> The bond of nature, all unkindness cease,
> And that among so few there still be peace:
> Else can you hope but with such num'rous foes
> Your pains shall ever with your years increase."
>
> (658–64)

The sailor invokes a generalized "bond of nature" as the element that should keep peace in the family of humanity. He also recognizes that, in both his own life and the scene before him, the sense of this ancient bond has been riven by the new laws of nation and family. The encounter itself bears out that the only bond that has any positive power is a provisional sense of engagement. In emphasizing the brotherhood of all, the lesson echoes the female vagrant's own wisdom and suggests that, in a belated fashion, she has communicated with him. In speaking this truth to the father, the sailor acquires a passing sense of calm. And at the sight of a stranger's tears for his bleeding son, the brutal father's anger subsides: "Such sight the father of his wrath beguil'd; / Relenting thoughts and self-reproach awoke ..." (653–4). The arguments of his wife, who has a much more obvious claim on his attention, have been unable to accomplish half so much.

It is typical of the world of "Adventures" that this brief space of meaningful interaction prefigures the sailor's undoing. In the scene above, the sailor witnesses a kind of resolution he comes to crave – atonement and forgiveness. He cannot communicate with the female vagrant because she cannot forgive him, but only unknowingly accuse him. Although the abusive father also cannot forgive him, their encounter at least can provide a situation whose outlines recall the kind of redemption the sailor seeks. At the sailor's behest, the father feels guilt and sorrow, kisses his child, and atones for his error.

The sailor's desire for forgiveness by a sanctioned authority – a desire for the resolution of marginality – peaks when he discovers that his wife is now a dying, homeless pauper. She is found by the female vagrant in a cart outside of town, where the driver has paused in his journey back to her home parish. The sailor and his wife meet once again, although the wife does not know the man before her is her husband. Her deathbed speech reveals to the murderer the extent of his culpability. Shunned by her community after the murdered man was discovered nearby, she seeks shelter in her father's house. Sickness has prevented her from completing the journey and she has been removed by the overseers in the parish where she stopped. The lack of an overt parish presence in "Salisbury Plain" has been supplanted by a heavy awareness of unsympathetic local authority.

The sailor's immediate response to her story is painfully predictable; it is also too late. "He cried, 'O bless me now, that thou should'st live / I do not wish or ask: forgive me, now forgive'" (773–4). She dies, "A sudden joy surpriz[ing] expiring thought" (777), but gives no clear indication that she has understood or granted the substance of his plea. The most he can garner is a sense of fading recognition. The narrator implies that there is expiation to be found in this scene, if the sailor would search for it: "A look was on her lips which seem'd to say, / 'Comfort to thee my dying thoughts have sent'" (781–2). This is not enough. Her husband's needs, conditioned by guilt and a fear of surveillance, demand a more formal, more sustained and less ambiguous feeling of atonement. This brief encounter fails to bear the necessary meaning. Since the sailor feels he has, in effect, murdered twice, he now completes the pattern established earlier of, as Foucault explains, being "caught up in a power situation of which [he is himself] the bearer." He turns himself in "Not without pleasure" and confesses "all which he had done" (812, 813). He is executed, hung in chains, and left to act as a sign of disciplinary force. The incident of the beaten boy proves the sailor's capacity for forgiveness and instruction. His own urge to receive the same from official authority in the end proves overwhelming: his valence finally is fixed, his confusion dispelled. The vagrant criminal has now been completely coopted by the society from which he has desperately tried, and failed, to distance himself.

In this revised poem, the female vagrant is now no stranger to guilt either. However, the story of her suffering offers an entryway into the poem's shrinking, but still discernible, space for marginal existence. Her uneasiness is not a function of the sort of crimes that haunt the sailor. She is rather plagued by the idea that the activities necessary to sustain her have somehow compromised the purity of her spirit. Near the end of her narrative, she describes the combination of begging and living off the land that have enabled her to survive. These activities, to her, smack of immorality in some ill-defined way. She does not invoke the technical jargon of the vagrancy laws, but it is clear that wandering and begging appear as evil to her as any member of Parliament would wish them to. Like her husband and like the sailor, she has internalized culture's knowledge of what constitutes good, acceptable behavior for someone in her position. In despair, the female vagrant emphasizes that she turned to her current life only as a last resort.

> I lived upon the mercy of the fields ...
> ... or what general bounty yields,
> Now coldly given, now utterly refused.
> The fields I for my bed have often used:
> But, what afflicts my peace with keenest ruth
> Is, that I have my inner self abused,
> Foregone the home delight of constant truth,
> And clear and open soul, so prized in fearless youth.

> (541–9)

Her sense that vagrant life is immoral prevents her, when she returns to England, from taking up "the beggar's language" (477). She almost dies of hunger because she cannot ask others for money. The virtuous antithesis to vagrancy is significantly imagined by her as a "home delight" (548), an idea whose hold retains its grip on her despite her domestic history.

One incident in her story shows a way around her guilt and the sense pervading "Adventures on Salisbury Plain" that the vagrant's room to maneuver is being eliminated. Taking to the road, she sees a small group sitting about a fire. She describes them as a "wild brood," and attributes to them a quality sorely missed in her narratives: selfless generosity (503). They give her their society, food and a resting place. It becomes clear that this is a band of vagrant burglars. They masquerade as traveling potters and peddlers, returning at night to rob houses they have visited earlier. They are exactly the people that vagrancy laws are supposed to guard against. Far from seeming cowed by Georgian law, though, they seem gleeful when describing to her the unconstrained flow of their lives, punctuated by periodic gatherings with fellow vagabonds.

> "But life of happier sort to me pourtrayed,
> And other joys my fancy to allure;
> The bag-pipe dinning on the midnight moor
> In barn uplighted, and companions boon
> Well met from far with revelry secure,
> In depth of forest shade … "

> (514–21)

The female vagrant declines the travelers' invitation to join them; robberies "were not for me, brought up in nothing ill" (530). She cannot accept this anarchic alternative to confining, conventional life. This refusal is hardly surprising, given the weighty guilt she feels even about the minor crime of vagrancy. But even she cannot help seeing the good in them; they act not with guilt but with merriment, their interactions with each other depend on respect, not fear, and they are the only people in her account whose kindness is not conditioned by duty or an expectation of something in return. They are, in fact, the only truly happy people in the entire poem. The female vagrant admires them as we admire those who act as we would like to, but cannot.

> "My heart is touched to think that men like these,
> The rude earth's tenants, were my first relief:
> How kindly did they paint their vagrant ease!
> And their long holiday that feared not grief,
> For all belonged to all, and each was chief…"

> (505–9)

The hope of sustaining marginality is not, in "Adventures on Salisbury Plain," totally extinguished. The position embodied in "Salisbury Plain" by the protagonists is represented now by these generous, warm-hearted vagrants who are nevertheless thieves.[38]

A related defiance of social norms occurs a final time, in what might seem an unlikely place. The last stanza, with its description of the tormented sailor dead at last, hanging in chains, is undeniably tragic. Yet the response of those who come out to see the displayed corpse is more complex:

> They left him hung on high in iron case,
> And dissolute men unthinking and untaught,
> Planted their festive booths beneath his face;
> And to that spot, which idle thousands sought,
> Women and children were by fathers brought. ...

(820–4)

Rieder assumes that the profiteers and those patronizing them are representative of a "seriously deformed community," and show how the spectacle of terror maims the moral sense (326).[39] But perhaps, in this society, being unthinking and untaught is not undesirable. The merchants, unfazed by legal spectacle and on the move like the thieving potters, represent a mentality that official regulation and surveillance cannot quite comprehend, much less completely contain. Appropriately, the state execution is designed for the education of family subordinates, the women and children. Yet for others the event is a business opportunity, not a moment for reflection and fear. As for the thousands, their motives for witnessing the body's fate are dismissed as idle, the term used to describe the poor and vagrants. Rather than unequivocal evidence of depravity, their imperviousness to the scene may partake of a resiliency, or a refusal to be encompassed by norms, that the sailor could have learned from. In his study of public execution, V.A.C. Gatrell generally argues against the view that irreverent or unruly scaffold crowds converted an execution into a challenge to authority. He adds, "If there was a carnival element at executions, it was witnessed narrowly in the hubbub and movement of people and in the commercialization of the event" (94). The taverns that opened early, the pie men and gingerbread sellers, the activity of the spectators, worked against the state's assumption of solemn supremacy at the scaffold, and even in the courtroom, which could be a noisy and indecorous place.[40] When Wordsworth and Coleridge attended the Carlisle assizes in 1803 for the trial of John Hatfield, the "Keswick Imposter," a hungry Coleridge did not scruple to signal it was time to go by "hallooing to Wordsworth who was in a window on the other side of the Hall – *Dinner!*" (*Notebooks*, 1432). Despite growing obstacles, the power of such irreverence makes an appearance through the traveling profiteers and vagrant thieves of "Adventures on Salisbury Plain."

3

Life During Wartime in *Lyrical Ballads*

In the opening stanzas of "The Thorn," the narrator offers a puzzling description of three natural objects: a thorn, a pond, and a hill of moss. The speaker intrigues us by emphasizing how these items partake of multiple, and at times opposing, intangible qualities or physical properties. The thorn is associated both with infancy – it is "Not higher than a two-years' child" – and advanced age – it "looks so old and grey" (5, 4).[1] The small, muddy pool nearby, never completely dry, is neither a proper pond nor dry land. And the adjacent moss heap's resemblance to "an infant's grave in size" is qualified, since no grave was ever "half so fair" (52, 55). Finally, the speaker explains what distinguishes these three items:

> At all times of the day and night
> This wretched woman thither goes,
> And she is known to every star,
> And every wind that blows;
> And there beside the thorn she sits …
> And to herself she cries,
> "Oh misery! oh misery!
> "Oh woe is me! oh misery!"

> (67–77)

We in time realize that the pathetic woman, like the natural objects, occupies a series of marginal positions. Just as the thorn is both infantile and ancient and the pool at times is only a puddle, she is an innocent who is also morally tainted, an enigma to long-time neighbors who expect to know her well, and, as the lines above suggest, a vagrant who nevertheless has a home. Martha Ray has a hut, but she is hardly ever in it. Instead, she spends much of her time journeying to and sitting by the thorn at its mountain-top site. A

94

domiciled woman who is nevertheless out "At all times of the day and night," Martha Ray is both community member and mysterious wanderer, both neighbor and alien. Like the thorn, pond, and moss heap, she defies easy classification.

Through such ambiguities, Martha Ray resembles the wanderers of Wordsworth's earlier poems, and her late-night wanderings and mysterious thoughts recall the disorder traditionally associated with homelessness. But she also exemplifies a new figure in Wordsworth's corpus – the quasi-vagrants of *Lyrical Ballads*. For unlike the homeless of "Salisbury Plain," Martha Ray repeats the same journey, over and over, through a familiar landscape for a highly ritualized purpose.[2] The bounded character of Martha's journeys is in keeping with her neighbors' desire to map her life story through reference to a fixed set of legal and moral coordinates. Describing the plight of the homeless through a transparent third-person narration, the Salisbury Plain poems use generally realistic accounts of vagrant life to address how social polyvalence undermines systems of opposing political or moral binaries. *Lyrical Ballads* shifts the focus to how the homeless are perceived by the communities through which they pass, a development explaining the volumes' deployment of first-person narratives and lyrics. In the process, traditionally ambiguous perceptions of wanderers give way as communities tend to construe them in absolute rather than contingent terms. While the situational peculiarities and personal idiosyncrasies of Wordsworth's speakers occasionally preserve the unstable cultural valence of the homeless, that instability increasingly is resolved by observers into the certainty of innocence or guilt.

The speaker of "Tintern Abbey" rejects this situation by creating a self and memory characterized by diffusion and flexibility. Just as the river Wye reminds him of times past yet itself seems unchanged, the speaker exists at a temporal crossroads where past, present and future alternately coexist and cancel each other out. The final "home" the poet accepts is the unpredictable repository of the female memory, whose nature blurs the boundaries between domesticity and homelessness, brother and sister, and truth and fabrication. However, "The Thorn" elaborates on the obstacles to identifying vagrancy with marginal social or political contexts, and the clearly defined needs of the neighborhood are the signal feature of "The Old Cumberland Beggar." The vagrant's loss becomes the community's gain. The cyclical wanderings of Martha Ray and the

Cumberland Beggar are manipulated so as to fulfill a larger cultural purpose. The observations and tragic stories fashioned out of their experiences by others serve a crucial, normalizing function in local life. The development of such narratives shows how vagrancy can become useful to communities and debilitating only to the homeless themselves.

This chapter brings to light the impact of growing popular support for the French war and the Tory government's crackdown on dissent on Wordsworth's changing representations of vagrancy by the late 1790s. By 1797, national panic at the prospect of invasion was accompanied by a diminished tolerance for social disorder and virulent suspicion of strangers like the homeless. Attending to biographical and historical detail reveals how the first two editions of *Lyrical Ballads* document the local benefits of this suspicion and the mechanisms for its circulation. By showing how Wordsworth's poetry describes an altered political climate, such a reading necessarily revises scholarship identifying *Lyrical Ballads* with a retreat from public concerns.

MARTHA RAY'S FACE

Rebuffed by her lover, Martha Ray of "The Thorn" goes mad and becomes a wanderer. Her neighbors are ignorant of the motives behind Martha's actions after she is abandoned, but they demand certainty. Consequently, they struggle to resolve their confusion over her bizarre behavior into a conviction about her guilt as an infanticide. This response amounts to a defense of static interpretive categories central to social order, like guilt and innocence, whose adequacy is called into question by uncertainty over Martha Ray's conduct.[3] Such uncertainty appears almost contagious, permeating perceptions of her physical surroundings (the thorn, pond, and moss heap) as well as her biography.

In his study of abandoned women in poetry, Lawrence Lipking suggests that representations of these women have political implications, since they frequently stand for a group, comprised of both men and women, that is injured and oppressed.[4] Verdi's operas, for example, allegorize the anguish of an occupied Italy through the "yearnings of a heartsick woman" (Lipking, 11). Italy and the abandoning lover are conflated; in her grief, the heroine cries out for her country's return to its people, as well as her lover's return to his sweetheart. Such buried critiques exist "almost everywhere when people are forbidden to discuss their complaints openly" (11). Poetry about abandoned women thus serves as a coded commentary on the situation of the politically subjugated and alienated.

Martha Ray is one of several women in *Lyrical Ballads* who have been abandoned by husbands, fiancés, or lovers. But desertion does not stop there. Friends and relatives also shun these women, whose experiences and behavior exclude them from respectable family life and the larger home of a welcoming community.[5] Emphasizing this larger sense of abandonment in concert with Lipking's thesis, Martha Ray's plight refracts an important truth about the British provincial milieu of the late 1790s. Small communities increasingly were intolerant of anyone and anything resisting easy social or political classification. In showing how Martha Ray's neighbors situate her enigmatic actions within a plot about baby murder, Wordsworth throws into high relief the process by which communities persecuted suspect Britons during the invasion scare of 1797. Victims of local paranoia included not only those known to be critical of the war effort, but also outsiders whose conformity to popularity accepted loyalties and values was unclear. The poet himself was well aware of this public mood. After he moved to Somerset, his unorthodox behavior confused villagers as to his precise political orientation – was he radical or loyalist? Guilty or innocent? Defending the integrity of these traditional binaries, Wordsworth's Alfoxden neighbors resolved their uncertainty by accusing him of being a French spy. In contrast to "Salisbury Plain," the restrictions on freedom in "The Thorn" stem less from an atmosphere of government-engineered repression than from local prejudice. Connections between Wordsworth and Martha Ray further imply that the poet's rejection in the West Country made him feel unmanned, or vulnerable as only a woman could be. "The Thorn" subtly draws on the power of vagrant behavior in particular to generate uncertainty in observers, but departs from Wordsworth's earlier work in stressing the observer's need to resolve that uncertainty. Martha Ray's wandering is essential to her ambiguous relation to the community; that ambiguity, in turn, induces neighborly suspicions about alleged crimes. Ultimately, she narrowly escapes being hanged on the strength of local gossip. Likewise, Wordsworth's itinerant habits, his newness to the area, and his associations with radical activists led Somerset villagers to suspect the poet and his sister of French sympathies and insurrectionary objectives.

This approach rectifies two related difficulties in the mass of criticism on this poem. Most commentators locate in "The Thorn" a shift from Wordsworth's early, supposedly radical humanitarianism to an apolitical interest in the creative process, a view usually supported by ignoring or downplaying Martha Ray's plight in favor of the speaker's psychology. Accordingly, Stephen Parrish's influential reading argues for the poem's significance as an imaginative product of the narrator's mind (100). More recently, James Averill still concludes that the ballad's goal is to show how sentimental poems are composed (168). In his summary of criticism on "The Thorn," Patrick Campbell notes the result of such studies: "At times Martha, the 'wretched woman' of the tragedy, has been as much an object of rejection by the critics as by her lover Stephen Hill" (84). Scholars who do discuss Martha's troubles, such as Helen Darbishire (43) and Mary Jacobus (*Tradition*, 244–8), do so in generalized, apolitical terms of love and loss. The tendency to treat this poem apart from its context continues up until this writing.[6] Nicholas Roe views *Lyrical Ballads* specifically as a reaction against Wordsworth's earlier political poetry; the 1798 collection shows how "the political imperative is succeeded by imaginative receptivity as the dominant mode of Wordsworth's writing, and the social victim [is] gradually transformed into a figure of monitory wisdom" (*Radical Years*, 142). The poem's origins in the loyalist revival of 1797–8 and the history of vagrant infanticide require us to consider Martha as an actual outcast rather than an imaginative stimulant or timeless sufferer.

The early parts of Martha Ray's story, presented in a factually clear and precise way, show that she was not always an enigma to her community. Without qualification, the narrator tells us her name and how she was betrothed to Stephen Hill 22 years ago. He straightforwardly relates how Hill abandoned his fiancée for another woman he also had promised to wed. As Martha's behavior becomes more complex, however, the narrative about her becomes more obscure. After her abandonment, Martha's pain and sense of loss cause her to go mad.[7] In its capacity to alienate family and friends, insanity itself can be construed as a kind of inner vagrancy; personality changes can convert familiar, even loved, people into elusive strangers.[8] In the narrative about Martha Ray, this conversion is registered through the introduction of speculation about her – indicated by the mantra "they say" – when the village believes that the fire of madness "almost turn'd her brain to tinder" (132).

Soon, her opaque mental state is complemented by physical movement: "She to the mountain-top would go, / And there was often seen" (135–6).

Early on, the narrator acknowledges the effect of Martha Ray's new isolation and wandering ways: her life after her abandonment is a riddle resisting articulation. At points, he resists the urge to fill the gaps in her story with gossip: "I cannot tell; I wish I could; / For the true reason no one knows" (89–90). But like the community of which he is a part, the narrator is not content with half-knowledge. His obsession with discovery manifests itself in the relation of mundane details that many have considered a blot upon the poem; we are told of the pool, "I've measured it from side to side: / 'Tis three feet long, and two feet wide" (32–3).[9] Martha Ray cannot be sized up so easily. So in the absence of facts about her, the inhabitants have resorted to the invention and guesswork that dominate the poem's narration. In his tale, the speaker increasingly fills the lacunae in Martha's story with local accusations of concealed crimes.

Over the years, an entire mythology has evolved regarding Martha Ray's life after her abandonment. "[T]hey say" that after the faithless Hill deserted her, Martha Ray went mad (129). "They say" she then began to make her journeys to the thorn (133). "They say" that six months later she appeared to be pregnant (133). Finally, many believe that she then committed infanticide: "some will say / She hanged her baby on the tree, / Some say she drowned it in the pond ..." (214–16). Lest we take all these suppositions as truth, one crucial stanza belies their certainty:

> ... what became of this poor child
> There's none that ever knew;
> And if a child was born or no,
> There's no one that could ever tell;
> And if 'twas born alive or dead,
> There's no one knows, as I have said. ...

(157–62)

In other words, many aspects of Martha Ray's story after her abandonment are pure conjecture. People do not know whether her child was born dead or alive, or whether miscarriage or abortion occurred instead. However, villagers now believe the old stories. In the absence of more authoritative information, gossip has come to be regarded as fact.[10] The shady line between fact and fiction extends to Wordsworth's choice of a name for his female vagrant. The mother of Wordsworth's friend Basil Montagu, the real-life Martha Ray, was murdered by a jealous lover in 1779. Editors Brett and Jones find it "completely inexplicable why Wordsworth should have chosen the name of his friend's unfortunate mother" for "The Thorn" (291). The confusion, however, would seem precisely to be the point here: the conjecture and excitement over the original trial of Martha Ray's murderer, which the editors say "received considerable publicity," accords with the reception of Wordsworth's character in her community (291). Endowing a fictional character with the name of a woman who in fact had born a bastard (her son Basil) furthers the interpretive challenges at the poem's core.

In the course of the poem, the narrator does dispute the prevailing myth: "But kill a new-born infant thus! / I do not think she could" (223–4). Still he more frequently reaffirms the rest of the village's belief in Martha's crime; people disagree as to her method – some say she hanged the baby on the thorn while others argue that she drowned it in the pool – "but all and each agree, / The little babe was buried there" (218–19). The narrator's own investment in some version of this plot is betrayed by his opening description of the thorn, pool, and hill, where the thorn is explicitly compared to a child and a (grave) stone and the hill to a grave. Here, he also lays the groundwork for the infanticide charges he will later relate; the thorn is described as if it is being punished by nature for witnessing or participating in some secret wrong. Mosses clasp the tree

> So close, you'd say that they were bent
> With plain and manifest intent,
> To drag it to the ground;
> And all had joined in one endeavour
> To bury this poor thorn for ever.
>
> (18–22)

And like the rest of the village, the narrator actively avoids Martha, a point meriting further examination momentarily. The villagers assume a connection between socially condemned, or even criminal, activity and community ignorance about vagrants. Martha Ray's fundamental crime is not bastardy or infanticide but rather

her position as a mysterious stranger, an abandoned vagrant woman. Since so little is known of Martha Ray the crazy wanderer, almost anything can be suspected of her. Eventually, the absences in her story are filled in by the body of a child whose birth itself is theoretical. In local eyes, her insanity and the erratic travels that grow out of it create the uncertainty that makes the charge of infanticide credible.

The village's process of reasoning in "The Thorn" reflects a well-established bias in English law. Since Tudor and early Stuart times, a constellation of statutes had linked crimes like vagrancy with other offenses, such as bastardy and infanticide. In the early modern period, bastardy and infanticide statutes resulted from the widespread belief that the growing mass of homeless people was far more likely to engage in extramarital sex than to support any resulting offspring.[11] Anne Wallace has shown that well into the eighteenth century, walking women found "their peripateia translated as sexual wandering" (29) – a bias still evident in our use of the term "streetwalker" for prostitute. Leaving an infant for the parish to support, or simply stifling it after birth, were old options for wandering women. Yet in early Stuart times, these acts became punishable under new laws associating sexual immorality and baby murder with the increasing numbers of vagrants (Hoffer and Hull, 12).[12] The statute concerning infanticide in the Georgian period actually dated from the reign of James I. The law punished not infanticide *per se*, but concealment of birth.[13] A mother who concealed the birth of a child later discovered dead was assumed to have killed it, unless she could prove otherwise.

Like the law, Martha Ray's neighbors are interested less in the crime of baby murder than the sense that something has been hidden or is missing, a feeling of absence that stems from her vagrant ways. However, Wordsworth's depiction of Martha's neighbors is peculiar in light of the way bastardy and infanticide had come to be treated in the poet's own time. Georgian attitudes toward sex and its consequences were noticeably more tolerant than those of the previous era. The medieval practice of commencing sexual relations after betrothal resumed in the eighteenth century. The result was "far more pre-nuptial intercourse (usually followed by marriage) and a ... simultaneous increase in the proportion of couples who failed to marry after pregnancy occurred" (Stone, 395). After 1780, bastardy rates showed sharp increases. Poor unwed mothers still faced intense local pressure, but on financial more than moral grounds; the parish's real interest was in finding someone to maintain the child.[14] The same practical tolerance influenced the administration of infanticide law. While there is no evidence that infanticides decreased in the eighteenth century, the courts ceased to convict defendants based on the Jacobean statute. By mid-century, to obtain a conviction the state had to prove the baby was not born dead. In most cases, the accused had concealed her pregnancy and the birth, but juries simply did not care. The same era that demonstrated a new tolerance for pre-marital sex viewed infanticide law as unduly severe. When trials occurred, they were still the privileged subject of newspaper coverage and local gossip, but less because of moral outrage than sensational titillation.[15] The Jacobean statute against infanticide was repealed in 1803.

Consequently, the fervor of Wordsworth's villagers seems somewhat anachronistic, especially given their actions near the poem's end:

> And some had sworn an oath that she
> Should be to public justice brought;
> And for that little infant's bones
> With spades they would have sought.

(232–5)

A female vagrant suspected of infanticide would have faced local condemnation, but her chances of being "to public justice brought" were declining. Her chances of being convicted were even slimmer. As in "Adventures on Salisbury Plain," one has the strange sense of a time warp. Rather than the 1780s or 1790s, the poem recalls a much earlier period when the residue of puritan morals still much influenced decisions to prosecute these cases.

The use of anachronism becomes intelligible, however, in light of the larger context that usually accompanied zeal against infanticide. In James I's reign, the need for infanticide law suggested how economic and demographic changes were destabilizing once close-knit villages. As hardship forced competition among villagers for food and work and created a growing class of homeless laborers, charges of infanticide in the courts escalated. These were allegations "which earlier generations had kept within the confines of the community. Infanticide allegations bespoke the breakdown of this community" (Hoffer and Hull, 27). Whether or not these allegations were justified is beyond the scope of this study; historians and sociologists long have lamented the problems in tabulating accurate statistics on such crimes. Rather, the point is that the way communities treated these accusations changed. Villages ceased to resolve such charges through informal proceedings and consensus, going instead to the official courts. As with witchcraft prosecutions, the handling of infanticide charges is a useful index for hostility to vagrants and the social instability they represent.[16] In the early modern period, the increasing social and political disorder fueling infanticide anxieties eventually was confirmed by nothing short of civil war.

In "The Thorn," infanticide's importance suggests the impact of disorder on a later era, for elements of the turmoil of Caroline England recurred in the 1790s, a decade racked by food shortages, crime, and political agitation. The laws most indicative of trouble in Wordsworth's time concerned crimes against the state, not newborn infants. At the level of political allegory, however, infanticide serves as a mirror image of treason: the murdering mother seeks to destroy her offspring, while the treacherous citizen aims to subvert the authority of the patriarchal state. Either scenario indicates a critical breakdown in the stability of the family, the state, or both. By 1797, early modern infanticide accusations and Georgian treason charges shared at least one trait: in small communities, such allegations indicated acute general worries about economic hardship and national security. Accordingly, the village's anxieties in "The Thorn" recall the provincial paranoia over traitors prevalent in the late 1790s. As the poem intimates, such a regional environment can foster suspicion and hostility among even long-time neighbors.[17]

Such suspicion was very real during Wordsworth's Alfoxden year. Government pressures on the political opposition assumed new intensity later in the 1790s. A botched French invasion of Wales in February 1797 gave conservatives another opportunity to initiate treason prosecutions and restrict constitutional guarantees. The invasion itself induced a series of false sightings of French ships throughout the west coast (Emsley, *British Society*, 56).[18] During the same period, naval mutinies diminished Britain's ability to defend its coastline. In response, the Pitt ministry redoubled its efforts against anti-war and reformist elements: propaganda vilified the war's opponents, and mutiny became a capital offense. In February 1798, government agents rounded up leaders of the United

Irishmen, a secret society pursuing Irish independence with French help. By April, militant members of the London Corresponding Society supporting the United Irish and radical changes at home also had been apprehended. The underground networks revealed by these arrests justified the re-suspension of Habeas Corpus on 21 April 1798. Many arrested now were held without trial until the Peace of Amiens in 1802. According to Marianne Elliott, "Attacks on government policy by the opposition in the face of such revelations were depicted as tantamount to treason" (189).[19]

The measures of 1797 and 1798 differed from those taken earlier in the decade in one crucial respect. Pitt's Two Acts had generated a notable public outcry. In the 1794 treason trials, the defining court proceedings for the first half of the decade, acquittals reflected the doubts many British citizens harbored about Pitt's domestic and foreign agendas.[20] Four years later, popular acceptance of another wave of repression signaled a sea change in the public's view toward the war and the measures Pitt was enacting to continue it. Invasion fever meant that the government could pursue potential French sympathizers and anti-war activists with assured parliamentary and public support.[21] The public's mood enabled Pitt to demand "the public commitment of as many as possible to the war and his government and the besmirching of anti-war opponents" (Cookson, *Friends*, 167). To escape persecution, many leaders of the reform societies either withdrew from public life or emigrated by the end of 1797 (Albert Goodwin, 414–15). Another alternative was capitulation to government power followed by re-entry into community life and affairs, a path chosen by many socially prominent people who had opposed the war. For businessmen or anyone else interested in the goodwill of his neighbors, the pressure to choose reaction over reform or equivocation was overwhelming (Cookson, *Friends*, 178).[22] One court case underscores the effect this political climate would have had on Wordsworth. In January 1798, classical scholar Gilbert Wakefield was charged with seditious libel for his *A Reply to some Parts of the Bishop of Llandaff's Address to the People of Great Britain*. Wakefield's case was one of four in the 1790s subject to the *ex-officio* information, a draconian method of indictment that bypassed the grand jury.[23] Virtually everyone connected with the publication of Wakefield's anti-war, anti-Pitt tract was implicated in this case. In the end the author, publishers Joseph Johnson and Jeremiah Jordon, and a bookseller were all convicted of libel. The conviction was a landmark event that effectively silenced the opposition press in London (167).[24]

Loyalist sentiment was sweeping across the country in the same months that "The Thorn" was taking shape in Wordsworth's mind. The poem was composed just as Pitt was taking advantage of yet another suspension of Habeas Corpus by arresting the government's critics.[25] Even in his provincial retirement, Wordsworth well may have been aware of the Wakefield case, which concerned a pamphlet like his "Letter to Llandaff" and profoundly affected the publishing world and his own friend and former publisher, Johnson.[26] By the time of the composition of "The Thorn," Wordsworth also knew from personal experience that many ordinary people had adopted the official view of permissible behavior and sympathies. Unlike his friend John Thelwall, Wordsworth became a political suspect not through the government's spy network but through the aegis of his neighbors. The Spy Nozy incident, memorialized first in Coleridge's *Biographia Literaria*, shows how the invasion scare made informers out of provincial gentry and laborers. In 1797, government spy James Walsh was sent to the West Country to follow up a report by a Bath physician about French spies living at Alfoxden. A remarkable chain of hearsay, reminiscent of the gossip in "The Thorn," led to Walsh's visit. The Bath doctor's information came from his cook, who in turn had heard the news from Charles Mogg, a former Alfoxden servant. Mogg had gotten his details from Thomas Jones, who lived near the Somerset home. Jones, Mogg, and Christopher Tricky, who lived at the Alfoxden dog pound, had considered the Wordsworths suspect for weeks: they were strangers curious about the navigability of regional rivers and they often spent their evenings wandering about the countryside. The Wordsworths did not declare themselves opponents of the government; their neighbors had little evidence of William or Dorothy's political affiliations. But as with Martha Ray, local uncertainties about the Wordsworths were resolved through speculation based on what was clear: the Wordsworths' proclivity for a good ramble when such activities might have military applications. Infamous reformer Thelwall's visit to the Wordsworths in August added to local suspicions, and a consensus emerged among Mogg, Jones, and Tricky that the Wordsworths were French agents reconnoitering for another invasion attempt. David Simpson has discussed the resurgence of what he calls localism among Britain's bourgeoisie at the century's end, an "ethic of staying in place [that] marked off the vernacular speakers and the relatively immobile from the international travelers and cosmopolitans" (*Academic Postmodern*, 142). Simpson explains how localism became a kind of patriotism for those outside Britain's ruling orders after 1789, targeting a ruling "subculture that like to speak French, to travel, and to imagine itself as belonging to a worldwide citizenry" (142). Any stranger to Somerset would likely have been viewed with suspicion in these years, but Simpson's analysis suggests how this tendency would have been compounded by Wordsworth's itinerant background, his friends, and his unfamiliar Northumberland accent, which his Somerset neighbors seem to have inferred was French. Like Arthur Young in France in 1789 (see Chapter 1), Wordsworth in 1797 found that "French" was less a national designation than a kind of code for the forbidden, the threatening, the unfamiliar.[27]

After a brief investigation, Walsh concluded the Wordsworths were not a French menace but isolated, disgruntled English people. As a result, the Home Office took no action against them. But Walsh's letters and subsequent events show how harshly the Wordsworths were judged by their neighbors. The government agent wrote:

> Mogg spoke to several other inhabitants of the Neighborhood, who all told him, They thought these French people very suspicious persons, and that They were doing no good there. And that was the general opinion of that part of the Country. The French people kept no servant, but they were Visited by a number of persons, and were frequently out upon the heights most part of the night.
>
> (Quoted in Roe, *Radical Years*, 250)[28]

Hostility to the new residents made Walsh's job easy: talkative villagers eagerly shared their antipathies and beliefs. As Stephen Gill points out, "suspicion of strangers, envy of the people in the great house who seemed not to need to do honest work, mistrust of [Thomas] Poole, who, it was believed, had tried to introduce Paine's sedition into Stowey – all fueled the gossip" (*Wordsworth*, 127). In the end, the Wordsworths were hounded out of Alfoxden, not by the government but by local opinion. Walsh's inquiries cemented rural prejudice against the Wordsworths, and by the end of the summer they were informed that they would have no chance to renew their lease when it expired in the coming year. Like the villagers of "The Thorn," Wordsworth's neighbors saw themselves as upright subjects trying to bring criminals to public justice.

The Wordsworths' letters during the Alfoxden year are largely silent on this sequence of events, although mention of the situation is made as the moving date of midsummer 1798 approaches. The necessity of leaving the area crops up in letters from both William and Dorothy dating from early March, the same time that Reed believes the poet was beginning "The Thorn." A hint of the local animosity emerges in Dorothy Wordsworth's letter to Mary Hutchinson, dated 5 March 1798, which announces the move and laments that "there is little chance of our getting a place in this neighborhood" (*Early Years*, 199). Coleridge's correspondence from the same period is less oblique. In April 1798 he writes Joseph Cottle, publisher of *Lyrical Ballads*, that

> Wordsworth has been caballed against so long and so loudly, that he has found it impossible to prevail on the tenant of the Alfoxden estate, to let him the house, after the first agreement is expired, so he must quit it at Midsummer; whether we shall be able to procure him a house and furniture near Stowey, we know not. ...

> (*Collected Letters*, 403)

A letter written nearer in time to Wordsworth's arrival in the area expresses greater anxiety. Coleridge advises John Thelwall not to move to Somerset, because of the "Very great odium T. Poole incurred by bringing *me* here ... Wordsworth came & he likewise by T. Poole's agency settled here – / You cannot conceive the tumult, calumnies, & apparatus of threatened prosecutions which this event has occasioned round about us" (343–4). Coleridge feared for Thelwall less because of any Home Office action than because "riots ... might be the consequence" (344).[29]

A familiarity with these events makes it hard to read "Simon Lee," a poem based on an encounter with the aptly named Christopher Tricky, without irony.[30] The Spy Nozy incident also reveals similarities between Martha Ray's isolation and Wordsworth's position as a suspect stranger among reactionary, resentful neighbors. In both cases an itinerant life and unclear motivations encourage accusations of crimes, including infanticide and treason, which were associated with vagrants. Martha Ray's madness and wandering make her suspect – "at all times of the day and night / This wretched woman thither goes" – as do the Wordsworths' mysterious interests and walks "'out upon the heights most part of the night.'"

If "The Thorn" mourns the breakdown in community tolerance during the late 1790s, it also suggests some uses for suspicion that were quite in keeping with Pitt's objectives. Though Wordsworth's note explaining the background of "The Thorn" appears only in the 1800 edition of *Lyrical Ballads*, the poem as first published makes it quite clear who the real stranger is: the narrator himself. Martha Ray's trajectory within the community has been the exact opposite of the person through whom we learn her story. She begins by being an accepted, respectable member of her community. The narrator enters the village as an outsider with an itinerant past of his own, or as Wordsworth's 1800 note has it, a sea captain who has "retired upon an annuity or small independent income to some village or country town of which he was not a native, or in which he had not been accustomed to live" (350).[31]

Tellingly, it is during his first days in the region that his initial (and perhaps only) encounter with Martha Ray occurs. He knows that she goes to the thorn because he has seen her there himself.

> For one day with my telescope,
> To view the ocean wide and bright,
> When to this country first I came,
> Ere I had heard of Martha's name,
> I climbed the mountain's height:
> A storm came on and I could see
> No object higher than my knee.

> (181–7)

The situation that ensues is reminiscent of the meeting of sailor and female vagrant in "Salisbury Plain" but elides that poem's sympathetic conversation between travelers. As a storm begins, the sea captain runs toward what he thinks is a crag that will afford him shelter. In this poem about the difficulty of seeing others clearly, it is appropriate that rain and mist prevent the narrator from perceiving until the last minute that he has seen not a crag but a miserable woman sitting on the ground. Although at points in "The Thorn" he claims to sympathize with her, at this key early moment in his retirement he declines to comfort or even acknowledge Martha. He tells breathlessly that

> I did not speak – I saw her face,
> Her face it was enough for me;
> I turned about and heard her cry, "O misery! O misery!"

(199–203)

What is wrong with Martha Ray's face? We are not told, beyond the fact that it is "enough" to make the narrator recoil. This enigmatic formulation highlights the problem of finding meaningful terms for, or of finding conventional meaning at all in, Martha's appearance and actions. The narrator reacts to her, but this is not described in a way that grants us access to his or her feelings or motivations. He has not heard her story yet, so his reaction cannot stem from fears about her supposed crimes.

The narrator's mysterious initial response to Martha subsequently is resolved into intelligible binaries: in the poem he expresses suspicions about her guilt or, more rarely, a belief in her innocence. This is fortunate for him, since it marks the beginning of his incorporation into the region where he has retired. Given his seafaring, itinerant past and interest in observing the landscape, this is a process which otherwise could have been difficult. In 1797, Wordsworth's innocuous gestures of exploration – which included observations of the sky through a telescope – were construed by his neighbors as treason.[32] The retired seafarer, as marginal a figure as his creator, might be a naval war veteran or a French spy; his mysterious origins and motivations (why does he want to observe the sea through his glass?) do not resolve his status and would attract the kind of local suspicion that engulfs Martha Ray and the poet. The narrator's initial ignorance about Martha, the apparently privileged subject of local conversation, implies he is already in danger of becoming isolated from his adopted community.

The encounter above, however, smooths his path to acceptance. In his reluctance to talk to the mysterious Martha Ray, whose very physical makeup seems indeterminate in the storm (is she human or stone?), he shows himself to be like his neighbors. In the aftermath of this encounter, he can develop an opinion about her. Having such an opinion is another hallmark of community membership, and by contributing to the collective version of Martha's story, the narrator gradually integrates himself into the structure of local life. The ultimate evidence of this process lies in the form of the poem itself. Unlike Martha, the narrator is talking not to himself but to someone new to the area. The newcomer asks questions at various points, provoked by the narrator's innuendos and eager to learn more. Then, the narrator advises his listener to visit the thorn himself, that he may develop his own opinion to voice during these discussions.[33] The narrator tells the newcomer,

> I wish that you would go:
> Perhaps when you are at the place
> You something of her tale may trace.
> I'll give you the best help I can. ...

> (108–11)

This exchange shows that Martha Ray's isolation has become intensely useful to this region. Gathering and presenting bits of her story is an ongoing process, providing an initiation procedure for newcomers and allowing old timers to reassert their place within the community. The narrator states that as recently as last Christmas, Old Farmer Simpson added a new wrinkle; during the last weeks of her pregnancy, Martha seemed momentarily to become lucid so that before labor "Her looks were calm, her senses clear" (154). It is hard to believe that at this point anyone can have anything new to say about Martha Ray. Simpson is one of the three people in the poem mentioned by name, a fact that shows how information, or speculation, about Martha has come to be associated with stature in the village. It is in keeping with the rest of the poem that this new claim clarifies a previously enigmatic aspect of Martha, her mental state. So while Martha has traveled farther and farther from the center of her community, the narrator increasingly has become accepted until he is an authority on her life. Neighbors who express themselves in terms of the acknowledged poles of opinion – here, concerning guilt or innocence – are embraced. Martha Ray, whose confusing behavior resists these categories, has become a pariah.[34] This situation recalls provincial hostility during the loyalist revival not only to the government's critics, but to people whose political allegiances and activities were unclear.

This reading of the sea captain complicates a simple identification between Wordsworth in 1798 and the pathetic

Martha Ray. Like his female protagonist, the poet is avoided, and for similar reasons; but she begins as an accepted villager, a position Wordsworth never attains at Alfoxden. Like his narrator, he enters a community as a stranger with hopes of peaceful retirement. But the resemblance between the poet and his narrator fades after the latter's encounter with Martha Ray. By turning his back on the female vagrant, the speaker is choosing to ally himself squarely with the local interests inimical to her. Wordsworth's persecution at Alfoxden escalated in part because he was incapable of making a statement or gesture that would have definitively disproven local fears about him – he remained a politically ambiguous figure. His reservations about events in France had not made him into an admirer of Pitt. The most historically accurate foil during the invasion scare for the speaker, then, is less Wordsworth himself than those who conformed to loyalist sentiment during the late 1790s.

In such a politically polarized climate, the poem implies, the mechanics of the community-building process ensure that outcasts remain isolated. For a newcomer, the first step in gaining local acceptance is a wholesale rejection of mysterious, as well as openly disruptive, people. Martha Ray says nothing when first confronted with the narrator. It is only when he turns from her that she cries out in despair. This brief encounter implies that the real source of her misery might be not Stephen Hill or a regretted murder, but neighbors that shun her as her fiancé did in the past. Her solitude now is reinforced by villagers too fearful of her erratic behavior even to engage her in conversation. She is never given a chance to tell her story, although she may be willing to do so.[35] The speaker tells his listener to visit the thorn only on those rare occasions when Martha Ray is at home:

> Pass by her door – 'till seldom shut –
> And if you see her in her hut,
> Then to the spot away –
> I never heard of such as dare
> Approach the spot when she is there.

> (96–9)

That her door usually is open suggests that Martha wants company, but that it is denied to her. Speaking to her might disprove accepted parts of her story and threaten the power of her tale to bind together the village.

For similar reasons, the location of the supposed infanticide requires careful handling. Village custom permits superficial examination of the thorn and its surroundings because this activity reinforces, or at least does not undermine, local suspicions. Accordingly, we are told that a view of the pond's surface shows "a baby and a baby's face / And that it looks at you" (228–9). The narrator relates without inhibition his measurements of the pond. Digging deeper, however, is more dangerous and ultimately forbidden – akin to asking Martha Ray about her past, rather than speculating about it in her absence. Such dangers surface in the poem when, in a righteous frenzy, some residents decide to dig up the moss heap and find the bones they believe are there. Then, the speaker asserts that "... the beauteous hill of moss / Before their eyes began to stir," shaking the ground "for full fifty yards around" (236–7, 238). Needless to say, this event prevents the villagers from pursuing their project. Widespread acceptance of this vignette also ensures that the story and its normalizing function within community life are safe. The wrong kind of certainty can be as unsettling as ignorance. After all, what could be worse than digging up the moss heap and finding ... nothing? As it is, all can still maintain that "The little babe is buried there" (241) and, like Farmer Simpson, contrive additional trivia when it suits them. By supplementing superstition with speculation, the villagers prevent any theories from being definitively disproven. Indeed, Wordsworth's 1800 note to the poem presents it as an exhibit "of the general laws by which superstition acts upon the mind" (Butler and Green, 353); the circulation of that superstition turns out to have quite worldly uses.

Wordsworth's life in Somerset ended when he left for Germany in September of 1798 with Dorothy and Coleridge. The reason for the Wordsworths' visit to the continent usually is explained in terms of a vague desire to continue in Coleridge's company. Soon after arriving in Hamburg, the group split up; Coleridge continued on to Ratzeburg while William and Dorothy settled in isolated Goslar. Gill remarks that brother and sister seem to have embarked from England "with no clear purpose, beyond a lukewarm desire to learn the language, and had been fretting about money from the moment they landed" (*Wordsworth*, 157). The poet's experiences at Alfoxden, though, suggest a reason for renewed travel apart from delight in Coleridge's ready conversation. In the end, Wordsworth left the strife and suspicion of the West Country in a way that Martha Ray could not. He felt compelled to do so, after the pause in his travels at Alfoxden, by neighbors who believed that his ambiguous, itinerant ways made him unfit to end his journeying in Somerset.[36]

THE OPEN ROAD AS THE HOUSE OF INDUSTRY

Late in life Wordsworth maintained that "Old Man Travelling" was "an overflowing from 'The Old Cumberland Beggar'" (Curtis, 57). Accordingly scholars have concentrated on the latter, or as Wordsworth himself suggests, the primary work. So secondary has "Old Man Travelling" become that, in their widely distributed edition of *Lyrical Ballads*, Brett and Jones include as a gloss on the poem a critical quotation that clearly deals with "The Old Cumberland Beggar" and his repeated rounds.[37] Wordsworth's statement of priority is peculiar considering that lines designated as "Old Man Travelling" were composed first and that the old man rather than his more celebrated cousin appears in the first edition of *Lyrical Ballads*.[38] In fact, the Fenwick note and the critics who have accepted its assumptions erase the severe dissonance between the two texts, while only dissonance can explain the need for continued composition. There might seem little need to publish an overflowing; a correction is another matter. As a revision of "Old Man Travelling," "The Old Cumberland Beggar" shares "The Thorn's" emphasis on the community's role in defining the individual, even as the later poem portrays that process much more sympathetically. This shift is enabled by reducing the beggar to an imbecile collection of purely physical responses – the reduction Martha Ray's neighbors could never quite achieve. The interchange between self and other at the heart of "Tintern Abbey" surfaces here in a ghostly form, not through the beggar's perceptions, but through the reflections his poverty casts on the minds of benefactors. The beggar paradoxically seems both all body and nothing but the embodiment of an idea, a concept that is processed by different social classes in different ways. Criticizing the legislative objectives of national politicians by reference to local experiences, "The Old Cumberland Beggar" accords with the realities of Georgian vagrancy law and its enforcement. Along the way the beggar

becomes nothing more than perception, preventing the develop-
ment of the ambivalent response that a three-dimensional character
would produce in observers. In the end, the beggar is neither victim
nor criminal; he is only an occasion, an opportunity for giving
charity. The poem's debate then is not really about the valence of
the beggar, but about the value of the responses he induces in
others.

A brief review of "Old Man Travelling" will clarify through con-
trast the issues at stake. Unlike the Cumberland beggar (or Martha
Ray), the aged traveling father of the shorter poem is confronted
and speaks within the poem. This difference points to a broader dis-
tinction: "Old Man Travelling" is directly critical of official authority
in ways the longer poem is not. In the last six lines of "Old Man
Travelling," pared down to four in 1800 and omitted entirely by
1815, the speaker asks the traveler the nature of his journey. The
response is scathingly simple:

> "Sir! I am going many miles to take
> A last leave of my son, a mariner,
> Who from a sea-fight has been brought to Falmouth,
> And there is dying in an hospital."

> (17–20)

The poem's style and content ally it with the early Salisbury Plain
poems. The destructive agent is society and the war its govern-
ments make; the damning knowledge of this state of affairs comes
from an ordinary person battered by greater powers. Such com-
mentary itself was considered unpatriotic, even seditious, in the
years that Britain's rulers and provincial population became united
by fear of invasion and domestic radicalism.[39] That the son received
his wounds in a channel sea-fight responds to popular anxiety gen-
erated during the late-1790s invasion scare.

The poem's implicit critique of authority gains force from the old
man's long, unsupervised journey. The government has not only
killed the son for serving his country faithfully, but also might well
classify his father as a criminal for making this trip. In this regard,
the poem's author is a problematic figure. He may be a sympathetic
listener, but he has all the overseer's lines – "whither he was bound,
and what / The object of his journey" (15–16). The poem's abrupt
ending leaves this tension pointedly unresolved. The poem's chal-

lenge to governmental control and popular sentiment is strength-
ened by the fact that the old man's arrest or punishment are
unlikely. His statement and traveling might be considered action-
able, yet the very situation motivating his errand makes his legal
status ambiguous and punishment improbable. The father's mobil-
ity and blunt words challenge convention, but arresting him for
vagrancy while he travels to see a dying veteran would be unpopu-
lar. The vagrant's disruptiveness is underscored by his effect on
youthful observers: "the young behold / With envy, what the old
man hardly feels" (13–14). The father's age and experiences exempt
him from some limitations of younger people. He is said to be
unfettered by pain, by an awareness of the effort of walking, or by
the need for patience. The poem unites the traveler's escape from
outside interference or inner strain under the feeling of "peace"
earned in old age (13).[40] The young cannot imitate him, lacking the
experiences and motivation that make the journey legally possible.
Their inability to share in his freedom only increases the force of his
example. The old man's power makes others aware of their weak-
ness and envious of his strength. Young people long for his power
to baffle socially and physically conditioned limitations.

   These are precisely the small subversions that are perfected out of
"The Old Cumberland Beggar." Unlike the nationally defined
journey of the "Old Man Travelling," the Cumberland beggar's
movements are governed by an orderly routine involving a single
village. At the outset, we are informed that the beggar belongs to a
class of paupers "who confined themselves to a stated round in their
neighborhood, and had certain fixed days, on which, at different
houses, they regularly received charity" (205). The beggar's encoun-
ters with others define him in subtle but important ways. Though he
does not appear to receive public assistance, in his own fashion he
relies on parish assistance. The upper classes, embodied by the
horseman, help support him, and the second verse paragraph
depicts other examples of informal outrelief, the loosely structured,
often spontaneous aid that proponents of workhouse schemes
sought to eliminate.[41] The tollgate keeper, when she sees the beggar
coming, "quits her work, / And lifts the latch that he may pass"
(35–6). The post boy contributes by turning his cart to the roadside if
the vagrant does not move aside. These small acts are not systematic
or the result of policy yet are important in facilitating the beggar's
survival and make him dependent on parish goodwill in ways the
traveling father or the speaker of "Tintern Abbey" are not.

Further, while the traveling father voices his motives and "Tintern Abbey" is an extended monologue, people's engagement with the beggar never deepens beyond the exchange of food for complacency: he repeatedly is said to be in "solitude" (15) or "a solitary man" (24, 44). The combination of superficial familiarity and a deeper isolation allows the beggar's village to view him as an object, a servant of local custom and unity. The potential challenge to stability encoded in his homelessness is transformed into a prop of community.[42] This process parallels the one at work in "The Thorn," where Martha's estrangement endows community gossip with a normalizing function.

Finally, where "Old Man Travelling" invites us to question the pursuit of the French war, "The Old Cumberland Beggar" does not, a fact easily verifiable by a survey of criticism. Historicist scholarship has focused on relating the longer poem to the bitter debate over the poor laws in the late eighteenth century.[43] These analyses (like the poem itself) can obscure the larger cause behind the 1790s poor law controversy. The poor rate skyrocketed because the war with France had brought crippling taxes, high food prices, unemployment, and inflation. This explains why politicians like Pitt and Samuel Whitbread and philosophers like Bentham sought new laws to both relieve and restrain the increasingly desperate lower classes. The cause of poor law reform gained ground at the same time that the radical London Corresponding Society and trade unionization were being outlawed, suggesting that the goal behind all these initiatives was a desire to contain the social and political unrest of the 1790s (Emsley, *British Society*, 84–5). As "Old Man Travelling" suggests, the search for more effective control over the poor was tied to a larger quest by the Pitt ministry for control over the peace movement and reformers.

To the extent that "The Old Cumberland Beggar" does address these issues, it casts the beggar as Pitt's accomplice rather than his critic. The essence of Wordsworth's appeal is that the beggar and the vagrant existence are not simply "nuisances" to be swept away by "Statesmen… who have a broom still ready in your hands" (70, 67). For the people he affects most profoundly are precisely the uneducated laborers hardest hit by the economic disruptions of the war. He compels the better off to a "kindly mood" (84) and to sympathy "with a world / Where want and sorrow" are (107–8). Singled out for consideration, however, are "the abject poor" (135) who

Long for some moments in a weary life
When they can know and feel that they have been
Themselves the fathers and the dealers out
Of some small blessings, have been kind to such
As needed kindness, for this single cause,
That we have all of us one human heart.

(141–6)

By giving the beggar scraps from their own meager tables, the "poorest poor" suddenly feel akin to their better-off neighbors. The explosive potential of economic and social difference is subsumed by the knowledge that every person ultimately values generosity and loving-kindness. Subsequent lines show a poor villager giving "One unsparing handful" of meal to the beggar (151). The narrator calls attention to the exact amount of her gift because it is such a sacrifice for her. Yet the reminder the beggar brings, of both his own destitution and her want, only results in her "build[ing] her hope in heav'n" (154). This response could only comfort authorities fearful of the real rage among many by the late 1790s over the astronomical price of the very flour this woman gives away. From 1799 to 1801, poverty hit the English northwest with new severity, and food riots broke out in Birmingham, Lancaster and Wigan (Gilmour, 428–30).[44] The prose headnote informs us that the beggar's rounds are confined to a single neighborhood, but the range of his travels is nevertheless broad, binding together individuals and groups who might not even see themselves as part of the same community: "farms and solitary huts, / Hamlets, and thinly-scattered villages" (88–9). The beggar virtually creates and defines singlehandedly the neighborhood he circumnavigates. His homelessness does imply a certain power to wander, but his value to the community (the justification for his vagrancy) depends on his careful regulation of it. He must appear at certain, expected times to act as the "record which together binds / Past deeds and offices of charity / Else unremembered" (81–3) and to qualify for the charity that this awareness produces. His assiduous fulfillment of this function makes the beggar seem considerably more industrious than the "sauntering horseman-traveller" (26) who gives him alms or the speaker, who composes this poem "in my walk" (1).

Despite these qualifications, "The Old Cumberland Beggar" does endow its subject with a limited independence from popular values and government mandates that the speaker feels is worth preserving. The beggar's regulated power entails suffering which many critics have winced at; yet his trials should be measured against the pains of forced national service represented in the Salisbury Plain poems.[45] In his vagrancy, at least he has a choice of servitude. Insofar as he may "*where* and *when* he will, sit down / Beneath the trees, or by the grassy bank," the beggar is free from the mental terrors that afflict Wordsworth's sailor vagrant. So "Long as he can wander," he should be allowed to (165). The beggar's physical hardships only become a problem when the narrator considers how domesticating him – literally, putting him in a state-run "home" – would eliminate his community function and hasten death through "that pent-up din, / Those life-consuming sounds that clog the air" (173–4). This is the life that "Tintern Abbey" identifies with the city, and that broom-wielding statesmen, in a metaphor recalling Wordsworth's earlier equation of home with danger and repression, would force on the beggar.[46]

Though Wordsworth derides a newer conception of the workhouse mandating labor for those within its walls, throughout the eighteenth century the poorhouse was described through the rhetoric of a coercive home. In the Fenwick note to the poem, the author states that its origins lay in his childhood memories of such a homeless man, but such men were only part of the Lake District poor (Curtis, 56). When Wordsworth was born, his hometown of Cockermouth had supported a poorhouse for thirty years. Like other creations of its type, the Cockermouth home was to provide work for able-bodied inmates and housing for the infirm or sick, all within a clearly delineated regimen. Activities, amounts and types of food, and work hours were prescribed; drunkenness, disobedience, and personal possessions were forbidden. Everything except bedding and some clothes were to be sold for the inmate's maintenance when he or she entered the workhouse. As was common in such documents, the Cockermouth workhouse charter phrases the Master's relation to the inmates in specifically paternalistic terms. In a typical example, the document states that "The Master [may] bring as many of his family as can be conveniently spared from the service of the House to Church or permit them to go to their usual place of worship every Sunday morning and afternoon." This view of workhouse relations completed the obliteration of the poor person's unique origins and desires that was the aim of the vagrancy laws.

On one level, the poem would seem to embrace precisely such an obliteration of identity. The ironies of "The Thorn," which encouraged scrutiny of the community's and the speaker's motives, have vanished in favor of a speaker whose unapologetic claims about the uses of the beggar's isolation appear in deadly earnest. Robin Jervis methodically demonstrates how carefully the poem's opening denudes the beggar, step by step, of any meaningful interior life, thus reducing him to "a proper object for contemplation" that can offer "no resistance to the invasive gaze of the poet" ("Wordsworth", 208). Mark Schoenfield also comments on the pervasive visual imagery of the text, identifying the beggar as something of a moving panopticon who monitors the behavior of the villagers as well as regulating his own peregrinations. But Schoenfield locates more than monitory force in that gaze, for in the poem "sight is transformed from an activity to a location, a property over which the beggar has a right of occupancy against the claims of the Statesman and his statutory Poor laws" (168). The beggar's re-grounding of domestic and local affections therefore "establishes his right to nature's eye" (168), the claim of the poem's final two lines. Insofar as this argument suggests that the beggar's settlement lies in local perceptions of him, rather than in actual residence, Schoenfield might appear to be making a distinction without much of a difference. But the difference illuminated by his discovery is more than may be immediately apparent, for while residency or landownership are material facts, perceptions can be idiosyncratic and subject to change. In "The Thorn," this was the source of what by the end seemed little less than outright persecution. "The Old Cumberland Beggar" makes a few modest moves toward recuperating perception's whims, however, as an agent for the preservation of polyvalence. As Jervis notes, the dehumanization of the opening seems to deny the beggar even the one human heart that later is extended to everyone else – he is not even allowed to receive gratification from scattering "the crumbs in little showers" (18) for the birds, though this would appear to be a more humble instance of the already rustic assistance habitually offered to him by the poorest of the poor. Like that charity, the beggar's offering is to an extent involuntary, the result of the trembling of his "palsied hand" (16). Yet the speaker registers this act as "waste," not charity, and implies that the beggar might even beat off the sparrows who timidly approach but know to stay beyond "the length of half his staff" (21). This speaker's reading of these details changes in the course of the poem. He concludes his exhortation to the officious Statesmen by casting this very same behavior as evidence of the kind of volition that the "eye of Nature" (188) makes room for but that the life of the workhouse will not. Let him sit where he will, "and with the little birds / Share his chance-gathered meal" (186–7). While the sharing might be involuntary, still the result of that palsied hand, situating this appeal amid the beggar's ability to situate himself holds out the possibility at least that he willingly shares his crumbs with the gathering birds. This revision in the speaker's interpretation of this act is small, but its appearance in a poem whose argument is the centrality of acts so inconspicuous that they could be forgotten should not be ignored. If the concluding lines construe sight as a space that can be occupied, it is a space whose instability makes it potentially more accommodating than the status derived from property. Depending on the eye of the beholder, the beggar might be thought to "know and feel" that he has been the bestower "of the small blessings" (142, 144) after all, even if his objects are only the smallest mountain birds.

The polemic of "The Old Cumberland Beggar" implicitly gainsays the wisdom not only of workhouses, but also of the long prison terms for those ambivalent about or defiant toward government measures. Those incarcerated, particularly in the wake of the 1798 loyalist revival, were often held for years without ever being charged by the authorities. This situation was made possible by the suspension of Habeas Corpus from 1795 through the early 1800s. A potential check on the use of vagrancy law in conjunction with the repression of sedition, the legal tradition of Habeas Corpus forcefully encoded how closely movement and political freedom were linked in Britain. Habeas Corpus – in medieval Latin, "You shall have the body" – were the words beginning a writ that required the state to present the accused in a court and to offer charges justifying investigation and imprisonment. Habeas Corpus reversed the burden of proof voiced in the vagrancy laws. According to the latter, movement had to be justified by the person engaged in travel. Stability was assumed to be the norm. Under Habeas Corpus, freedom *to move* was an assumed right, and "restraint" via arrest and imprisonment had to be justified by the authorities through a specific and reasoned charge of criminality. Freedom to move and freedom from arbitrary government oppression were inextricably linked. Influential Georgian jurist William Blackstone articulates the standard view of the rights secured by Habeas Corpus: "this personal liberty consists in the power of locomotion, of changing situation, or moving one's person to whatsoever place one's own inclination may direct, without imprisonment or restraint, unless by due course of law" (I. 130). He goes on to call Habeas Corpus a natural right and to identify it as one of the defining separations between English law and France's system of *lettres de cachet* and unspecified terms of imprisonment. Blackstone displays an acute understanding of how losing the body's power to move, precisely because it is a humble power, is a more meaningful measure of the erosion of personal liberty than more dramatic injuries.

> To bereave a man of life, or by violence to confiscate his estate, without accusation or trial, would be so gross and notorious an act of despotism, as must at once convey the alarm of tyranny throughout the whole kingdom: but confinement of the person, by secretly hurrying him to gaol, where his sufferings are unknown or forgotten, is a less public, a less striking, and there-fore a more dangerous engine of arbitrary government.
>
> (I. 131–2)

Blackstone does acknowledge that suspending Habeas Corpus may be necessary in times of national crisis – "in these the nation parts with its liberty awhile, in order to preserve it for ever" (I. 132) – but he reassures the reader that such a measure can be authorized only by Parliament, not by the crown alone. He concludes this discus-sion by reiterating the guarantee's central importance, calling it a "second *magna carta*, and stable bulwark of our liberties" (I. 133). Blackstone discusses vagrancy as an offense under the category of idleness. As this classification implies, for him the real evil of the homeless is not their physical mobility but the economic support they siphon off from communities that assist them. Citing "prover-bial" wisdom from China, he contends that "... though the idle person may shift off the want from himself, yet it must in the end fall somewhere" (IV. 169). Wordsworth will specifically address the value of Habeas Corpus in the Vaudracour and Julia episode of the 1805 *Prelude*. But to the extent that "The Old Cumberland Beggar" is an extended argument that the beggar is anything but idle, his right to move should be constitutionally guaranteed.

This backdrop connects the logic of the workhouse condemned in "The Old Cumberland Beggar" with that of other kinds of corrective facilities, including the prison or even the transportation colony. We are explicitly told that placing the beggar in a "House, misnamed of industry" would render him little better than a "captive" or prisoner (172, 173). A belief in basic English liberties dictates his right to move freely – within agreed-on limits. The very existence of the anti-workhouse polemic in the poem displays the poet's sense of how common assaults on even moderate instances of somatic and ideological wandering are in the current political climate. "The Old Cumberland Beggar" aims to preserve the remaining marginality yet embodied by such figures. The events of 1798, and Wordsworth's own experiences in Somerset, illustrated how the scope of those limits was shrinking, subject to swings in local feeling and circumstance.

Ultimately, the beggar's representation is balanced delicately between marginality and community, between movement and stability, and between a potential challenge to the government and the non-coercive support of its domesticating objectives. While he is a "record," a seemingly unchanging reminder of past deeds, his effect on his neighbors relies on a curious blend of custom and conscious thought:

> The mild necessity of use compels
> The acts of love; and habit does the work
> Of reason, yet prepares that afterjoy
> Which reason cherishes.
>
> (91–4)

The process described here is partly mechanical, yet the mechanism exists to provide material for "reason," which like "theory" was a term implicated in the radical polemics of Paine, Godwin, Frend, and Thelwall. For Wordsworth, only active mental engagement in the end justifies the existence of the mechanism at all. James Chandler's argument that the poem accords with Burke's defense of habit as a mechanism for social stability neglects this insistence that the villagers' customary gifts are accompanied by active mental apprehension (83–9).[47] Such an interplay dominates descriptions of the beggar's effect on others. The same process imparts valuable knowledge to "lofty minds," who then "Will live, and spread, and kindle" (98, 101). The potentially dangerous energy generated by the "mild touch of sympathy" is to some degree counterbalanced by the beggar's repetitive movements and the mental associations they engender. If he stands as a "silent monitor" (115) of charitable deeds, the thoughts he calls up are nevertheless "transitory" and "to no one give the fortitude / And circumspection needful to preserve / His present blessings" (116, 120–2). The homeless can only momentarily make one aware of one's good fortune. The repetitive nature of his own travels does not enable him to fix the villagers' thoughts into a circular routine that would evoke the schedule and paternalism of the workhouse, or literally make them "circumspect." Memory is sparked, but not governed exclusively, by a process of association. On a social level, the result is a loosely spun sense of decentralized community less prone to tyranny than national government control would be.[48]

The significance of defending marginal mental and cultural space for the individual's physical and ideological wanderings emerges again in the second edition of *Lyrical Ballads* in "The two April Mornings." The speaker is on a walking trip with Matthew, but their journey is repeatedly arrested by a paralyzing string of mental associations. As Matthew views a distant cloud bank, he stops without explanation; when later questioned by the speaker, he stops again, finding it impossible to walk and talk of his state of mind at the same time. The difficulty is that the cloud

> Brings fresh into my mind
> A day like this which I have left
> Full thirty years behind.

                    (22–4)

That day was characterized by a similar series of pauses guided by a memory even farther in the past. On the day thirty years ago, Matthew stopped while passing the churchyard where the grave of his daughter lay, unable to continue his journey without contemplating his loss.

The final, most eerie repetition then occurs. On that day in the past, turning from his daughter's grave, he sees a child standing with "A basket on her head." Like the girl bearing a pitcher on her head in the spots of time sequence of *The Prelude*, this child is a signal of some extraordinary mental occasion, but not one that demonstrates how the mind is lord and master. Instead, this double of Emma – or perhaps a vision of her, since we are not even sure the child, who neither speaks nor is spoken to, is real – petrifies the course of Matthew's thoughts. His sense of loss becomes acute at the same time that he is fascinated with this living image of the dead: "I look'd at her and look'd again; / – And did not wish her mine" (55–6). Matthew has stopped twice in the poem's frame and once in its inner story; these two lines describe his thoughts and physical movements becoming locked in a cycle of repetitions dictated by painful and unchangeable memories.

"The two April Mornings" attends to the consequences of memories and associations so tyrannical that nothing, not even reason, can alter or color them. The living child Matthew beholds may trip "with foot so free" (50), but at the poem's end Matthew himself remains standing with even his eyes "fix[ed]" upon the cloud bank that initiated his memories. Nothing can change the character of his loss in those unmoving, because they are so very moved, eyes. His hidden obsession converts experiences that are superficially related to yet actually distinct from his daughter's death – a cloud bank that resembles one years ago, a child who in fact is not his own – into signs of his daughter and her death. Matthew's mindset both terminates his journey and stalls the poem written about him. In the last stanza, we are left to infer yet another April mourning. The speaker tells us

> Matthew is in his grave, yet now
> Methinks I see him stand
> As at that moment, with his bough
> Of wilding in his hand.

> (57–60)

The speaker has acquired Matthew's habit of thought, and the result is a concluding image of such fixity that it is hard to tell Matthew out of the grave from Matthew in his grave. The concluding image is a vision of Matthew halted at the moment of his recollection. The walking tour, and the poem, can never get beyond this moment of suspension. The fact that memories of the dead initiate such moments intimates how close to death this cycle of repetitions really is.

In contrast, the Cumberland beggar's compromise between stasis and mobility by 1800 is codified as a type for the process of poetic composition. In the 1798 advertisement for *Lyrical Ballads*, Wordsworth expressly takes on "that most dreadful enemy to our pleasures, our own pre-established codes of decision" (*Prose*, 1: 116).

He begins the 1800 preface on the same note, stating his indifference toward gratifying "certain known habits of association" (122). By tempering convention with individual imagination, the poet hopes to imbue his work with vitality: his themes come from "low and rustic life" because there "the essential passions of the heart ... are under less restraint, and speak a plainer and more emphatic language" (124). At the same time the 1800 preface is colored by the knowledge, implied in "The Old Cumberland Beggar," that pressure on social as well as aesthetic marginality is growing. Vagrant emotions themselves are subject to the principles of human psychology and the discipline of regulated artistic practice. There are "primary laws of our nature" which govern "the manner in which we associate ideas in a state of excitement" (122–4). That is to say, some habits or restraints are so powerful that they govern even mental states, like excitement, which would seem to admit of few laws. Material for poetry comes from the emotions, but only when they have been recollected in tranquillity.

THE BORDERS OF PERCEPTION

"Tintern Abbey" traditionally is recognized as the poem in which Wordsworth discovers the subject that makes his work great: loss, realized in time and through memory, is redeemed by an ongoing sense of personal growth and outward fellowship.[49] The relation of these topics to political or social contexts, however, has been among the most heated debates in Romanticism; Johnston summarizes the view of many in remarking that "Where one stands on 'Tintern Abbey' makes a big difference in Romantic scholarship" (*Hidden*, 591). Historicist critics have tended to cast the poem as fragile and deceptive, avoiding historical fact in favor of a superficial harmony. Other commentators have defended the timelessness of its personal and humanistic themes.[50] What follows is, in part, an attempt to explain the origins of this critical binary, which lie in the contradictory rhetoric of the poem itself, positioning the lyric self alternately as unchanging or as enmeshed in multiple temporal continuums. The speaker's right to successively adopt these seemingly opposed positions, as well as variants on them, is the implied argument of the work. While "Tintern Abbey" does not address social events as explicitly as the Salisbury Plain poems, for example, its objective does carry the residue of public events. More particularly, this text seeks to safeguard homeless polyvalence from the menace of political sectarianism by locating the terms of debate in one man's wandering spirit. Fred Randel has argued that "those who appear homeless in this poem are not restricted to a marginal group of capitalism's most impoverished victims, but are equivalent to the poet and his contemporaries, who have been let down, as he believed, by existing institutions" (384). In a text about living among the ruins of political and social promises, the poet of "Tintern Abbey" also is keenly aware of his own incompleteness, of the fragmentation of personality that prevents him from definitively affirming a unified experience of life time. This sense of fragmentation usually has been interpreted as a crisis, a perception the speaker fails to or succeeds in (depending on the reader's ideological orientation) allaying. While the poem repeatedly enacts a drama of advance and retreat over the continuity of personality and the recovery of memory, the speaker uncovers advantages as well as burdens in confronting the irregularities in his own identity. The incompleteness of individual consciousness enhances his awareness of connections with outer forms and other people, for only in the continual modification of those connections are the shifting contours of our lives, what existence can mean to us and to others, rendered.

The most destructive response to this state of affairs turns out to be immersion in certain kinds of social settings that ironically accentuate, rather than bridge, differences between people and therefore the individual's sense of fragmentation. The poem's central fault line between youth and age finds a counterpoint in the fracture between self and society, and in this way Wordsworth gestures toward the political divisions that by the close of his Alfoxden days had made him an alien in his own country. Locating in the poem the substitution of a professional poetic role for that of a knowable individual subject, Thomas Pfau remarks that the "tranquil restoration" professional membership secures for the speaker "can also be read as a political trope, that is, as substituting the Tory ideal of 'virtual' representation for the radical and evidently unattainable ideal of 'direct' representation" (130).[51] Rather than see the speaker's worries over unified identity as signaling the death of the individual political subject, Randel views the poem's diffusion of consciousness through all things as a reaction against "the recent efforts of both France and Britain to crush dissent." He explains, "'Tintern Abbey' is Wordsworth's declaration of independence from exclusivist models of cohesiveness and from the institutional structures that promote them" (396). My own variation on this theme compels modification of the view that the poem finally rejects "any political position that suppresses freedom and denies to individuals the right or power to think independently" (Randel, 388). Rather than clearing a space free from connections or commitments, the poet's fragmented sense of identity juxtaposes continuity *alongside* rupture. The individual's incompleteness only strengthens one's reliance on a mesh of intersections between times, people, and ideologies, in addition to those between humanity and the material world. The result is less a sense of unrestricted freedom than a highly nuanced network of interdependencies essential for self-understanding, social perpetuation, and political dialogue transcending the "unintelligib[ility]" with which the poet quarrels.[52]

"Tintern Abbey," like "The Thorn," focuses on a vagrant whose wanderings are cyclical. As in "Salisbury Plain," written during the poet's original visit to the Wye valley, the vagrant of "Tintern Abbey" speaks for himself. During a dilated pause in his travels, he enunciates his own experience of victimization by and isolation from the communities through which he has passed. Also as in "Salisbury Plain," the homeless speaker of "Tintern Abbey" in the end finds an alternative to such treatment in moments of camaraderie with a fellow traveler. In this respect, the poem incorporates the insights of other *Lyrical Ballads* showing the vulnerabilities of the homeless in the face of community exclusion and pressure. In "Tintern Abbey" the wanderer creates a micro-community with a family member whose memory will provide a home for them both. Consequently, the vagrant speaker enjoys the love and association denied to Martha Ray. Memorializing such love in memories that are fluid, accretive, and at times unreliable emancipates that feeling from the confinement characteristic of the home or the routines supporting it.

Yet "Tintern Abbey" also expands on the vagrant's significance in ways earlier poems cannot, largely due to the lyric's focus on individual consciousness and memory. This focus enables Wordsworth to make his understanding of marginality as a place of overlapping perceptions the basis for an aesthetic grounded in what we "half-create, / And what perceive" (107–8). If the literary form most suited to this awareness is the lyric, its most local incarnation is the allusion; appropriately, Wordsworth footnotes the above line, perhaps the poem's most famous, as bearing "a close resemblance to an admirable line of Young." The same note immediately muddies this literary debt, however, since Wordsworth cannot remember "the exact expression" that he claims inspired him (119).[53] The line both is and isn't Young's (as compared to the endless quotations peppering *An Evening Walk*); Wordsworth's perceptions of the world both are and aren't his own; and he both is and is not the same man who trod this path five years ago. He is not, in other words, Matthew, who in "The two April Mornings" cannot escape his past and the one relation, to Emma, that defined everything else for him. Wordsworth's decision to develop this dynamic through the meditations of a wandering speaker cements its connection to the volatile valence of homelessness.

In a move familiar to the reader of *Lyrical Ballads*, the 1798 collection's final poem begins by identifying homelessness with isolation and repetition. Initially, the speaker standing over the Wye valley seems separated not just from society in general but from any other human presence: the deep isolation of this moment calls up "thoughts of more deep seclusion" (8). As if such solitude were not enough, representations of disguise also permeate this isolated spot. The green fruits of trees "lose themselves" among the green landscape, and even the hedgerows are "hardly" discernible, so well do they blend in with a background that is semi-cultivated (13, 17). The uniform tint of the valley promises to immerse even the farm cottages sprinkled in the distance, for these are "Green to the very door" (18). The adjective "wild" appears three times in the first section, always as an affirmation of how secluded or unsocialized the scene is. Finally, the speaker's doubles, the region's "vagrant dwellers," are themselves camouflaged by the "houseless woods," their presence possibly imaginary and only conjectured from the smoke that winds up from the dense forest (21). Yet the uniformity of the scene gives way before the speaker's continual eye for difference amid the sameness. In an amazing feat of recall, he knows that he now reposes under "this dark sycamore," presumably the exact same one he rested under in 1793. The hedgerows and cottages, difficult for others to differentiate, for him are "these" (16, 17) hedgerows and cottages, remembered from times past.

Wordsworth's most sustained verse meditation on his vocation since *An Evening Walk,* "Tintern Abbey" conveys an even stronger realization than before that any sense of one's isolation or uniqueness is necessarily temporary, and that the same mechanisms that appear to segregate individual experiences can be, or perhaps inevitably are, conceptually configured so as to bridge them as well.

Accordingly, the cliffs promoting thoughts of deep seclusion in the opening simultaneously "connect / The landscape with the quiet of the sky" (7–8). The speaker heralds the "sweet inland murmur" (4) of the Wye, but the poet's choice of a river as his renovating source imports Heraclitean overtones of inevitable variation, and despite the opening insistence on repetition we will indeed see that one can't step into the same waters twice. A note to the poem justifies the river's stable, "inland" sounds by explaining that the "river is not affected by the tides a few miles above Tintern" (116). The very clarification of the water's isolation at this turning registers the river's overall implication in the larger motions of sea and moon. Even the time of year invoked in the opening section requires that we both notice isolation's charms and bear in mind that they are not absolutes. The farms are green to the cottage door now, but those unripe fruits will ripen and the harvest will be taken in, leaving barren fields devoid of comforting camouflage. The poem's extended description of mid-summer throughout the opening lines at once insists on the passage of time – those five summers and five winters, the continuous observation that all these sights are experienced "again" (2, 4, 9, 15) – while granting the existence of only one time, the eternal summer that almost occludes the proceedings of the calendar year. There are other seasons, other times, in the Wye valley, but we and the speaker know them by inference rather than by verified experience.

Sections two, three and four all describe difficult or problematic situations and then present remembrances of the "sylvan Wye" as a solution (57). Significantly, these situations are often presented as moments of confinement, even oppression, as a result of contact with the forms of organized society. In the past described in section two, urban bustle minimized rather than facilitated human contact, as the speaker has found "in lonely rooms" (26–7). But then, as in the present, vagrant consciousness circumvented the speaker's sense of physical, as well as temporal, isolation; the speaker looks at the Wye now and the Wye in the past; the speaker next looks to the absence in between now and then, when the country was not "As is a landscape to a blind man's eye" (25). The locodescriptive eye has become the lyric I, and physical experience becomes the basis for consoling daydreams. These daydreams are not simply the somber meditations of earlier eighteenth-century introspective poetry; they become fuel for other feelings and actions.

The fact that we cannot know these feelings or actions directly, since both are "unremembered" (32, 35), does not prevent them from being "that best portion of a good man's life" (35). The continuum between action and thought, material and spiritual, memory and forgetting, creates a series of negotiations whose resolution is deferred by the poem's ongoing rhetoric of assertion, qualification, and revised declarations. The diffusion of action into unremembered deeds is paralleled by the ensuing dispersal of consciousness, as the physical being is "almost suspended," yet the "eye made quiet" continues to operate, allowing us to see into the life not of an undefined entity but of the quite material, as well as completely open-ended, "things" (46, 48, 50). The same language, and some of the same terms, recur later when the speaker describes

> ... something far more deeply interfused
> Whose dwelling is the light of setting suns,
> And the round ocean, and the living air,
> And the blue sky, and the mind of man,
> A motion and a spirit, that impels
> All thinking things, all objects of all thought,
> And rolls through all things.
>
> (97–103)

The pantheistic overtones accommodate both the diaspora of identity and its innumerable incarnations in countless physical and psychological processes. Memories acquired by thoughtless youth are altered by the adult, organizing imagination located in a version of natural communion. One might expect Wordsworth to use a metaphor of burial or imprisonment, traditional ways of securing a treasure. But in "Tintern Abbey" such a response would be no improvement over the very psychological and physical isolation the speaker is fleeing. He takes the exact opposite approach, constructing identity not only through reference to a treasured past but also by disseminating the self in the present so that the particles of selfhood can never be pinpointed, much less gathered and disciplined. The description of this transformation necessarily lacks detail; the vagueness of this faith gives the speaker power because he and his beliefs fail to follow a culturally defined script of development.

There is a "dwelling" here for personality and thought, but it is no more substantial than sunlight and no more controllable by outside

forces than the oceanic tides. In " ... Poetically Man Dwells ..."
Martin Heidegger advances a similar claim for Hölderlin's poetry,
arguing that it shows how dwelling can mean something very differ-
ent from residing in a home or single place. For Heidegger, poetry is
the measure of humanity's dwelling, which itself is defined as a
measure of one's relation to God and the heavens; poetry becomes a
verbal manifestation of this upward gaze toward the infinite that
even the weariest laborer engages in. Like Wordsworth describing
his relation to nature, Heidegger finds the description of this con-
nection, or dwelling, between people and the godhead as mysteri-
ous and beyond physical qualities as God himself; it "does not
consist in a clutching or any other kind of grasping ..." (224). Albert
Wlecke identifies "Tintern Abbey" with such a phenomenological
mystery and diffusion: in the poem's paradoxical dwelling, "the
mind itself moves beyond a fixed attachment to a specific location,
pours and spreads itself throughout the space of the visible cosmos
(and finds expressive form for this action through a catalog of
dwellings, the terms of which ... do not really localize)" (7). In more
practical terms, the advantage of such a posture lies in its power to
baffle modes of perception or political rhetoric that cannot see
beyond predetermined modes of apprehension and ideas of loyalty.
In "Tintern Abbey" the unintelligible world is cast away only to be
regained in a more fundamental sense, as its constituent elements
are available once again for the speaker's perusal and interpretation.
It is this larger dynamic, in addition to claims for the specific powers
of the Wye, that the speaker explores and champions.

Temporally, then, marginality here means a simultaneous
acknowledgment that life is composed of discrete experiences and
that those experiences are connected, even as they are also (some-
times quite) separate. The poem enacts this understanding through
its descriptions of psychological states, but it also realizes this belief
at the level of a rhetoric that explores such consciousness purely as a
series of hypotheses and reversals. To see the poem's turnings, like
those of the Wye, as a tortured drama of self-assertion and doubt is
thus to somewhat miss the point; the pattern of belief followed by
doubt followed by changed belief offers all three positions, as well
as all sites on the continuum between them, as possibilities in the
progress of the speaker's journey. A poem with only the assertions
and none of the doubts would be as stifling as the "lonely rooms"; it
would be purged of the kind of polyvalent perception that is not
the poem's problem but its prescription. At its most general,

"Tintern Abbey" is about the right to change one's mind. Again and again (as the opening reminds us). The speaker's belief in this right constitutes the "abundant recompense" (89) that has been praised by humanists and criticized by materialists, modern opponents whose ideological roots extend to the very political camps to which Wordsworth was responding. For all its raptures, the youthful self Wordsworth mourns, even as that self continues to live on in memories (a true loss of temporal continuity would be to have no memory at all), was limited by his indifference to any "remoter charm, / By thought supplied, or any interest / Unborrowed from the eye" (82–4). *The Prelude* will call sight the most despotic of the senses, a view "Tintern Abbey" anticipates by tying dependency on sight to containment within narrow physical and temporal confines. The speaker's stumbling attempts to describe his earlier self may partly reflect on his current inadequacies, or they may point to the failings of his earlier self. For how can a consciousness who sees the logic of negotiation everywhere render a self of purely sensory apprehension and appetites? There simply may not be that much material to work with, from the perspective of his older self. The very fact that he cannot meaningfully describe its particulars makes way for a positive evaluation of his maturity. That said, the speaker's relation to that earlier self is clearly more substantive than his despairing claims would have us believe. After telling us he "can't paint" who he was, he provides some of the most powerful and descriptive passages in the poem to do precisely that.

That Wordsworth identifies loneliness and isolation with social life in general and city dwelling in particular posits the city as a metonymy for the domestic political climate created by government policies. Wordsworth's own brush with government surveillance came in the provinces, but urban residents were particularly vulnerable to official oversight, arrest, or harassment, and the seclusion of a prison stay lacked the possibilities for interaction implicit in the speaker's situation. In the city, meaningful interchange is supplanted by the din of political grandstanding and public panic. Examining urban representations in Wordsworth, Coleridge, and Lamb between 1797 and 1801, Lucy Newlyn alludes to the political significance of the city in "Tintern Abbey" since "the detail is not just physical, it is also painful: the life-consuming sounds had clogged the air ... capable – but for imagination's power – of smothering and denying liberty" (413–14).[54] Later imagery continues to locate the speaker's fear less in the changes in belief he accommodates than the powerlessness to make such changes, a powerlessness the text repeatedly couches in metaphors of weight. In a tactile pun, oppression often is figured as a kind of physically burdensome pressure.[55] Through the speaker's memories of the rural Wye, "... the heavy and the weary weight / Of all this unintelligible world / Is lightened" (40–2). Section three expands on the experience of subjugation as a physical encumbrance, as "the world" is blamed for "the fretful stir / Unprofitable, and the fever" that "hung upon the beatings of my heart" (53–4, 55). The music of humanity can "chasten and subdue" (94), but it does not stand in the way of the ensuing "elevated thoughts" and "something far more deeply interfused" that continue to argue for the connections as well as the differences between varieties of human experience. Neither "harsh nor grating" (93), the music distinguishes itself from "the calls to arms of both sides in the propaganda wars of the 1790s" (Randel, 391) as well as from the discordant noise of towns the poem criticizes. The individual's capacity for interfusion, and the actual somatic movements that are analogues for the process, become occluded in certain social contexts. When Wordsworth describes the 1793 visit to the Wye, he quickly qualifies his assertion of nature's importance by admitting that he was "more like a man / Flying from something that he dreads, than one / Who sought the thing he loved" (71–3). While the details of Wordsworth's activities in the summer and fall of 1793 remain unavailable to biographers, these lines insinuate that the earlier trip was motivated in part by a desire to avoid London and the government crackdowns that were making life there heavy indeed for the politically outspoken. Gill cites the crown's political intolerance as a likely motive for the western tour of 1793: "Oppressed by ... unthinking conservatism, as well as intensely worried about his personal position, Wordsworth must have felt trapped and impotent during his time in London" (*Wordsworth*, 73–4). Similarly, we might explain the line "The time is past" (84), atypically conclusive in this poem about uncertainty, by reference to Wordsworth's subsequent encounter with a government spy in 1797. After the poet's persecution and eviction in what, compared to London, seemed provincial isolation, the area would have lost any association with deliverance from "something that he dreads."

This hypothesis gains force from the few lines in "Tintern Abbey" that provide detailed cause for the speaker's periods of despondency. In the final section where he addresses his sister, he offers their companionship as proof that

... neither evil tongues,
Rash judgments, nor the sneers of selfish men,
Nor greetings where no kindness is, nor all
The dreary intercourse of daily life,
Shall e'er prevail against us ...

(129–33)

Johnston observes the peculiarly "narrow but intense range of expressions for human evils" that appears in "Tintern Abbey" ("Politics," 12). These lines, a compressed description of malicious gossip and its effects, acquire new significance in light of Wordsworth's experience among hostile neighbors in Somerset. The much commented-on significance of the poem's dating, 13 July 1798, recalls defining events of Wordsworth's youth, particularly the day he landed in France in 1790; 13 July (1797) was also the date he and Dorothy Wordsworth moved into their Alfoxden home (*Hidden*, 522). Walsh's letters show how little Wordsworth was understood or accepted by his Somerset neighbors and reveal much about a political atmosphere in which unfamiliarity with the locals and nocturnal walks could be construed as treason. Such innocuous details of quotidian existence became "dreary" when they became material for hostility and accusation. These lines are concomitant with the sudden introduction of Wordsworth's sister into the poem, whose presence here may reflect the fact that she was ostracized at Alfoxden alongside her brother, while he made much of the 1793 tour of the west alone.[56]

Despite fears about being isolated amid society, the speaker of "Tintern Abbey" concludes by reasserting his inevitable bond with at least one other person. Dorothy Wordsworth here is ideal for Wordsworth's purpose, since a sibling incarnates the ambiguities the poem has been centered around: they share the same bloodlines but remain different people. As Pfau explains, Dorothy's status as the poet's replica makes her the ideal audience; she incarnates a reconciliation of subject and object (124). The tensions in this juxtaposition persist, however, fueling the conclusion's descriptions of Dorothy as first an extension of the poet, and then finally as someone whose experiences he cannot control or predict. The key again is memory, as was also the case in "The Old Cumberland Beggar," but while the beggar's value resides in reminding people of specific charitable acts "Else unremember'd" (83), in "Tintern

Abbey" the process is more important than the content. In the final section, the speaker shifts focus from his own past, both separate from the present and continuous with it, recoverable in some senses yet inaccessible in others, and instead looks forward to his sister's future that is similarly pitched between what can be predicted and what cannot. In keeping with the rest of the work, Dorothy Wordsworth's future memories could be oddly forgetful, since memory's workings do not operate with mechanical consistency. Individual will and reflexive mental processes are sometimes at odds and sometimes united in purpose, and memory's vagrancy endows it with an indeterminacy, an uncertain mixture of truth and fabrication that is half-created, half-perceived.[57] Temporally, this combination translates into the speaker's concluding view of his sister as a combination of his past and her future: she is "what once I was" (121) and what she will become. This dynamic is less a time line than a time web, where disjoined moments abut each other, coming together in the person of the sister. This overlap of competing times enables the speaker to affirm a unity of identity that honors disjunctions between different periods of human physical and mental development. Dorothy Wordsworth is with him as he is, but she also is him as he was, and she will be him as he is at this moment. The multiple temporalities of memory, operating on the logic of both/and rather than either/or, provide a conduit for perception that escapes the limitations implied by the speaker's idolatry when nature was all in all to him. Not grounded in a specific location, the mature memory embraces continuity between past and present, but this cannot be achieved by one person alone, a fact that gestures toward the undeniable fissures segregating one time of life from another.

The camaraderie between brother and sister is situated within a larger context of actual physical wandering and an awareness of its hardships. Those travails are portrayed as essential preparation for the particular kind of mnemonic capacity Wordsworth believes it is urgent for his sister to possess in the future. He urges

> Therefore let the moon
> Shine on thee in thy solitary walk;
> And let the misty mountain winds be free
> To blow against thee …

> (135–8)

The "therefore" indicates the power of communion to fend off the hard words the vagrant attracts, replacing them with the conviction that "all which we behold / Is full of blessings" (134–5). Like the vagrants of Salisbury Plain, William and Dorothy are earlier figured as "dear, dear Friend[s]" (118). An unavoidable counterpart to this intimacy is the possibility of Dorothy's later isolation or solitude, and of William's later death, though the poem teaches that such separation, like everything else, is contingent rather than absolute. Dorothy's physical environment compels our awareness of interchange between body and spirit, of the connection between the gains of vagrant ambiguity and the costs of physical hardship. Unlike the Cumberland beggar, Dorothy does not have to endure the exposure to the elements the speaker describes. Instead, she is exhorted to "let" the moon shine and the winds blow on her, or in other words to relinquish a measure of her own comfort. This is what meaningful companionship with people, and nature, requires of us. It is the difference between thoughtless youth and the mature listener to humanity's sad music, which expands in addition to subduing consciousness.

The familial bond between William and Dorothy, as opposed to the impromptu sympathy of "Salisbury Plain," ensures that their future separation will be mediated.[58] In the present, this bond converts Dorothy into her brother's double rather than his companion:

> … in thy voice I catch
> The language of my former heart, and read
> My former pleasures in the shooting lights
> Of thy wild eyes. Oh! yet a little while
> May I behold in thee what I once was …
>
> (117–21)

Dorothy's vibrancy may account for the speaker's ability to describe his own youth, despite his early disclaimer that such a feat is impossible. The poet's dependence on her here illustrates again that the self is not autonomous, but is constituted over time in its transactions with others. Several readers have found Wordsworth's use of his sister troubling, denying her an autonomous existence or individual desires.[59] The totality of the poet's identification, and the depth of the speaker's longing, seem to deny her a separate identity at all, replacing a model of interchange between two subjects with one of simple domination. His passionate desire also suggests that the "abundant recompense" defended earlier in the poem fails to console us when faced with an image of what we have lost but another still possesses. At this juncture, the speaker's feelings objectify the sister and seek to appropriate her qualities by converting her into a kind of picturesque commodity that one can "catch," "read," and "behold" (117, 118, 121).[60] The echoes of confinement here recall the descriptions of city and social life that disturbed the speaker earlier in the poem. Although he is impelled by admiration rather than hostility, his desire to preserve her as a reflective double of his own best qualities smacks of its own kind of subjugation.

In her revisionary reading of Wordsworth's relationships with women, Judith Page argues that although "the male poet denies his sister her own story," he "demonstrates his dependence on her, even as he constructs his myth of male development" (47). This awareness of dependence is formally underscored by the sharp juxtaposition of Dorothy Wordsworth, who initially appears as the poet's tool, with the poem's other female, "Nature [who] never did betray / The heart that loved her" (123–4). The description that follows reasserts the importance of outside influences on his development and life, since the agency that Dorothy seems to lack is promptly redistributed to nature, who "leads," "informs," "impresses," and "feeds" the adult mind (125–8). Reminded of this dynamic, and facing a renewed comprehension that volition can divide, as well as unite, people – remember the dangers caused by those "evil tongues" – the speaker concludes with an altered assessment of Dorothy's significance, one that honors the differences and inevitable distance between them, even as it reasserts a connection between them as friends and siblings. It is now that he envisions her alone, on her "solitary walk," and that he can consider her living after he himself has died (136). A bond between them remains, but in the end this bond makes way for individual progress and decay. In the imagery of "Tintern Abbey," she remains a vagrant to the end, but her mind

> Shall be mansion for all lovely forms,
> Thy memory be as a dwelling-place
> For all sweet sounds and harmonies; Oh! then,
> If solitude, or fear, or pain, or grief,
> Should be thy portion, with what healing thoughts
> Of tender joy wilt thou remember me,
> And these my exhortations!

> (141–7)

Female memory becomes the homeless home of "Tintern Abbey." It is there that the sweet harmonies of mediated, if arduous, life will persist. Page contends that this imagery "prefigures the ideal of Victorian domesticity" (47), but this reading persuades only if we take "prefigure" in the most general sense. This dwelling place lacks the hermetic intimacy essential to the Victorian, or even Georgian, domestic ideal, instead enabling an awareness of outside burdens as well as joys.[61] It is precisely this crucial flexibility that allows for memory and the self's reconstitution throughout human life, a flexibility mirrored in the passage's temporal dispersion, looking ahead to when Dorothy will look back. The speaker's altered perspective on his sister, from a reflection of himself to a home for a variety of experiences, some of which he cannot even anticipate, results in a new image of Dorothy as agent and presence. Though he predicts that she will "remember me," he eventually allows for the possibility that she ultimately may remember little more of him than the fact that, for one moment, "... on the banks of this delightful stream / We stood together" (151–2). Dorothy as the housekeeper of memory has the advantage over the female vagrant of "Salisbury Plain" in that she is less encumbered by subordination and destructive possessiveness, a position summarized by the poem's concluding continuities and disjunctions between the poet's "many wanderings," the "many years of absence," and the multiple ways the memories of the Wye can be dear: "to me[,] for themselves, and for thy sake" (159–60).

A revision of poems that grew out of Wordsworth's last tour of the west in 1793, "Tintern Abbey" invokes and qualifies the conclusions of the Salisbury Plain poems. The poem's concluding encounter is not simply a temporary affair, between strangers who will never see or perhaps even think of each other again. Although the vagrants of "Tintern Abbey" also are conscious of a hostile society, they remember their moments of communion and sympathy and these remain an enduring, as well as a volatile, comfort to them. Their fellowship and the contingent relationships the speaker witnesses within the outside world and between it and himself allow for the mental flexibility and the physical mobility to which resistance was building in the heavy world of the 1790s. The victimization of the vagrant in "The Thorn" generated the dialectical acknowledgment of community power and prejudice over all individuals in "The Old Cumberland Beggar" as well as the enduring assertion of the individual's role in interchange in "Tintern

Abbey." The narrators of Wordsworth's 1802 poems concerning the homeless will acknowledge transformations in that role at a time when to outward appearances pressures on the marginal were in retreat.

4

Suspicious Lives: Delinquency in the 1802 Poems

In a comment particularly pertinent to Wordsworth (and indeed to most Romantic writers), Foucault explains the central role that biography played in an important innovation in nineteenth-century police: the development of the concept of delinquency. This rubric replaced the amateur constable's mission of apprehending criminals, guilty of a discrete offense, with the professional policeman's diagnosis of delinquents, individuals whose predilection toward crime – whether they actually had violated a law or not – was verified by a "slow formation ... shown in a biographical investigation," carried out from the "triple viewpoint of psychology, social position, and upbringing" (Foucault, *D&P*, 252). Investigators policing delinquency associated details about an individual's life seemingly irrelevant to a particular offense with a tendency to commit crime – a practice that in our own time has been rationalized in the profession of the criminal profiler. The twentieth-century identification of certain types of crime with social isolation, regularly disseminated through the newcast cliché for murder suspects, "s/he was a loner," is one obvious example of the kind of link legal professionals make between crimes and character traits with no obvious, causal connection. Delinquency enters British policing practice not through a desire to circumvent the actions of violent criminals, for example, but in response to the vagrancy problem in London during the 1790s and early 1800s. Of course, biographical information always had been important in the practice of vagrancy law; a wrenching (or damning) personal history often affected how or if the homeless were punished. But laws in 1792 and 1802 anticipated the concept of delinquency by expanding the inquiry into vagrant behavior in a particularly overdetermined way, codifying the criminality not only of certain behaviors but also of a suspicious *reputation.* This formal authorization of community perception alone as a basis for arrest and punishment would gradually be accompanied by theorizing about the criminal mind and its tendencies, enabling professional investigators to predict illegal behavior. Policing could become preventative rather than simply reactive, as it had been in the eighteenth century.

The Peace of Amiens (1802–3), a welcome intermission in Britain's war with Napoleon, provided the unlikely backdrop for these developments. To many observers, the truce seemed to engender an atmosphere of more open and free debate on issues like political reform. Yet the new permissiveness was grounded in the fact that the government's most troublesome critics largely had fallen silent. Vagrancy laws criminalizing a dubious reputation demonstrate how the returning confidence in stability among the nation's ruling classes ultimately served to metastasize, rather than allay, the elite's fears of political subversion. The laws' expansion of vagrant criminality to include delinquents justified the extension of an embryonic government bureaucracy that sought to manage a range of illegal or undesirable behavior. The "suspected persons" law of 1802, which points to the advent of modern criminology in Britain, was administered by government employees, London metropolitan magistrates and constables, whose expertise and government salaries made them among the earliest professional enforcers of British law. These events form an unexamined frame for Wordsworth's poems about the homeless composed during the spring and summer of 1802. In "Alice Fell" and "Beggars," Wordsworth casts himself as not only a professional writer but also a kind of investigator of the poor and their conditions. Potentially a social monitor, he employs elements of official investigative method, but his unpredictable responses to lies and other "suspect" behavior are by turns sympathetic, charitable, and willfully self-deceiving. The absence of anyone else in the poem who could serve as an untainted, professional observer means that the borders of delinquency cannot be policed because no one can claim to stand outside it, to be legally and morally pure. "Resolution and Independence" addresses the new laws' implications specifically for Wordsworth's understanding of his poetic vocation as a marginal condition akin to homelessness. His initial failure to reconcile the wandering poet's aesthetic power with mental or emotional control, or with the more worldly goals of financial security and social respectability, taints his perception of his artistic talents as delinquent, as culpable for their implication in poets' feckless reputations and dangerous mental instability. These same doubts and fears, however, make the poet too unreliable to be a source of testimony against himself. Through his subsequent reactions to a homeless old man, the poet thoroughly differentiates himself from the legal professional by finally identifying with his subject, a man whose sound mind and defense of his way of life offers both poet and vagrant protection against reductive formulations of guilt. All of these poems set out to baffle consistent application of the kind of investigative outlook presupposed by the early nineteenth-century professionals directed to monitor the homeless and other subversives; in the process, Wordsworth attempts to validate the marginality of homelessness and by extension other kinds of suspect behavior. That Wordsworth attempts such a position at all, in light of the first-person accounts of *Lyrical Ballads,* speaks to the fact that the peace did bring real improvements in Britain's social, political and economic climate. That he feels such a defense is necessary underscores the superficiality and fragility of those same gains.

WAR AS PEACE

When it was finalized in March 1802, few saw the Peace of Amiens as much more than a needed ceasefire between two spent antagonists. Yet Pitt's resignation from the government a year earlier, after George III balked at his proposal for Irish Catholic emancipation, had perceptibly mellowed the British political environment. Henry Addington's new ministry made the peace with Bonaparte, and until the treaty's collapse in May 1803, Addington tolerated opposition to a degree unknown for a decade. The general elections of the summer of 1802 featured several contests where candidates branded their opponents as Jacobins (Hone, 133), but there was no attempt to renew the suspension of Habeas Corpus, and many arrested in the repressions of 1798–9 finally were released. The 1795 Seditious Meetings Act was allowed to expire, permitting critics of the government to hold legal meetings (94). Even the November 1802 discovery of Despard's plot to seize the Tower of London and the Bank of England did not produce a crackdown like that following the alleged attempt on the king's life in 1795. Emsley explains, "… Addington did not use the discovery of the plots as an excuse for unleashing an anti-Jacobin witch-hunt. While Addington was no liberal, both mainstream Whig and more radical opponents admitted that under his government the wounds left by Pitt's repressive policies were soothed" (*British Society*, 95), and other wartime measures, such as the income tax, were discontinued.

This newly open atmosphere, however, partly reflected the comforting awareness among the powerful that both the numbers and energy of their opponents had fallen off sharply. The disintegration of the reform movement in the late 1790s had been striking. From 1799 to 1801, ministerial measures led many radicals who retained their convictions either to emigrate – destinations ranged from Hamburg to India – or retire from public life altogether. Others became disenchanted with the cause of reform and of France when Napoleon seized power on 10 November 1799 (18 Brumaire). The Peace of Amiens itself further damaged the opposition's cause by destroying a main rallying point, the government's prosecution of the war. As the treaty was finalized, even seasoned radical leaders often were "more concerned to reconstruct their businesses and private lives, than to actively consider ways for promoting political change" (Hone, 100). Increasingly, France appeared more as a threat to be feared than an example to be admired, especially after Napoleon was elected consul for life in 1802 and his imperial ambitions were beyond doubt. As the contested Middlesex election of 1802–3 showed, in the early years of the century most reformers advanced their agenda (insofar as they did so) through polite, legal opposition rather than by seditiously challenging a government and a nation still fearful of invasion.[1]

And while Pitt was (temporarily) out of power, the governmental bureaucracy that had responded to the French and Jacobin threats persisted and in some cases expanded. Suggestive in this light was the enactment of 42 George III, c. 76, signed into law on 22 June 1802 and debated in Parliament during the spring months. The statute re-authorized and extended the provisions of the Middlesex Justice Bill (32 George III, c. 53), passed in 1792, which according to Elizabeth Sparrow had established police offices throughout metropolitan London "quite simply to prevent the possibility of revolution"; this bill's provisions for summary justice reflected the belief that "revolutionary intentions were… so heinous as not to require the ordinary process of justice through the courts" (363). A heartfelt conviction of Georgian Whig gentlemen, ever wary of challenges from above (the crown) as well as from below (the mob), was that

Britain's only policing force should be composed of landed, unpaid local residents like themselves. While its innovations may seem modest, the Middlesex bill testifies to the ways in which that long-held view underwent transformation in the face of political and social change, particularly in the capital.[2] The Middlesex Justice Bill and the Alien Act (1793) sought to regulate mobility across parish and national borders and presupposed a causal connection between such mobility and political subversion. These laws consequently were of a piece with the revised vagrancy act of 1792, examined in Chapter 2, that sought to standardize punishments for vagrants and began to transfer power away from amateur constables and justices of the peace toward paid officials, such as masters of houses of correction. The 1802 revision of this earlier police bill enables the ongoing operation of the seven police offices set up a decade before, and attempts to ensure a disinterested (read bribe-resistant) force of JPs, appointed by the king and paid £500 a year tax-exempt (a specification pointing to another agency – the Treasury – whose power had ballooned during the war). Constables too were to be salaried, as well as reimbursed for expenses.

Also re-authorized in the 1802 law was one of the most contested provisions of the original bill, which had recommended one group in particular to the attention of metropolitan officials: "ill-disposed and suspected Persons and reputed Thieves," who "although their evil Purposes are sufficiently manifest," have managed to defy arrest in the past. If one witness swears to the "evil Fame" or criminal reputation of the accused, "and such person or Persons shall not be able to give a satisfactory Account of himself or themselves, and of his or their Way of living," the accused will be punished as a rogue and vagabond (Tomlins, 427). In 1792, Charles James Fox's speech in Parliament singled out this section, showing that he recognized its affinity with precisely the tactics of continental despotism abhorrent to Britain's gentry. Fox argued that to arrest a man on suspicion, without reference to a specific act, "was against all the principles of criminal justice whatever – repugnant to the very essence of the law of England" (quoted in Philips, 170). In his study of Georgian vagrancy, Nicholas Rogers sees in this provision the beginnings of a sea change in the treatment of Britain's homeless, who began to be associated less with particular occupations or activities than with a psychology of deviance that foretells Foucault's articulation of the delinquent in France. Rogers explains how during the late eighteenth and early nineteenth centuries policing [became] the main arbiter of vagrancy and the central agency for its resolution. Vagrancy could no longer be left to local discretionary action; it required [in the words of magistrate Patrick Colquhoun] "a systematic superintending policy calculated to check and prevent the growth and progress of vicious habits and other irregularities incident to civil society." As a result, the social boundaries of vagrancy were extended beyond the act of vagrancy itself; they began to include forms of deviance in anticipation of begging. The preventive paradigm ... moved hesitatingly beyond the offender to the delinquent. It tended to establish, in Foucault's words, "the criminal as existing before the crime and even outside it." Nowhere is this clearer than in the extension of the vagrant acts to "suspected persons," the notorious "sus" law.

(145)

The renewal of such initiatives in the peacetime year of 1802, with none of the accompanying outcry of 1792 and at a time when political tensions appeared to be diminishing, illustrates the indirect yet powerful ways in which ruling-class anxieties informed government policy. Although opposition to professional police continued for decades, the precedent for such a force was now in place.[3]

Colquhoun's *A Treatise on Indigence* (1806) would make perfectly clear the connection between the seemingly humble offense of vagrancy and the urgent need for a force of policing professionals, a force that could be used to suppress any number of subversive activities. Citing with annoyance the current inconsistencies in the way vagrants are processed by the law, Colquhoun (a disciple of Bentham) faults both the law itself and those who administer it. The 1744 vagrancy act comes in for rough treatment in the *Treatise* as anachronistic, unnecessarily brutal, and confusing. The statute itself is less a modern legal document than a sloppily compiled palimpsest, in which "some of the offenses, which appear to have been copied from ancient statutes, are also long since obsolete" (Colquhoun, 70). In other words, bearwards – individuals keeping bears and exhibiting their tricks for pay, cited as vagrants during the Stuart era – are not as common on the public roads or as threatening in 1803 as they were in 1640. In addition to updating such provisions, Colquhoun openly champions the "new principle in jurisprudence" encoded in the 1792 and 1802 laws, which punishes someone "*for threatening to commit an offense,* not of a criminal nature, and before he actually commits it" (78; emphasis in original). However, such an innovation alone will not reduce the crimes, or the potential for crime (itself now a crime), of the homeless. For "the cause of these evils may be traced principally to *one source.* There exists in this country nothing in the shape of a systematic superin- tending police ..." (82–3).[4] The incipient criminality of the vagrant thus both justifies and defines the mission of the new notion of police. Ultimately, Colquhoun wants to create a national board within the Home Office that would superintend "*general and internal police*" (89). Glossing Colquhoun's similar proposals in his earlier *Treatise on the Police of the Metropolis,* which went through seven editions, David Philips observes that the lower classes "could no longer be personally supervised by the squire or the master; it now required *institutions* – a 'Central Board of Police', a 'Pauper Police Institution'... to carry out the necessary surveillance to ensure [in Colquhoun's words] 'the blessings of true Liberty...'" (177). It was precisely this interest in prevention that would justify the creation of Britain's modern police force in the 1830s.[5] As Colquhoun understood, such a modern force would have systemat- ically to deploy "*intelligence, labour,* and *investigation,* aided by a *thorough knowledge of facts*" (90). "Intelligence" here refers both to the mental capacity required of investigators and the network of informants whose spying could monitor offenders' whereabouts and activities.

This apparatus for managing vagrancy has obvious applications for policing political disloyalty. The move toward the conversion of innocence (the absence of proof of a discreet illegal act) into delin- quency (focusing on reputation or tendencies) is of a piece with the gradual erosion of marginality throughout the 1790s in the arenas of both treason and vagrancy law. Escalating accusations flying between conservatives and reformers came to obliterate almost all distinctions except one: beyond agreement, all was treachery. The terrifying innovation in the 1795 Treasonable Practices Bill was its unprecedented association of treason not just with action, but with the threat of actions as articulated in language. In related fashion, the 1802 suspected persons provision pressured the spectrum of response toward the homeless, as both criminals and victims, that underlay parish attitudes towards vagrancy throughout the eight- eenth century. The new law gathered to the category of criminal a widening sphere not just of illegal acts, but the threat of such behavior. The objective was to replace the case-by-case judgments meted out by local officials with legal mandates consistently enforced by impartial professionals: the stipendiary magistrates and constables created by the Middlesex Justice Bill and re-commissioned in 1802 were sought out as adept and respected experts on crime, consulted by ministers, Parliament and police reformers in times of crisis (Emsley, *Crime*, 222).

Wordsworth confronts the implications of developments such as the 1802 bill through a series of poems discrediting its assumptions. Brian Goldberg has argued that during the 1800–2 period, Wordsworth (particularly in the preface to *Lyrical Ballads*) presents the poet as a hybrid, a genteel professional who is simultaneously a gentleman with a classical education and (in an anticipation of nine-teenth-century standards) a trained expert who exercises his talents for pay. In Goldberg's view, Wordsworth's famous 1801 letter to Charles James Fox substitutes for the vanishing statesmen, formerly charged with maintaining social and domestic affections, "the pro-fessional poet, whose own expertise is transformed into a new kind of property which bears 'virtue' and status for the poet and conse-quently for the nation" (345). Insofar as they offer speakers as atten-tive observers of vagrants' situations and options, "The Sailor's Mother," "Alice Fell," and "Beggars" validate Goldberg's view of a poet whose professionalism derives in part from his power to trans-late the experiences of children, the poor, and other marginals into language suitable for consumption by the higher ranks. In addition, the poet's response to the poor is repeatedly set at odds with the kinds of professional legal evaluation prescribed by the new statute. "The Sailor's Mother," the first poem in this sequence, endows a wandering woman with the dignity of royalty; occupying two opposing statuses at once, her character perplexes the drive to col-lapse her diverse qualities into a charge of feckless intent or criminal action. "Alice Fell" and "Beggars" shift the emphasis from the vagrant to a speaker whose interrogation of the homeless belies the professional's power to define a rationally knowable delinquency predicated on the acquisition of biographical information. Even in situations where the charge of delinquency would seem clear, this knowledge does not consistently dictate the poet's response or behavior. The speakers in all these poems retain a privileged per-spective that enables interrogation and judgment, but judgment depends less on adhering to a received set of standards than on idiosyncratic evaluation and intuition. To the extent that this is part of what constitutes the poet's own professional role, his vocation is a direct affront to the emerging objectives of professional criminal practice. The real delinquents, ultimately, are as much Wordsworth's speakers as anyone else in these poems, a state of affairs that "Resolution and Independence" calls attention to by meditating on the poet's failure to be the pure, disinterested observer who alone could pronounce a verdict of guilt or innocence. In the end, however, it is precisely this failure that saves him by allowing an elusive instant of identification with a homeless man who defies the law's preconceptions about such people.

In some respects, "The Sailor's Mother," composed on 11 and 12 March 1802, rehearses the situations that will become the focus for "Alice Fell," "Beggars," and "Resolution and Independence." As in "Alice Fell," a woman clings to an object as a source of comfort. As in "Beggars," she asks for alms while telling her story to the speaker. As in "Resolution and Independence," the speaker offers us initial impressions of the woman which are then juxtaposed, and perhaps debunked, by the conversation he subsequently has with her. If the old man's and Alice's vagrancy is mitigated as an offense because they are compelled to wander – the leech gatherer by the lack of leeches, Alice by her trapped cloak – the sailor's mother has an even more compelling excuse. Like the "Old Man Travelling" of *Lyrical Ballads*, she has lost a child to the war, and is on the road but headed home, having collected and sold most of his few possessions. The most direct of the poems discussed in this chapter, "The Sailor's Mother" offers a useful baseline in representations of the vagrant against which we can measure complications Wordsworth will introduce in both speakers and the homeless in the poems he will compose in the following days.[6]

Discharged sailors were allowed to beg on their way home without being arrested as vagrants, and as the poem was written in 1802, the armistice was swelling the numbers of such individuals and their relatives (such as this woman) visible on the road. Indeed, the many unfavorable reviews of the 1807 *Poems*, in which the poem first appeared, do not single out "The Sailor's Mother" as unpatriotic, as Charles Burney had done in his 1798 review of "Old Man Travelling." This task instead has fallen to contemporary critics, who have argued that the first stanzas advance some form of patriotic or nationalist agenda.[7] The speaker begins by comparing the woman to a "Roman matron" (6) and boasting that "Old times thought I, are breathing there; / Proud was I that my Country bred / Such strength ..." (8–10). Gene Ruoff contends that these sentiments are subsequently deflated by the speaker's encounter, which shows his initial conception unequal to this woman's experience and burdens (112–13). The speaker's impressions seem doubly mistaken if we consider the allusion in these stanzas to Burke's portrait of Marie Antoinette in *Reflections on the Revolution in France*. As Don Bialostosky notes, phrases such as "lofty thoughts" and "Roman matron" echo Burke's depiction of the French queen. Burke writes:

> I hear, and I rejoice to hear, that the great lady, the other object of triumph, has borne that day (one is interested that beings made for suffering should suffer well) and that she bears all the succeeding days, that she bears the imprisonment of her husband, and her own captivity, and the exile of her friends, and the insulting adulation of addresses, and the whole weight of her accumulated wrongs, with a serene patience, in a manner suited to her rank and race, and becoming the offspring of a sovereign distinguished for her piety and her courage; that like her she has lofty sentiments; that she feels with the dignity of a Roman matron; that in the last extremity she will save herself from the last disgrace, and that if she must fall, she will fall by no ignoble hand.
>
> (169)

While this representation places woman as courageous and dignified, women in the *Reflections* occupy a vexed position. Burke deplores what he feels is the undue power and insolence of women in the National Assembly, even though they are there only as spectators. Female influence on and physical interactions with the deputies are described in ways that give the proceedings almost a sexually debauched air: the women "sometimes mix and take their seats among" the representatives, "domineering over them with a strange mixture of servile petulance and proud presumptuous authority" (161). In recalling the royal couple's removal from Versailles to Paris, Burke again features the grotesque behavior of female onlookers: "the horrid yells, and shrilling screams, and frantic dances, and infamous contumelies, and all the unutterable abominations of the furies of hell, in the shape of the vilest of women" (165).

But woman as emblem of the worst excesses of revolutionary liberty is mirrored by woman as greatest standard-bearer of the old values of modesty and forbearance. This, as the extended quotation above indicates, is the role of Marie Antoinette, whose behavior in the *Reflections* is the object of even greater admiration than that of her husband. Louis XVI smarts under his injuries as a sovereign and a husband; indeed, he is perhaps affected excessively, for he "felt much on" the removal from Versailles (169). Marie Antoinette, by contrast, is unruffled and serene, as stoic as a Roman matron. Bialostosky argues that this allusion in "The Sailor's Mother" erases "the distinction between beggar and queen by transferring the terms of admiration from the latter to the former" (*Wordsworth*, 68). To go further, the response of Wordsworth's speaker, who is recalled from his "lofty thoughts" (13) by the actual speech of the woman, implies that true worth is not to be found in those like the French queen who have endured reversals of fortune. More admirable are those who always have endured the daily hardships of poverty, those who never have been wealthy enough to purchase a substitute for their children in military service, those who are compelled to sell virtually all their loved ones' possessions simply to finance a desolate return from an empty house. It is not that the sailor's mother is as virtuous as a queen; rather, she is virtuous in a way that a queen could never be. Marie Antoinette lived for years in palaces of state, and was guillotined on 16 October 1793 as the "widow Capet"; the dramas implicit in such a zenith and nadir may outshine but cannot meaningfully equal the quotidian suffering and self-denial of the life of another casualty of war, the sailor's mother.

The open-ended form of the poem prevents us from seeing the mother as a feckless delinquent. Partly, this stems from the speaker's initial response to her: he sees her begging, but the connection he establishes with her is based on an exchange of words, not money, an exchange in which the speaker himself rather than the pauper seems to be beneficiary. He asks only one question, "'Beneath your Cloak / What is it you are carrying there?'" (15–16), a query which substitutes for the loose change she seeks; this is "the first word I had to spare" (14). Rather than complain about what we might see as his lack of charity, she answers openly and at length; she has nothing to hide, after all, and when it comes to words, she is richer than he is. And she has the last word, frustrating any expectation that the speaker will tell us how to interpret this narrative by commenting on the pauper's behavior or psychology. Does he reward her tale with nothing, with alms, or with a lecture on her situation? His initial musings make the latter unlikely. Yet the poet's refusal to cap her story by closing the frame he opens in the beginning – by representing his offering her money, a homily, even just a sympathetic reaction – reflects Wordsworth's resistance to appropriating the story of the sailor's mother for any predetermined purpose, benevolent or hostile. Her narrative may confirm his initial, fanciful impression of her, or it may discredit it since she at the end seems to lack the stoicism of Burke's Marie Antoinette. Her answer supplants all of this, however, pointing to the professional poet's willingness to do what no officer of the law could: let the story stand apart from judgments of virtue or vice. This becomes clearest in the speaker's refusal to pronounce on the poem's most controversial point, the mother's decision to keep the bird. A hostile observer could attack this decision since by selling it she might have gained the funds necessary to avoid begging. The woman herself admits as much when she despairs over her choice – "I, God help me! for my little wit, / Trail't with me, Sir! he took so much delight in it" (35–6)! The poet confirms the differences between his investigative method and that of the law by ending the poem on this note, neither approving nor condemning her own ambivalence about retaining the animal. The complexities of human psychology defy abstraction into larger narratives about suspicion and innocence.

In the considerably more elliptical "Alice Fell," a young girl's emotions prove even more mystifying to a speaker who learns the limits of conventional narratives about poverty, wandering, and relief. The narrator subjects the girl, traveling alone, to what we can describe as an impromptu vagrant examination. In the language of the laws, he asks her for an account of herself: "wither are you going, Child, / To night along these lonesome ways?" (33–4). Seemingly a good girl, she replies with her name, rank and settlement, revealing herself an orphan dependent on the parish of Durham. Commenting on the potentially coercive nature of the speaker's questions, Bialostosky argues that Alice's greatest fear concerns not her cloak but discovery of and punishment for her wanderings by a hostile adult – a danger she parries by diverting the pompous but well-meaning speaker's attention and eventually getting him to buy her a better cloak than the one she has lost (*Making Tales*, 138–43). If Alice wants to be secretive she is less successful in her answers than Bialostosky allows, for she divulges the pertinent (in the eyes of the law) information about herself that the narrator seeks. Against Bialostosky's reading of Alice's brevity as resistence to the narrator's power to question her, William

Olejniczak notes the "extremely formulaic" nature of eighteenth-century vagrancy justice, and the typical "monotony and brevity of the written exam report" ("English," 633, 634). The narrator's laconic report of Alice's answer may simply mimic the minimalist rhetoric of official documentation.

Although her answers speak to the criteria authorities used to judge such cases, what is significant is that something in Alice persistently remains beyond the power of legal paradigms to process or evaluate. Alice is a strange, "half-wild" thing, and the narrator's efforts to reconstruct her situation and emotional state through his questions never feel completely successful (35). The bitterness of her grief, insisted upon in stanza after stanza, suggests that something in her is indeed past relief, past any corrective or comfort the narrator can offer.[8] Alice's psychology, according to Foucault one of the three main elements in establishing delinquency, remains opaque through most if not all of the poem. These complications are prefigured by the narrator's early struggle to locate Alice within a stable representational idiom. In a throwback to the gothic touches of the Salisbury Plain poems, before he confronts her directly she is only a voice, one that seems to envelop the chaise and man who hears her:

> As if the wind blew many ways
> I heard the sound, and more and more:
> It seem'd to follow with the Chaise,
> And still I heard it as before.

(5–8)

Alice is both everywhere and nowhere; the narrator alone hears her crying outside the coach, and he twice has to force the post-boy to stop in order to discover the source of the cries. The post-boy himself is oblivious to Alice's moans, let alone her existence, though he is alert enough to his passenger's presence to stop at a "word" from him (10). This sense of Alice as all spirit, if she is even that, then is supplanted by an image of Alice in her poverty, as all body; the cloak she and the narrator pull from the wheel seems fit only for dangling from a "garden scare-crow," making its possessor seem a hollow form rather than a human being (28).[9] Insofar as Alice is *only* her grief, Wordsworth's representation of her reconciles the seemingly contradictory images of disembodied voice and scarecrow body by presenting her grief, inexhaustible and voiced through sobs, as a form that can't be translated into a linear biographical narrative or to a psychological type. We call this a narrative poem because the speaker labors to shape Alice's life into a sequence of cause and effect, but like the cloak caught in the workings of a rotating wheel, her "wretchedness" (39) circles about as if it "could never, never, have an end" (40).

Aiming to contradict his sense that Alice is "past all relief" (37), the narrator finally responds with an unconventional mix of material assistance and imaginative speculation.[10] Imagination supplements practical intervention in her unfathomable despair, revealing that the poet has his own methods to ensure that Alice, and his poem, aren't just going nowhere. Escorting her to Durham and translating her circular and prelingual grief into a recognizable, if highly abbreviated, biography of loss and recovery – "Of Alice and her grief I told" (54) – the narrator takes concrete steps to reintegrate Alice into the parish structure, buying her a new cloak and validating the "account" she has given him of herself. But the poem is haunted by the knowledge that the success of his efforts remains arguable: the hyperbole of his injunction to the host of the inn – "As warm a cloak as man can sell!" (58) – betrays the narrator's understanding that the cloak is only a part of the total relief Alice requires. This interpretation is fueled by the ambiguity of her final emotional breakdown while still inside the carriage. She tells the narrator that she belongs to Durham, and then, he claims, "as if the thought would choke / Her very heart, her grief grew strong" (46–7). He goes on to identify the source of the choking thought as the cloak: "all was for her tatter'd Cloak" (48), and she cried "As if she'd lost her only friend" (51). Her response is hardly so obvious, and "the thought" that chokes seems just as likely to refer back to her recollection that she belongs to Durham (whose stewardship here certainly seems remiss) as to the cloak. The larger problems that underpin Alice's despair – the deaths of her parents, the poverty that will always keep her riding outside the coach, whether she has a new cloak or not – loom large here and cannot be remedied by a single charitable act. If the depth of Alice's mind can never be plumbed, the narrator falls back on his own imaginative projection of her story's resolution. He remains to the last fixated on her cloak, but the necessity of continuing his own journey requires him to imagine the orphan the next day with her gift: "Proud Creature was she the next day, / The little Orphan, Alice

Fell!" (59–60). The actual moment of relief cannot be witnessed and recorded but only surmised.

This process reveals the formative role the narrator's hopes and values play in the way he construes Alice's situation and prospects. After what we have seen and learned, "Proud" seems more a projection of the narrator's own self-satisfaction at his efforts than an accurate description of the enigmatic Alice herself. Essentially, Alice drops out of the final stanzas of the poem, and we are left with the speaker's optimistic rendering of a fantasy conclusion. Objectively, we do not know how the episode really ends, because the speaker does not stay to ascertain the conclusion. In substituting his musings for a happy scene where innkeeper and narrator dress Alice in her new cloak (for example), the poem makes the narrator's psychology at least as important, perhaps more important, as what happens to Alice and the money the landlord receives. The narrator's surmise is materially based – he can only imagine Alice's transformation if she has a new cloak – and yet also an invention (more or less probable, depending on one's faith in the landlord) standing in for ongoing, practical involvement in the child's case.[11] This is not to downplay the narrator's real charity. The point rather is that his intuition of her mental state – she ends, he imagines, not the wretched vagrant but the Proud Creature – is entirely a product of his own mind. The question as to whether Alice remains past relief, or prone to crime, is unanswered and, the poem implies, unanswerable.[12] The final image of Alice, however, may argue that the narrator's candidly self-involved behavior is actually superior, though it cannot decipher Alice's feelings, to an approach based on systematic, objective criteria. The speaker acts as an individual charging another individual, the innkeeper, to act on his behalf, rather than, for example, recommending Alice to the care of local authorities.[13]

The challenges of interpreting the apparently simple story of Alice's fixation on her cloak, at once very material and psychologically opaque, certainly undercut official expansion of the notion of criminality to include the suspect. The workings of Alice's mind remain obscure, and the psychology of the gentleman speaker, rather than the vagrant, is all the poem can fully disclose. "Beggars," written immediately after "Alice Fell," adds still more variables by exploring the problematic psychology of even "respectable" men.[14] "Beggars" differs from "Alice Fell" and "Resolution and Independence" (or "The Leech-Gatherer") in that in it we are confronted with a family whom the speaker feels impelled to judge the morality of because they openly ask for his assistance on the basis of their travails. To this extent, he appears more representative of an official, monitory figure than the speakers of the other texts. He tells us that the stately beggar woman he encounters in the first part of the poem is lying; he tells the boys themselves in the second part of the poem that *they* are lying. He seems interested in making distinctions between truthfulness and falsehood, and, we would expect, consequently between deserving and undeserving recipients of charity.

Of course this is not really the case. In fact, the speaker paradoxically seems very concerned to call our attention to his power to make moral distinctions even while disregarding them as a valid basis for action or judgment. This problem of explaining the speaker's conduct speaks to the difficulties of systematically applying a consistent grid of legal and ethical imperatives in judging the act and actors of vagrancy. As in "Alice Fell," these difficulties partly grow out of the enigmatic nature of the vagrant. The speaker's attempts to size up the woman are complicated by her racial difference, "Her face was of Egyptian brown" (9), and by his claims that these beggars are indeed actors, that vagrancy itself is an act or a ploy whose theater of disguise can never be completely sounded. As Thomas Frosch notes, the text begins by presenting a person who is a walking contradiction, a woman as tall as a man, whose head lacks a bonnet but who wears a long cloak in the heat, and who is a stately beggar. Some of these qualities contribute toward a faint undercurrent of potential menace in this encounter; she is taller than even a tall man, which presumably means she stands well over the narrator, and her association in the speaker's mind with the Amazons and with bandits calls up images of assault and robbery as well as sexual or picaresque independence.

The real actor (if not a very good one) may be the speaker himself. The uncertainty surrounding his character and intentions are finally much more troubling than the vagrants he encounters. The very credentials he cites as qualifications to evaluate this woman and her claims reveal disquieting similarities between himself and her. For proof of the unbelievability not only of her story, but also of her simple existence, the narrator gestures toward his own lifetime of rambling: "In all my walks through field or town, / Such figure never had I seen" (7–8). His contention that she resembles a gypsy, an Amazonian queen, and a Grecian bandit's wife may demonstrate more about his "romantic" imagination than about her. He argues that her unspecified injuries must be fabrications because "on English land / Such woes thought I can never be" (15–16), mounting an almost risible defense of the established social and political order. By 1802, after nine years of war, economic crisis, and political oppression, a commoner telling a story of "grief after grief" (15) would have been all too believable. The poem's alterations to Dorothy Wordsworth's original account of this incident in her journal point up the speaker's questionable behavior. Wordsworth's sister gives bread to the female pauper whose story she believes, and later when on the road she denies help to the young boys whom she recognizes are deceiving her.[15] Wordsworth's speaker rewards the female liar because he finds her sexually attractive; she gets alms from him "for your beauty's sake – you are a woman brave" (17). Although he parades before us his understanding of the difference between truth and lying, his ultimate disregard for such distinctions casts into doubt who the liar actually is here; can we trust such a person's assessment of what is true or not, given the criteria on which he bases his actions?[16] How reliable is a social monitor who calls the children of a gypsy mother "sweet" even as he recognizes that they are telling him a lie (32)? The instability of his ethical disposition explains the caprice, if not the outright moral dubiousness, of his charitable impulses. His inclination to employ judgment, if not his power to judge itself, wanders as much as the man himself "In all [his] walks" (7).[17] When the poem was published in the 1807 *Poems*, it very appropriately was the lead text in a section entitled "Poems composed during a tour, chiefly on foot," though we know that Wordsworth actually composed the work while home at Grasmere. That the speaker is more like the vagrants he encounters than he admits is reinforced by Wordsworth's decision to use the same verb, to spy, when describing the speaker's sighting of the boys and their first contact with him (20, 25).

The speaker's suspect identity occludes any decisive view of the woman or her children, and their motives and history not only remain unpsychologized but become irrelevant in the poem. Biography appears only as a series of lies on the part of the beggars, the speaker, or both. The speaker's own elliptical mental processes do not clarify the components of his evaluation or the process by which he arrived at his judgment. What we are left with is a discrete encounter that seems to make no generalizable statements about vagrants, about poets, about gentleman walkers, or much of anything else. Frosch remarks on what he feels is the unsatisfying character of the poem, that the transformative experiences we expect from Wordsworth's encounters make no appearance: the mental vertigo created in the poet's mind by *The Prelude*'s blind beggar or the discharged soldier, for example, is absent here (625). Frosch's sense that the speaker, and we, don't seem to have learned anything reinforces the cryptic nature of this encounter and the man through whom we access it: society lacks reliable, transparent observers capable of or interested in determining where guilt, abstracted from a specific act, ends and where innocence begins.[18] The idiosyncratic response of the speaker refuses to be dislocated by interpretation or by effect from its source materials, making it useless as a point of departure for theorizing about the suspect nature of vagrant criminality even as deception – by the speaker, by the woman, by the boys – is very much at the center of the poem. The poem's lack of resolution leaves the possibility of any transformational experience with the reader, and like the man in "Anecdote for Fathers," we may want to wring a more conclusive answer out of the speaker about the importance of this experience. But unlike that poem, "Beggars" implies that lying is not taught but is part of our makeup, entangling both the (perhaps) respectable and the (certainly) homeless in a web of suspicion.

"MIGHTY POETS IN THEIR MISERY DEAD"

The dubious character of Wordsworth's speakers as well as those they confront in these poems doesn't bode well for the new laws' mission, leaving the poet's methods as a non-judgmental alternative for portraying the workings of the psychology of potential criminals. In "Resolution and Independence" poetry itself comes under fire: the very activities of creative imagination now appear economically fruitless and spiritually self-destructive. This crisis in Wordsworth's feelings engenders a fear that he is on his way to becoming a psychological type, the mad, poor poet, whose end in disgrace and despondency is predetermined by the reputations of other authors who have gone before him. In part, this poet is saved from the charge of delinquency, a charge predicated in 1802 above all on reputation, by the irony that as the penumbra of legal suspicion expands beyond the empirically verifiable act, anyone can be suspect, leaving no untainted accuser to do the judging. Finally, the speaker's power to identify with a homeless old man presents him with a surprising alternative to the pattern of happiness and collapse he fears, showing the limits of evaluation based on expectation and suspicion. In this way, the imaginative engagement of the poet divulges still more deficiencies in the JP and the lawyers' aspirations toward impartial, procedurally based roles.

The poem opens by affirming the speaker's ability to register external stimuli as they really are, a power assumed by the new thinking about professionalized police. His inner state directly reflects the uncomplicated joy he perceives in animals and even in the earth itself. But the nature of these sensations renders confidence in him as an objective observer precarious; although he reports on the situation and actions, he emphasizes what is subject to interpretation – their emotional content. "All things that love the sun are out of doors" (8), the hare is mirthful, the sky rejoices. The reliability of the speaker's reflections on these sensations are called openly into question when his understanding of what he sees is affected by cryptic melancholy from within himself: "Dim sadness, and blind thoughts I knew not nor could name" (28). A return to an awareness of the external world – the skylark, the hare – cannot dispel this depression, which now takes the form of uneasy speculation over the future character of the poet's life because it has been so profoundly vagrant. The character of those early companions, the hare and the bird, changes, and they are companions no more; the speaker still hears them and sees them, but the moor has suddenly become "a lonely place" (52). No longer able to frame his travels in terms of the actions of the animals he observes, the speaker is suddenly seized by a belief proceeding solely from within, that his wandering life has been foolish and may be fatal. He will know poverty; he will go insane.[19] His initial attempts to stave off these fears – "Even such a happy Child of earth am I; / Even as these blissful Creatures do I fare" (31–2) – will be further cast into doubt as just another example of how poets "deify" themselves before inevitably plunging into the despair soon to follow (47). In the space of a few minutes, the source of the speaker's impulses has been reversed, and he questions the prudence as well as the morality not of a particular act, but of an attitude and the orientation of his entire life. He has become, in the language of modern criminology, a self-diagnosed delinquent, a man who is suspect to himself. He stands accused as a vagrant poet, a status which at the text's beginning seemed no crime at all, and the expanding borders of his sense of his culpability leads the speaker not just to interrogate his immediate intentions or desires, but to create a kind of criminal profile of the poet, whose guilty destiny is ordained by vocation and disposition.

Details of the speaker's own life are crucially supplemented by historical precedent to complete his understanding of the extent of his own damnation.

> I thought of Chatterton, the marvellous Boy,
> The sleepless Soul that perish'd in its pride;
> Of Him who walk'd in glory and in joy
> Behind his plough, upon the mountain-side;
> By our own spirits are we deified;
> We Poets in our youth begin in gladness;
> But thereof comes in the end despondency and madness.

> (44–9)

As the heavy use of capitalization indicates here, Chatterton, Burns and implicitly Coleridge, whose "Dejection" stimulated Wordsworth's composition, are invoked as specific types, as Poets. In this account, unaccountable high spirits are sure to be deflated by ensuing emotional agony that will rob the poet of his confidence, his wits, and his life. The vagrant is no longer associated with the unpredictable, the out of the ordinary; when he is a poet, at least, the trajectory of his life is a sure as the setting of the sun. It is this reputation that the speaker becomes convinced will follow him. Accordingly, while the questions concluding the previous stanza hold out some (though admittedly precious little) hope for another way out, with the declarative statements of lines 44 to 49 the poet, and the poem, seem to have abruptly come to an end.

That the poem does not end is due to the speaker's unexpected encounter with an old man. Some things can't be predicted after all, resulting from "peculiar grace, / A leading from above, a something given" (50–1). The old man will provide two invaluable services: he will divert the speaker's focus from self-accusation and he will demonstrate the error of allowing vocational clichés to shape self-image and expectations. Because homeless people often appear much older than they really are, it isn't surprising that the wandering man appears "the oldest Man … that ever wore grey hairs" (56).

Yet the speaker underscores the man's age throughout the text. He is "in his extreme old age" (72), whatever misfortune that befell him occurred "in times long past" (76), he is a "decrepit Man" (145), and Wordsworth calls him an "Old Man" six times in the poem. What he never calls him until the final line, despite the early title of the poem, is a leech-gatherer, or a beggar, or a vagrant, or a pauper. This language positions the old man at the end of his life narrative; as Keats said of himself dying in Rome, Wordsworth's old man seems almost to have entered into a kind of posthumous existence. The conventional narratives about criminal homelessness will not apply to this border figure "not all alive nor dead, / Nor all asleep" (71–2). As a posthumous character, his age situates him in a domain beyond the reach of received ideas about the destined end of those of his class and circumstances. Additionally, unlike the speaker, who is defined by what he does, compose poetry, the old man is just an old man who happens to be gathering leeches to scrape by.[20] It does not, we should note, take any particular skill to gather them, beyond a willingness to stick one's feet in ponds and allow the organisms to attach themselves to one's legs.

Jonathan Wordsworth has commented on the "obstinate physicality" of the old man, and the way in which the poet must "fight to subdue the Leech Gatherer's obtrusive physical presence" (*Borders*, 172). Such a battle is, however, beyond the speaker's power, and this is why the old man is the perfect antidote to his disorientation. In a letter to Sara Hutchinson about the poem, Wordsworth clearly felt the effect of the man's physicality still: "Good God! Such a figure, in such a place, a pious self-respecting, miserably infirm ... Old Man telling such a tale" (*Early Years*, 367)! The old man's irreducible physicality – the extremity of his condition, his age, his solitude on the moor, the physical basis of his work which, if successful, can literally suck what life that remains out of him – means he cannot be abstracted into a predetermined narrative about politics, the law, or occupational risk. The futility of any such attempt initially appears in the much commented-on similes of lines 64–70, where the old man is first compared to a stone and then even more inanely to a sea beast. In camouflaged form, these comparisons do address the speaker's query, "By what means [the old man] could thither come, and whence" (67). The freakish character of the figures of speech, however, tells us more about the effects of his doubts on the speaker himself than about the old man. The same speaker who connects a hare on a moor with the inevitability of poetic madness has no trouble seeing an old man as a sea monster. Both connections are symptomatic of a mind losing any sense of meaningful boundaries.[21]

The old man's irreducibility signals the speaker's need to rethink the way in which he has been interpreting the scene before him as well as the signs of his own life; the old man, who studies the pond waters "As if he had been reading in a book" (88), is the appropriate educator for the speaker's induction into a style of reading grounded in physical facts rather than fantastic apprehensions. The speaker's first comment, "This morning gives us promise of a glorious day" (91), is the early fruit of this process. He then asks the question re-illustrating the pull of the difficulties he must overcome: "What kind of work is that which you pursue?" (95). The grim humor of the poem is that this kind of question, under the criteria established in the new laws, has become almost useless in ascertaining guilt because the boundaries of vagrant activity have expanded to include whatever a group of witnesses agrees is suspicious. This explains the speaker's ongoing difficulty in attending to the old man's reply, constantly distracted as he is by intruding observations about the old man's style of speech, "a fire about his eyes" (98), and the speaker's own returning fears of "mighty Poets in their misery dead" (123). As a result, by line 124, the speaker still finds himself "not knowing what the Old Man had said." The old man is blissfully unfettered by such complicated mental interference, and patiently answers the same question twice in the way that he understands it, as a request for an account of his specific acts that earn him money to live. The answers are included in the text, but almost exclusively in indirect form, to prove to us that the speaker's sense of encroaching guilt has been managed; after the fact – we know it's after the fact because almost all the old man's responses are recorded indirectly – the speaker can recall the answers and even transcribe them. But in the short term, the old man's answers and the speaker's personal and professional concerns coalesce into a hopeless muddle for someone struggling to locate self and others in relation to broader guidelines of suspicion or innocence. Struggling to listen to the old man, the speaker finds that "his voice to me was like a stream / Scarce heard; nor word from word could I divide" (114–15). We are to take this statement quite literally; as the definition of the vagrant – "how is it that you live, and what is it you do?" – expands, dividing the suspect from the pure increasingly becomes problematic. The advancing periphery of guilt's boundaries overtakes each progressive attempt to segregate right from wrong. The poet's argument that we can't is the basis for his tacit attack on the law's confidence in the judgments of disinterested professionals trained to abstract concrete details from their worldly context.

Wordsworth's opinions on this point surface in his testy correspondence with the Hutchinson sisters about "Resolution and Independence." In a letter dated 14 June 1802, Wordsworth defends an early draft of the poem that seems to have included a good deal more of the details of the old man's biography and hardships. In this way, the early draft, "The Leech-Gatherer," demonstrates the resistance of individual biography to reduction to a type by presenting the old man's story at greater length and directly through his own words. Wordsworth's subsequent deletion of this material reflects not a decision to capitulate to delinquency's mode of biography, but rather a determination to show such a cognitive mode as little less than madness (the illness the speaker feels is almost upon him). This revision can be seen as Wordsworth's final, and not very gracious, rejoinder to his future sister-in-law in their argument over the quality of the poem. To judge by Wordsworth's response to her letter, Sara Hutchinson felt that the details of the old man's life actually worked to ensure a clinical distance reminiscent of the very legal paradigms that Wordsworth wanted to escape. The death of the old man's wife and children, his begging, his intention to supplement his income by selling religious books, specifics that Wordsworth found so affecting, induced at best mild interest, not involved compassion. Apparently quoting from the Hutchinsons' own letter, Wordsworth states that they found the poem "*very well*" after the leech-gatherer's introduction. He retorts, "this is not true, if it is not more than very well it is very bad, there is no intermediate state. You speak of his speech as tedious: everything is tedious when one does not read with the feelings of the Author" (*Early Years*, 367). He goes on to criticize Sara as an "*impatient* reader" whose "indifference" is not, as she has apparently tried to claim, immaterial, but clearly irks Wordsworth beyond saying. Perhaps most irksome of all was the knowledge that some of his most sympathetic readers had not only missed the point of the poem, but had been affected in the exact opposite way from that intended. The old man's sufferings induced not an emotional connection but a polite, dispassionate response that Wordsworth cannot second by being "indifferent" to the Sara's own reserve.

Wordsworth's letters on a very different topic during early 1802 confirm his stake in discrediting the new drive toward legitimizing "indifferent" professionalism as a cornerstone of modern legal judgment and practice. When James Lowther died on 24 May 1802, his heir announced that all just claims on the estate would be honored. As he worked on the poem that would become "Resolution and Independence," Wordsworth perceived that his family's inheritance might at last be paid. By the time the text was completed, 4 July 1802, the Wordsworths believed that Sir William, the new viscount, would resolve their claim (Gill, *Wordsworth*, 207). From May until July, the handling of the family's petition for the claim was Wordsworth's obsession; what he sought above all to avoid was to have the proceedings hijacked by legal professionals who would intervene between petitioner and lord. With impressive insensitivity he tells his brother Richard, himself a lawyer, that

> ... I have too much reason to be afraid that you are disposed to conduct the affair as a mere man of business. We see what Lawyers and Attorneys have done in it already; and depend upon it if you proceed according to the letter in this track we are ruined. Though the affair must be bottomed no doubt upon a right in Law, that right will be lost to us, and we shall draw no advantage from it whatsoever, if we do not constantly bear in mind that our hopes of success (both in the conduct and in the final settlement) must depend entirely upon our combining with this right certain principles of natural justice, and considering the affair as an affair betwixt man and man.
>
> (*Early Years*, 372)

The attorney originally responsible for the situation was, of course, John Wordsworth, Sr, whose pursuit of his professional duties on Lowther's behalf at the expense of his family's interest pauperized his children. In carrying out the baronet's commands, Wordsworth spent thousands of pounds of his own money, his children's patrimony, yet "there had never been any agreement ... as to payments or reimbursements" (Moorman, 7–8). Wordsworth distrusts the procedures and expertise of legal adjudicators because their supposed ethic of service masks a vertical power relation with their clients as suffocatingly paternalistic as any between lord and vassal. He begins his letter to Richard by berating him for the tone of a previous letter concerning their petition. The poet demystifies the nomenclature of the lawyer, claiming that Richard sounded "as if you were speaking to a child," not in the way that "Man ought to deal with Man" (*Early Years*, 371). The recurrence of this phrase later shows that Wordsworth does not conceive of himself as Lowther's inferior, yet he is keenly aware that he is neither Lowther's social nor economic equal. Involving lawyers and the courts, he believes, will only exacerbate this problem, since the formulaic jargon of attorneys grants them power without compelling them actually to address the facts of the case at hand. Wordsworth brushes aside his brother's calls for patience as just another element in the law's abstract formula, divorced from any intent to serve the client materially or resolve a specific dispute in a just fashion:

> But you must know as well as I that such exhortations are the common language of hackney men of business. "We must take time" "we must not be in a hurry." All this is a sort of mechanic rule they lay down, easy to adhere to: and thus they cheaply purchase to themselves the applause of being methodical, circumspect, and temperate men.
>
> (372)

Here Wordsworth appears to be what he had accused Sara Hutchinson of being, namely an "impatient reader." But the key difference between the lawyer's delays and the poet's "tediousness" is that the one proceeds from emotional detachment rationalized under the professional umbrella of method and circumspection, while the other develops from sympathetic involvement with the details of a fellow human being's life. It is this kind of involvement that both the lawyer's procedures and Sara's boredom are at odds with.

In his letter to Richard, Wordsworth goes on to argue that he and his siblings must present their petition quickly and directly, because this will play on Lowther's probable desire to curry favor among his new constituents on the eve of upcoming parliamentary elections. Wordsworth's emphasis on Lowther's motives within the understanding of a layman works to level the field of engagement between himself and the Lonsdale heir in ways that the attorney's procedures never could. The poet ends up as Lowther's peer in reasoning, if not in land holdings. Mark Schoenfield addresses this letter's leveling impulses, which "cannot be achieved by lawyers, but rather by writers who preserve the face-to-face character of conversation in their letters" (18).[22] Yet it is important to recognize that Wordsworth's rhetoric here treads a careful line between egalitarianism (natural rights, the face-to-face encounter) and deference: " … let me earnestly exhort you to avoid … a disposition to challenge Lord Lowther to try the affair in a court of justice" (*Early Years*, 370). By inserting themselves into this process, lawyers siphon off the resources and self-esteem of their clients without producing anything (like a settlement) in return; they are, in other words, leeches.[23] Professional legal training and skills are ultimately just a smoke screen whose abstraction and disingenuousness make them even less palatable than the older, uncamouflaged forms of power based on land and blood.

Insofar as his potential delinquency might attract the attention of a generation of legal agents armed with newly coined legal abstractions, the old man of "Resolution and Independence" is indeed a leech-gatherer. And the poem's speaker perhaps may be a leech in more ways than one.[24] But the obscure confusion of his self-consciousness invalidates the law's murky investment in suspicion and reputation, leaving us with only the "whole Body of the man" (116) in the case of both the poet and the old man. The speaker's attempts to divorce his understanding of the man from his immediate situation finally collapse in the final stanza when the old man does a simple yet unexpected thing: he changes the subject. This recalls the speaker from his most recent flight of fantasy, where

> In my mind's eye I seem'd to see him pace
> About the weary moors continually,
> Wandering about alone and silently.
> While I these thoughts within myself pursued,
> He having made a pause, the same discourse renewed.

(136–40)

In subsequently blending the original discourse – the details of his livelihood, presumably – with "other matter" (141), the old man interrupts the speaker's unfruitful, self-destructive commerce between the language of metaphoric abstraction and vagrant life. Significantly, we are told virtually nothing about these other topics of conversation; they are just "other matter." What really matters is that the focus has become not professional or moral definition or anxiety (either for a wandering poet or a homeless leech-gatherer) but the complexity of individual experience that cannot be adequately framed by legal or social categories.[25] The speaker's comprehension of this truth helps him to an enabling identification with the old man, an association the legal professional's code could never countenance but that the poet's creed finds value in. While his earlier identification with Poets as a class trapped him within a predetermined trajectory from gladness to suicide, the speaker's memory of this particular old man – "the leech-gatherer on the lonely moor" (147) – will provide a foundation for mediating even that biggest of abstractions, God, through tangible images of physical support: "be my help and stay secure" (146). The incongruity of finding a "stately" vagrant, or a gentleman who begs for proof of his own innocence and vocational potential from a homeless old man, is just one more indication of how the combinations of qualities we find in the world baffle schematic attempts to divine the human character. Rather than validate guilt's encroachments into the domain of innocence, the old man's particular mixture of criminality and victimhood confirms an expanded definition of marginality instead. His vagrancy is perpetuated by outside forces rather than simply by a desire to wander. The lack of leeches forces him to find them "'where I may'" (133), and in the end he defends leech-gathering as a perfectly "honest maintenance" (112). In its desire to defend the poet's creative powers on a similar basis, "Resolution and Independence" begins the exploration of Wordsworth's own biography that will develop into *The Prelude*'s main subject, the growth of the poet's mind.

5

Errant Thoughts and Social Crimes in *The Prelude*

The political situation in Britain during the 1790s receives scant attention in any version of *The Prelude*, especially when we consider the thousands of lines devoted in the 1805 and 1850 versions of the text to events occurring at the same time across the Channel. The one brief commentary on the conservatives who dominated British government during this decade attributes this omission not to indifference to domestic conditions but rather to the poet's still almost uncontrollable rage over them. In the 1805 *Prelude*, the narrator claims "this is passion over near ourselves, / Reality too close and too intense" (X.640–1). He adds:

> Our shepherds (say this merely) at that time
> Thirsted to make the guardian crook of law
> A tool of murder. They who ruled the state,
> Though with such awful proof before their eyes
> That he who would sow death, reaps death or worse,
> And can reap nothing better, childlike longed
> To imitate – not wise enough to avoid.
> Giants in their impiety alone,
> But in their weapons and their warfare base
> As vermin working out of reach, they leagued
> Their strength perfidiously to undermine
> Justice, and make an end of liberty.

> (X.645–56)[1]

By 1797, Wordsworth had experienced first-hand the reach of those vermin lurking underneath the floorboards – a metaphor for government informants. The excerpt works to contain the poet's anger by locating the events that caused it in the past. But the authorities who had authorized such tactics were continuing their use when these lines were written in 1804, with the added collusion of a country more worried than ever about the prospects of invasion from the continent.

The shaping force behind representations of homelessness in the 1805 *Prelude* is an awareness that this political climate still existed and was likely to exist for some time. In the first part of the poem's 1799 version, composed during Wordsworth's 1798–9 residence in Germany, he defiantly embraces vagrant acts because they seem to offer ongoing power to complicate the reductive assumptions of a restrictive cultural milieu. In the 1799 *Prelude*, vagrant behavior's legal polyvalence dramatizes how social norms themselves are often far from monolithic but rather liable to widely differing interpretations by people from various socio-economic strata. By acting in the social spaces where clear moral and political definitions become blurred, the wandering boy of the 1799 poem's first part evades supervision and punishment.

The second part of this poem, composed in England, and Wordsworth's extensive additions of 1804 interrogate this identification of homelessness with an empowering cultural ambiguity. Particularly in the 1805 *Prelude,* relatives, observers, and even the narrator increasingly fail to see vagrancy as a morally and legally confused category of activity. Rather, homelessness now is located conclusively on an existing grid of moral and legal practice. In times of national crisis, the vagrant's uncertain position in society makes him a tabula rasa on which the community can inscribe its most potent political fears and local prejudices. The second half of the 1799 poem acknowledges this understanding by struggling, with mixed success, to demonstrate its wandering, adolescent subject's obedience to natural tutelage and participation in community life and social activities. The 1805 text, incorporating material from 1799, begins along the same lines. Ultimately, the social pressure to define vagrancy's valence in readily intelligible, often politically subversive terms cannot be managed but only capitulated to. The persistence of a crisis mentality in Britain during the early 1800s leads the poet to expand his autobiography by casting himself as a wanderer sharing the revolutionary sympathies and subsequent disenchantment of his generation, rather than a young man skeptical of political and personal commitment.

POETRY, POWER AND THE JUVENILE DELINQUENT

While "Tintern Abbey" locates personal identity in a deliberately unspecified and displaced sense of being, the earliest versions of Wordsworth's autobiography mark developmental stages through a series of morally ambiguous acts. MS.JJ contains the earliest sequence of sustained composition toward what would become the 1799, two-part *Prelude*. Composed in Goslar from October to November 1798, MS.JJ draws strong connections between the narrator's youthful experiences of guilty pleasure and spiritual insight, between his moral and social iconoclasm and moments of liberation.[2] Tellingly, these experiences occur during pauses in the speaker's unsupervised wanderings; the boy passes from bathing in rivers to climbing mountains without interruption, mostly following only the guide of his own inclinations. Wordsworth's classes at Hawkshead commenced at 6:30 a.m., but we never see his boyhood incarnation studying.[3]

MS.JJ contains fragments describing boat stealing and ice skating which were later incorporated into the 1799 poem's larger autobiographical sequence. But in MS.JJ, the main sequence – a kind of ur-*Prelude* – contains only two extended episodes. Both are scenes of theft. The young boy, wandering over the Cumbrian mountains, first steals eggs from a raven's nest. Later we see him, unsatisfied with the catch of his own snares, robbing the traps of local hunters.

> Sometimes strong desire
> Resistless over came me, & the bird
> Th[at] was the captive of another's toils
> Became my prey, and then I heard
> Low breathings coming after me and sounds
> Of indistinguishable motion steps
> Almost as silent as the turf they trod.

> (JJ, 111–17)

Like the boat-stealing scene, which would be added to the main sequence in January 1799, trap-robbing seems "an act of stealth / And troubled pleasure" (JJ, 214–15).

Typically, the precise valence of trap-robbing for Wordsworth is unclear. His perceptions of an invisible pursuer imply a sense of guilt over an act he feels to be unethical.[4] This view is complicated by the fact that the boy feels anxious not when taking other people's catches, but in seeking his own; as he checks snare after snare, "hurrying on / Still hurrying, hurryin[g] onward, how my heart / Panted … " (JJ, 107–9). The silent, virtually undetectable walker behind the boy could be a psychological projection of disciplinary force or a dangerous accomplice, a stealthy double for a protagonist who is also short of breath. Similar ambiguities adumbrate the theft of eggs from the raven's nest. Although his goal of stealing eggs while "a rover" is "inGlorious" (JJ, 54, 57), the narrator tells us it is not necessarily a moral breach. After all, "the end / Was not ignoble" (JJ, 57–8). In the short term, an awareness of wrongdoing competes with the boy's experience of a precarious freedom while on his errand. The peril of hanging by "half inch fissures in the slippery rock" is compensated for by the boy's momentary feeling that perhaps he, like the raven, is capable of flight (JJ, 60). He feels "almost as it seemed / Suspended by the wind which blew amain" (JJ, 61–2). This moment of ambiguous physical suspension – am I falling or am I flying? – is a somatic accompaniment to moral uncertainties about his desire to take the bird's eggs.[5]

The two apostrophes that follow in the 1798 text ameliorate these initial uncertainties: they involve an awareness of chastisement and consequently of wrongdoing. The beings "that walk the woods and open heaths" (JJ, 69) do, after all, purify the heart and mind through "disc[i]pline" involving "pain & fear" (JJ, 77, 78). Yet the unspoken paradox is that to become pure one must first be sullied, making the childhood fall (or suspension) a fortunate one. The natural world, furthermore, is deliberately constructed so as to encourage the moral confusion that can make stealing seem momentarily acceptable. The beings of the lakes have

> Impressed upon all form the character
> Of danger & desire & thus [do] make
> The surface of the universal earth
> With meanings of delight of hope & fear
> Work like a sea.

> (JJ, 92–6)

This passage suggests an insoluble interpretive problem. Perception so aggregates desire and danger, hope and fear, and innocence and guilt that, as the trap-robbing scene intimates, to desire intensely is almost invariably to incur guilt. The boy hanging from the cliff while stealing eggs conveys the physical analogue of this equation: an experience of seeming to conquer basic physical limitations carries in its shadow the possibility of falling to one's death. By revealing the fluidity of our understanding of fundamental material categories like solids (the universal earth) and liquids (the sea), the quotation above manifests the adulterated character of all human endeavor and apprehension.

The child at the manuscript's center is a kind of model for the young vagabond: when he is not stealing, he wanders through the landscape at his leisure. The absence in MS.JJ of any scenes of home or indoor life indicates he virtually lives outdoor.[6] The psychological explorations enabled by the autobiographical form, however, invalidate the expansion of guilt aimed at by authorities intending to define vagrant delinquency. In the 1799 *Prelude* deviance is indeed everywhere. But rather than the crime expanding to include tendencies or behaviors that are not in themselves criminal acts, the acts of Wordsworth's juvenile delinquent peculiarly constrict, rather than expand, vagrancy's penumbra of suspicion. Because deviance at times appears to be everywhere, it finally can be located nowhere since it circulates within a psychic economy that includes innocence from and ignorance of evil. The moral play among all these elements technically makes the young poet a delinquent, but the vagrant's appropriation of the subject position – his open assumption of the power to (de)classify himself – dramatizes the power of aesthetics to unmask delinquency itself as another socially contingent category whose borders are liable to contraction as well as expansion.

The young boy's vagrant alienation partly reflects the intense isolation of the Wordsworths during their stay in Germany from the fall of 1798 to the spring of 1799. In Hamburg, for example, they were convinced they were being cheated at shops and by innkeepers – an ironic reversal of conventional fears that wanderers, rather than established community members, were prone to petty theft. The Wordsworths' very slow progress in the language and their lack of outside contact may have made these months seem hardly more congenial than their period of persecution at Alfoxden.[7] The poem's identification of wandering with theft also accords with English legal traditions that were reinforced throughout the 1790s. Vagrancy's criminality was due partly to the widespread belief that it invariably led to more serious offenses like stealing. In an era obsessed with the protection of property, vagrants were viewed as potential housebreakers and, conversely, housebreakers could be punished under vagrancy laws.[8]

When he steals game from others' traps or takes birds' eggs from the nest, the boy's behavior also recalls poaching activities the state had struggled to suppress for more than a century. MS.JJ's employment of poaching imagery reflects the view of the times: 39 and 40 Geo. III, c. 50, enacted 20 June 1800, reiterated an entrenched association of poaching with vagrant inclinations toward property theft and civil disorder.[9] One of the harsher game laws passed during the reign of George III, this statute allowed night poachers to be punished as vagrants: convicts could be whipped, incarcerated for as long as two years, and impressed into the military. Up until this time, a more typical punishment for poaching was a £35 fine or three months in prison. The mechanisms of vagrancy and poaching law overlapped in other ways as well; some justices of the peace used the settlement laws to extradite suspected poachers (Munsche, 87).

The childhood vagrancy of MS.JJ is especially threatening in that it facilitates a crime not politically innocent. The Norman game laws reserved the right to hunt deer, rabbits and specific kinds of birds for the king. A precedent-setting codification of this law, enacted in 1671, extended this right to substantial property holders. Animals designated as "game," including partridges, pheasants, moor fowl, and hares, could be hunted and killed by those with freeholds worth at least £100 per year or leaseholds or copyholds worth £150 year. Hunters also were entitled to follow animals onto others' lands if necessary, resulting in trampled crops and flaring tempers. Officials were empowered to search a person's house for snares, which Wordsworth's boy uses, traps, guns, and hunting dogs. Gamekeepers could confiscate the traps and shoot the dogs, for none of these items could legally be possessed by anyone except landlords and gamekeepers (McLynn, 207).[10] The persistence of poaching only intensified Parliament's desire to eradicate it; P. B. Munsche records no fewer than 25 major revisions of the game law during the reign of George III alone (171). In 1770, an act (subsequently made more lenient) decreed poaching at night was punishable by an automatic six months in prison. In 1803 armed poaching became a capital offense. An 1816 act recommended transportation even for an unarmed man caught with a net, and by 1827 "poaching crimes were accounting for one seventh of all criminal convictions in England" (Porter, 137). The ruling orders struck back with creative theory as well. The Cambridge jurist Edward Christian, for example, claimed a poacher's nocturnal ways must eventually turn him into a brutal primitive capable of the most feral deviance.

As the episodes of theft in MS.JJ suggest, however, in the eighteenth century far from everyone viewed poaching as a moral and legal transgression. In a conflict reminiscent of changing attitudes over infanticide legislation, there was widespread disagreement over the legitimacy of the game laws. Laborers believed hunting animals for food was a common right that, through the poaching laws, the ruling class had usurped for its own.[11] A yeoman lacking the property qualification felt perfectly within his rights to violate the law by shooting a pheasant on his own land, though he would likely see the poor venturing onto yeomen fields for the same purpose as poachers. Tenants, small freeholders, and tradesmen might be invited to join hunting parties organized by the local squire on his land. Although these guests lacked the property qualification, such outings generated valuable goodwill and were not in isolated instances considered illegal. Matters became still more complex after the 1750s, when the creation of bird preserves on the gentry's land led them to view game as they viewed deer, as private property. They became reluctant to share such commodities, and so hunting invitations to social inferiors fell off. Of course, this was unpopular: "it was not long before [those without the qualification] began to question the legitimacy of the laws which allowed the gentry to deny them a recreation – and a mark of status to which they felt entitled" (Munsche, 51). Finally, gentlemen were offended when yeomen assumed the privilege of the hunt without invitation, but resented lands forbidden to even the wealthy by ancient rights of royal franchise. Against the legal expertise of Christian, Blackstone argued that the entire network of game laws were vestiges of Norman tyranny that should be abolished. These conflicting viewpoints made any clear consensus on poaching's illegality impossible.[12]

One clear expression of the impatience of the middle sectors of society with the game laws was their growing appetite after 1750, especially in London, for the very animals reserved for the rich. After 1755, even qualified hunters were forbidden to sell game; the feeling was that the true, sporting gentleman would never hunt at night or for profit. It fell to those less encumbered by principle, professional poachers, to supply the huge black market in game generated by an unlanded but affluent middle class who wanted to become "gentrified" (211). Attempting to explain the boy's reaction to trap robbing in the 1799 *Prelude*, Jonathan Wordsworth observes that "The guilt [felt by the child] was no doubt disproportionate, but woodcock were a luxury food, fetching as much as ten pence apiece" (*Pedlar*, 42n.). Kenneth Johnston notes how the woodcocks and fish that Wordsworth caught and sold at market while a student at Hawkshead helped extend his small weekly stipend (*Hidden*, 45). While some late eighteenth-century professional poachers organized into armed gangs, many black-market suppliers lived in small villages and worked alone, relying like Wordsworth's narrator on stealth and skill rather than numbers and violence. It was precisely luxuries like woodcocks that urban residents were paying high prices for in the 1770s, 1780s, and 1790s.

The aristocracy's abiding affection for the game restrictions stemmed in part from the law's mission to force ethically murky actions into transparent categories of innocence and guilt. If a man lacked the property qualification and hunted, he was guilty. Such clarity was particularly useful in times of national crisis, when poaching was identified with more serious crimes. In 1723, the Waltham Black Act made deer stealing a felony, and doing so while armed or with a blacked face, a common method of disguise for poachers, punishable by death (Thompson, *Whigs*, 69). The act's swift passage owed much to Walpole's fear that the Waltham deer stealers were really Jacobites in disguise, preparing to join the Pretender's invasion forces soon to cross the Channel.[13] Passing an act that dealt clearly and harshly with poaching, from this perspective, was tantamount to successfully squelching rebellion. The law technically viewed deer as property rather than game, but the Black Act is an instructive precedent for feelings about the game laws as well.[14] In Wordsworth's own time, of course, the government's problem was Jacobins rather than Jacobites. Events in both France and England, however, reinforced the political importance of the game laws. In one of its first decisions, the French National Assembly in August 1789 had abolished the laws restricting hunting rights to the nobility.[15] Ensuing events in France led English conservatives to identify game law reform with Jacobinism, a view encouraged by the fact that such changes were in fact part of the English reformers' political program. For example, in *Peace and Union* (1793), William Frend called for the abolition of game laws (18–19). He also counseled, in the wake of Louis XVI's execution, that "It is in short no business of ours, and if all the crowned heads on the continent are taken off, it is no business of ours" (46). The poacher, a figure whose exact cultural valence had fluctuated wildly depending on circumstance, now became identified with nothing less than revolution. The upper class's enthusiasm for the game laws intensified in the face of John Christian Curwen's proposal to reform them, presented to Parliament in March 1796. A liberal-minded Cumberland squire, earlier in the decade Curwen had clearly stated his opposition to the French war. Curwen's bill was quite moderate in nature: to hunt, a yeoman farmer would have to purchase a three-guinea license, itself a considerable sum, and the penalties for repeated poaching or poaching at night actually would become harsher than before. He introduced the measure to the Commons by opining that Parliament had a simple choice: it could reform now, and retain command, or resist change and risk being trodden underfoot by a British revolution.

England's authorities were still reeling from the calamities of late 1795, including food riots and an attempt on the king's life, which had culminated in the first wave of laws against public assembly and criticism of the government. Pitt's speech against Curwen's bill implied that now was hardly the time to chip away at the system of deference and obligation the game laws traditionally had been a part of. It was worth reminding farmers and laborers that they owed what hunting they did enjoy, and a good many other privileges, to the largesse of country gentlemen. Further, it was a Georgian commonplace that the gentry's residence in the country-side stabilized rural England; in this time of crisis, this class's exclusive right to hunt was viewed as a well-deserved reward for preserving local security.

> By his paternal care of the poor, his supervision of local government and his hospitality to his neighbours, the country gentleman vindicated the wisdom and humanity of the existing social and political order. Moreover, without him as a guide, the lower classes would quickly fall prey to Jacobinism, the consequences of which were only too clear to everyone in 1796. The gentry's monopoly on game seemed, indeed, to be a small price to pay for such services.
>
> (Munsche, 130–1)

Curwen's bill was defeated on its second reading on 29 April 1796. Edward Christian's *A Treatise on the Game Laws* (1817) testifies to the persistence of this view through the early nineteenth century.

Christian chastises anyone who would see the aristocracy's right to hunt as dependent "only upon the fluctuating and occasional laws enacted by the Legislature of every country." Suggesting the contingent origin of such statutes "must, surely, be pernicious to the public quiet in all times, but more particularly when a spirit of insubordination and rebellion prevails amongst the poor classes. Such a spirit [this view] is calculated both to excite and to augment" (*Treatise*, 291).

The equation of activities like poaching with treason was of a piece with Wordsworth's experiences at Alfoxden scarcely a year later. His expulsion from Somerset illustrated how poorly the ambiguous position of a wayward stranger fared when the press was gagged, Habeas Corpus was suspended, and people feared invasion from the continent. As in "The Thorn," Wordsworth's West Country neighbors were incapable of observing his odd behavior at face value; it had to be secret evidence of something far worse. The first part of the 1799 *Prelude* invalidates this perspective, beginning with scenes of wandering and poaching in a struggle to reclaim the uncertain and the indeterminate as just that. It tenaciously asserts in the face of historical and contemporary pressure the narrator's own obstinate capacity for acts and beliefs that participate in the acceptable alongside the deviant or even criminal.

This project continues in the 1799 *Prelude* with the spots of time sequence. These memories of ethically equivocal, socially undesirable acts show how when "depressed / By trivial occupations and the round / Of ordinary intercourse, our minds ... are nourished, and invisibly repaired" (l.290–4).[16] Circumstances situating the speaker in a space where conventional moral registers of guilt and innocence overlap provide creative strength. The entire spots of time sequence is, like the vagrant child they portray, a kind of pariah. The narrator awkwardly acknowledges that the incidents "cannot here / Be regularly classed" (l.255–6), unlike the previously chronicled spurs to mental development. The spots of time were composed and incorporated into the poem sometime in December 1798 or January 1799. At this stage of composition the drowned man was grouped with the two other spots, though revisions would separate them. All three episodes concern the speaker's relation to a male authority figure whom he has disobeyed or who has died. The narrator's position is neither strictly criminal nor stainless; he does not cause the deaths or seem to deliberately disobey. Yet aspects of each episode carry a residue of guilt or fear of punishment. These moments all occur in the context of the young boy's travels: the physical act of straying from the planned path complements a more abstract deviation from acceptable behavior and viewpoints. Like Wordsworth's own professional development, the evolution of these moments has not been charted but is governed by "mischance" (l.304).

The middle scene describes how a wayward pony ride leads to the discovery of the gibbet where "A man, the murderer of his wife, was hung" (l.309). The intensity of the child's response may seem incommensurate with the rather straightforward sequence of events presented. Also suggestive is the remembered attachment to "honest James," the servant from whom he becomes separated (l.302). Another James, a servant in his grandfather's household, would be a tormenter rather than a helper to Wordsworth during the year he began the poem that would publicly announce his profession, *An Evening Walk*. In a 1787 letter to Jane Pollard, Dorothy Wordsworth details the petty humiliations to which she and her now-orphaned brothers were subject in their grandfather's house. Her description of the situation does not spare the help. James is singled out as ridiculing the children for their destitution and their modest needs: "... my Brs can not even get a pair of shoes cleaned without James's telling them they require as much waiting upon as *Gentlemen* ... " (*Early Years*, 4). She adds that James is "a particular favorite [with] my Uncle Kit, who has taken a dislike to my Br Wm" and that James "thinks [whi]le my Uncle behaves in this way to us he may do any thing ... " (4). These hostilities might have been forgotten by the winter of 1798. However, this seems unlikely given that in 1799, when Christopher Crackanthorpe (Uncle Kit) finally died, Wordsworth did not attend his funeral and declined to visit his aunt in her bereavement. Mary Moorman attributes this behavior to the poet's ongoing "deep grudge against his uncle for what he considered his unjust behavior to his nephews in their youth" (448). The memorable pony ride preceded by at least ten years the conflicts with this second James, which occurred after John Wordsworth's death when his son was in his teens. But according such a servant figure a place in the poem's chronology when virtually no one else is named remains strange when we consider the overlay of hostility tinting Wordsworth's memories of the Cooksons' household.

An awareness of this history makes it difficult not to read James' epithet, "honest," as an implicit rebuke to the Cooksons' notions of familial respect and courtesy. The second James' ridicule of the young Wordsworths effectively takes them down a rung on the social ladder; they require the same attention as if they were gentlemen, though they cannot claim that title in the wake of the loss of their inheritance. James' comment about cleaning the shoes rhetorically masks his own insubordination by ascribing it to the Wordsworths, who are claiming privileges that should be reserved for their betters. As the name of servants in both his father and grandfather's homes, James serves as a signifier for the expectations and arbitrary restraints that are Wordsworth's most galling inheritance. Losing James and finding the gibbet is tantamount to a momentary deliverance from those expectations and restraints: the relation of such bonds to the family indirectly surfaces in the episode through the executed man's crime, wife murder. For the murderer, hanging meant death, but this use of "hung" recalls its appearance earlier at the raven's nest, where the hanging narrator senses a rare kind of quasi-release. The presence of the Penrith beacon here also underscores the political, as well as moral, questions raised by early parts of the 1799 *Prelude*. Erected to warn borderers against Jacobite invaders and activated in 1745, the Penrith beacon situates the boy's rebellion against adults and family against a larger backdrop of civil war. The roles of Wordsworth's own family in the conflict, typically, bequeathed the poet a divided legacy. The Lowthers, and with them Wordsworth's paternal grandfather, had opposed the rebels, while Wordsworth's grandfather Cookson (his mother's father) had supported the Pretender. For Johnston, the Penrith beacon in *The Prelude* focuses the political and social ambiguities of the poet's childhood, including "which side – or which grandfather – was right" in the '45, an implicit debate that recurred during the family gatherings of Wordsworth's youth (*Hidden*, 40). A sign of confusion amid the scene's multitude of confused signs, the Penrith beacon signifies the persistence of personal and political history in the landscape but does not provide a key for deciphering the boy's, or the adult's, exact relation to that history.

Aesthetic empowerment is the gain, and anxiety and confusion are the price, of this experience.[17] After losing James, the speaker dismounts in fear before discovering the gibbet. The "visionary dreariness" (l.322) he subsequently perceives upon seeing the girl with the pitcher provides creative energy later in life, yet at the time the speaker in bewilderment "looked all round for my lost guide,"

James (1.323). A moment of imaginative transformation in which the ordinary becomes extraordinary is made possible by the throwing off of authority and wandering into possible transgression.[18] The boy's sin on one level is trivial; he wanders away from a servant. The scene he then stumbles upon implies that even small deviations from norms can, in extreme cases, culminate in the final journey to the gallows. The boy, obviously, is no murderer, but his vagrant adventure and the imaginative moment it leads to are mediated by an awareness of violence and punishment.

The two adjoining spots of time flesh out the connection between wandering, morally suspect acts, and poetic power. In the episode of the drowned man, the young boy walking near Hawkshead encounters an abandoned bundle of clothing near Esthwaite lake. As with the gibbet scene, the random nature of the encounter is called to the reader's attention. He only sees the clothes because, on a twilight ramble, "I chanced to cross / One of those open fields ... " (1.263–4). He watches for a swimmer but does not call for help or notify the villagers. A suspicion that a man is suffocating below the surface is displaced into the sinister "breathless stillness" which the youth feels encircling the lake (1.274). The poet goes on to report the later discovery of the body, which rises "bolt upright" during a search of the lake (1.278), but the suddenness of the motion has no counterpart of realized horror or sorrow in the youth's feelings. Instead, the death impresses upon a young schoolboy the possibility of "independent life" for both children and human memories (1.286). The drowned man's profession as a local schoolmaster and monitor of childhood contributes to this effect, and while other "distresses and disasters, tragic facts," influenced the narrator, this memory receives preferential treatment (1.282).[19]

When this episode is separated from the other spots and placed in Book V of the 1805 *Prelude*, the unsavory moral implications of the incident carefully are diffused. The child's composure is attributed now to a familiarity with the grotesque conveyed by books (1805: V.473–81). In the 1799 poem, however, the reader might formulate a different explanation. When the body abruptly surfaces, why should the boy respond with "vulgar fear" (1805: V.473)? He knows the day before that a body will be found. The facts of the case do not allow us to affirm that the boy had a hand in killing the swimmer; when he passed by the lake on the preceding evening, the man may have already been dead. Yet the speaker's behavior seems peculiarly detached in the face of the concern exhibited by other villagers, who the next morning assiduously dredge the lake for a body. For the reader, the boy's sense of power is purchased by a vague sense of complicity in the man's demise.

A similar scenario shapes the last spot, which concerns the death of the speaker's father. Again, the situation is framed by the narrator's tendency to stray from a set path or schedule. Anxious to return home at Christmas, the boy leaves the Hawkshead schoolhouse and walks a full mile and a half to anticipate the horses coming to take him that day: "Feverish, and tired and restless, I went forth / Into the fields, impatient … " (l.332–3). He climbs a ridge to gain a better view, but even here is not content with his station, for he looks "With eyes intensely straining as the mist / Gave intermitting prospects of the wood / And plain beneath" (l.347–9). As this portion of the episode ends, we never learn when the horses came or by which road. The point is the child's restless manner while waiting. At the time, the boy believes this small rebellion is brutally punished; he concludes that God kills his father to punish him for walking ahead in an unseemly eagerness to return home.[20] To the adult narrator, and to the reader perhaps, this notion now seems a mistaken childhood fancy; it is a function of the child's "trite reflections of morality" (l.358). But the force of the memory, and by extension the fact that it becomes a well for future power, owes something to the lingering sense that the son does share some culpability. The speaker's dismissal of his youthful "trite reflections" is sandwiched between two poignant claims for their authenticity, the last of which speaks of how, "with the deepest passion, I bowed low / To God who thus corrected my desires" (l.359–60). The language of the poem presents the young protagonist as guilty and innocent, eluding clear recognition much like the misty shapes he sees on the two roads approaching the school. Nothing the narrator sees on the two roads to Hawkshead indicates which route the horses will travel. Similarly, what in some circumstances might seem two clearly defined paths of guilt and innocence are here problematic. The episode ends suspended in an unresolved conflict between his two consciousnesses, the youthful one who believes himself guilty and the adult who finds himself blameless.

The second half of the 1799 *Prelude*, composed largely at the Hutchinson farm at Sockburn-on-Tees after the Wordsworths' return from Germany, deals with these questions in a changed way. The poem's latter half downplays the narrator's interest in vagrancy and its potential rebellions, emphasizing instead scenes where he is educated in restraint. The final stages of the poet's growth seek to demonstrate subservience to the idea of natural discipline, the philosophical poetic vocation, and English law and order. Proving such allegiance becomes the mission of the *Prelude* by late 1799, even as it was the objective of British authorities during the year Wordsworth returned from Germany.

The new extremes of the British political situation in 1799 may be measured by the passage of legislation forbidding trade unionization, or combinations. The Combination Acts were akin to the Two Acts of 1795, designed to restrict freedom of assembly and political opposition. To the government, trade unionists were either potential or practicing Jacobins, a suspicion justified by a 1799 report of the Commons Committee of Secrecy positing a conspiracy among British tradesmen and reformers, United Irishmen and the French (Emsley, *British Society*, 84–5). As a result, the London Corresponding Society and the societies of United Irishmen, Englishmen, and Scots were outlawed by name. On 10 March 1799, London officials moved against the intractable by arresting 20 men at a United Irish meeting in London, and 13 more believed to be their cohorts on April 9. The proofs of treason the government had hoped to obtain on the suspects themselves were missing. This was of little consequence, however, since Parliament renewed the suspension of Habeas Corpus before the summer recess of 1799.[21] Many of these men were held, uncharged, until the Peace of Amiens in 1802 (Hone, 91–2).

This atmosphere informs the attitudes of the 1799 *Prelude*'s maturing subject. In part two, he tries to bend his will to an enjoyment of others' society and to the dictates of natural tutelage. He now has companions on his boyhood wanderings and returns home at a journey's end, as opposed to the solitary, loosely disjointed experiences of the first poem's first part. At times, part two indicates that the accommodation required of the narrator is at worst a tolerable compromise. His instruction under two mothers – nature and the biological mother – still leaves him with "a quiet independence of the heart" (2.72). The infant babe passage describes the relation of the poet to nature as collaborative rather than subordinate: he "creates, creator and receiver both, / Working but in alliance with the works / Which [he] beholds" (2.303–5). Like parts of "The Old Cumberland Beggar," the lines work hard to show how one delicately can balance belonging and independence.

This mediated freedom is better than the pronounced marginality characteristic of the child in part one, or of the sailor and female vagrant of "Salisbury Plain." Their liberty entails a separation from human ties that can generate despair, a quandary the socialized infant of part two avoids: "No outcast he, bewildered and depressed" (2.291). By remaining connected with his mother, he is privy to a "filial bond" (2.293) that actually facilitates his cooperation with nature as an independent.

Nominal obedience to human guardians and to nature proves difficult to sustain. The narrator's young self still periodically lives in a grey zone where, in a kind of mental misspelling, subservience might become subversiveness. In part one, such uncertainty conveyed imaginative power. Because the rhetoric of part two seeks to replace doubt with something nearer to certainty, these mixed signals only produce confusion. Evidence of this emerges in a portrait of late adolescence:

> ... I still retained
> My first creative sensibility,
> That by the regular action of the world
> My soul was unsubdued. A plastic power
> Abode with me, a forming hand, at times
> Rebellious, acting in a devious mood,
> A local spirit of its own, at war
> With general tendency, but for the most
> Subservient strictly to the external things
> With which it communed.

(2.408–17)

The character and desirability of obedience to nature or society never are resolved here. The first four lines suggest a nobility in being "unsubdued" by anything; the poet's own mental inclinations are impervious to conventional expectations, or the "regular action of the world." As the description lengthens conflict deepens. The narrator is "Rebellious" and "at war / With general tendency," but goes on to claim that ultimately he is "subservient strictly" to normative notions of perception and authority.

Confusion continues when this verse paragraph concludes that the young poet's mind "bestowed new splendour" (2.419) on the sunset and controlled "A like dominion" (2.422) in the breezes, streams and oceans. By styling himself as the monarch of various natural phenomena, the narrator seems to cross the line between subservience and subversion. The child appears to usurp authority from nature rather than share power democratically or acknowledge the latter's superiority. Perhaps we are meant to see that serving nature can at times feel as if nature is in fact serving you. Yet the poem excludes any criteria that would tell us when we have slipped from one register of interaction, subservience, to another, subversiveness. Like the boy poised atop the blast stealing ravens' eggs, the adolescent position problematizes the distinction of right from wrong. This difficulty remains unsolved by the 1799 *Prelude*'s conclusion, impairing the narrator's ability to ascertain whether he has become a good pupil proceeding on the correct path or not. Is it that

> To unorganic natures I transferred
> My own enjoyments, or, the power of truth
> Coming in revelation, I conversed
> With things that really are?

> (2.440–3)

Are his perceptions of the external world evidence of his willful projections of his own desires, apart from any true manifestation of them? Or do his apprehensions actually result from sharing power with nature, from conversing with the world as it actually is? We, and he, remain unsure.

As in "The two April Mornings," also written in Goslar (Reed, *Early*, 34), this uncertainty appeals more than the spiritual stagnation in scenes where servitude seems entire. Part two begins with recollections of disruptive childhood games. They occur outside the routines of laborers and the aged, both of whom are asleep with exhaustion while yet the children's "revelry / Continued and the loud uproar" (2.12–13). These children seem indifferent to the adults who would or should supervise them. But this memory is introduced only for contrast; the adult narrator, no longer a deviant, wandering child, lacks the boy's sense of possibility. He now feels it is desirable, but impossible to give

> to duty and to truth
> The eagerness of infantine desire ...

> A tranquillizing spirit presses now
> On my corporeal frame, so wide appears
> The vacancy between me and those days.

> (2.23–7)

The tranquilizing spirit threatens to overwhelm the narrative enterprise of documenting continuous development. Tranquility emphasizes not continuity but breakage; when looking back at this childhood, the narrator seems "Two consciousnesses, conscious of myself / And of some other being" (2.30–1).

This sense of fragmentation partly comes from the changed landscape of Hawkshead, which the poet has recently discovered. In "Tintern Abbey" the unchanged terrain is an important catalyst in the narrator's recapitulation of his youthful self, and the 1799 *Prelude* notes with irritation the erection of a Town Hall on land that was formerly the boys' playground. The narrator seems peculiarly tranquilized in other passages as well. His praise of the moon, for example, concerns its identification with "patriotic and domestic love," affiliations seeming to necessitate a kind of psychic anesthesia (2.229). The narrator remembers,

> … I would dream away my purposes
> Standing to look upon her, while she hung
> Midway between the hills as if she knew
> No other region but belonged to thee,
> Yea, appertained by a peculiar right
> To thee and thy grey huts, my native vale.

> (2.231–6)

The moon here seems a model of the obedience and stability elsewhere praised; she acts as if she belongs to this particular village. This model exacts a considerable cost on its imitator. Like the unchanging moon, almost eternally poised between enclosing mountain peaks, the speaker is rooted to the spot of observance. His mind is restricted to a kind of trance-like worship, forgetting his own plans or preferences in favor of a mental torpor that, in valuing place and country, is reminiscent of Burke's little platoon of local affections. The presence of the grey huts intimates how communities can restrict one's ability to act through what neighbors may perceive as their "peculiar rights," a fact that energizes the previously discussed poems in *Lyrical Ballads.*

The consequences of tranquility seem most enervating when the narrator recalls rowing home across Windermere after bowling on a lawn across the lake. Having played with his friends, the speaker now returns home as expected. The children pause in their trip back to leave one boy to play his flute on a small island. This boy supplants the narrator as a wanderer preferring to defer the return home. The speaker's apprehension of this change that now he goes home while another stays out late results in a disturbing paralysis. As he hears the flute tones receding across the water,

> oh then the calm
> And dead still water lay upon my mind
> Even with a weight of pleasure, and the sky,
> Never before so beautiful, sank down
> Into my heart and held me like a dream.

> (2.210–14)

Because of his susceptibility to nature's power, the boy begins to resemble the drowned man he describes earlier. This moment, seductive though it is, insinuates that the ultimate reward for faithful service to nature and society may be spiritual stagnation if not physical death.

The poem's perspective on such events comes full circle in a concluding scene, where the speaker returns to a modulated version of the vagrancy of part one. Once again he remembers walking alone at night and garnering "visionary power" from natural stimuli (2.360). From such moments

> the soul
> Remembering how she felt, but what she felt
> Remembering not, retains an obscure sense
> Of possible sublimity to which
> With growing faculties she doth aspire,
> … feeling still
> That whatsoever point they gain, they still
> Have something to pursue.

> (2.364–71)

This statement returns us to the logic of the spots of time, and "Tintern Abbey." The content of individual memories may remain intact, but the independent workings of our minds cause the emotional meaning of those images to change over time. We are always in the process of creating our memories. Drifting layers of psychic sediment continually change the mind's composition and configuration, and in the end nothing is so vagrant as the act of creative memory itself.

This sort of activity, like Wordsworth's Alfoxden vagrancy, seems vulnerable when juxtaposed with a closing attack on Pitt's white terror and those who succumbed to it. Wordsworth includes this passage to illustrate how he, now nature's obedient pupil, has managed to retain a confidence in humanity others have lost. The probable example of those lacking the narrator's security complicates his own views about memory. In mid-1799, politician and philosopher James Mackintosh recanted his support for the French Revolution and the political philosophy behind it in his *Lectures on the Law of Nature and Nations*. In Wordsworth's term, he became one of the "good men" who had "fall[en] off we know not how / To selfishness" (2.481, 482–3). How are we to distinguish Mackintosh's recantation from the changing views of the *Prelude*'s narrator cited above? In effect, Mackintosh simply changed his previously favorable opinion of various political events and philosophers. Does this fundamentally differ from the speaker's own statements as to the way his own memory works? Might Mackintosh's soul too simply be "Remembering how she felt, but what she felt / Remembering not"? Years later in *The Spirit of the Age* (1825), William Hazlitt would criticize Mackintosh's lectures for ideas that "do not arise, as it were out of the subject, or out of one another at the moment" (157), adding that "There is no principle of fusion in his work" (158). The two-part *Prelude* suggests a similar disjunction in the narrator between memory and meaning, between the significance of an event and its import years later.[22] The poem's conclusion, immediately following the reprimand of Mackintosh, demonstrates anxiety over how to clarify the narrator's view in such a polarized context. Only to Coleridge, it appears, can the narrator speak "unapprehensive of contempt, / The insinuated scoff of coward tongues" (2.500–1).

Through reference to other texts, we might devise a way of reconciling the narrator's self-congratulation with his censure of Mackintosh. We might say, for example, that Mackintosh's difficulty (and difference) lies in his recklessly swaying from one extreme, radical, to the other, Tory, never achieving the poet's vaunted "independence of the heart." In this respect, Mackintosh might be a later version of the Burke attacked in Wordsworth's prose letter to the Bishop of Llandaff, who drunkenly swaggers from one side of the political roadside to the other. Mackintosh did claim that meeting Burke after the publication of his *Letters on a Regicide Peace* (1796) changed his own thinking about the revolution. But nothing in the 1799 *Prelude* encourages us to go so far afield, or provides us with any criteria for distinguishing Wordsworthian memory from Mackintosh's swings of opinion.

Once again the text, in trying to separate good men from bad ones, presents us with a situation liable to moral judgment that it cannot pronounce decisively on. Wordsworth was keenly aware of why this dilemma was troubling: if we resist allegiance to an accepted set of evaluative criteria we risk allowing the community to define us as it will.[23] In the 1790s, this meant possibly being seen either as a French-sympathizing traitor or a reactionary, regardless of one's true political beliefs. Yet if we do successfully relinquish vagrant independence for subservience to an accepted label, political or otherwise, part two implies that we risk something perhaps worse, spiritual stagnation. The unsavory choice the 1799 *Prelude* leaves us with, then, is either being perpetually misunderstood or being spiritually tranquilized. The vicissitudes of British politics during the French wars leave no other option. In the end, this is a choice the poem refuses to make. Its resolution awaits and explains the text's expansion into the thirteen-book, 1805 *Prelude*.

NAMING THE "CONFLICT OF SENSATIONS WITHOUT NAME"

As late as early March 1804, Wordsworth intended the revised poem on his life to become no longer than five books. Book I of this *Prelude* was to begin with memories of Hawkshead, and book V to conclude with the spots of time.[24] The French Revolution and the varied English reaction to it had, as yet, no place in the work. But by December 1804, Wordsworth was composing the 1805 poem's books IX and X, and in the process refining the biography that his Alfoxden neighbors already had begun to write for him. In its final form, this is the narrative that to varying degrees has structured assessments of Wordsworth's political career to this day. The 1805 books IX and X maintain that, in 1792, he had been a patriot, convinced of the Revolution's justice until the Terror. Then, he had turned to William Godwin's *Political Justice*, which had guaranteed the eventual triumph of benevolent, impartial Truth. Eventually, he also turned away from Godwin, whose philosophy was crippled by sterile rationalism. In 1805 he now emerged as an independent, "a sensitive, and a *creative* soul" (XI.256). In May 1805, Wordsworth would make an oft-quoted comment to Sir George Beaumont expressing worry over the burgeoning length of *The Prelude*, admitting that the poem was assuming "an alarming length! and a thing unprecedented in Literary history that a man should talk so much about himself" (*Early Years*, 586). Seizing on this comment, critics have assumed that in writing his lengthy autobiography, Wordsworth was transgressively breaking with literary decorum. In a representative pronouncement, Mary Jacobus contends:

> At once an endless beginning and always an afterword to the life it narrates, Wordsworth's autobiography seems not to have a proper place at all. It belongs nowhere and has no fixed character, redundant to the non-existent text which its title is supposed to "prelude." In short, it is an impropriety, and one properly suppressed during the poet's lifetime.
>
> (*Romanticism*, 189)

Wordsworth's reservations over the burgeoning length of the poem, however, only point to the importance of the additions he made in 1804 and 1805; what he was adding was simply too crucial to be left out. Aware of the alarming dimensions of his life story, Wordsworth nevertheless continued work on the books covering the 1790s.

　　In dealing directly and at length with the French Revolution's impact on British society, this material does something new in Wordsworth's verse. Perhaps most importantly, it clearly and self-consciously situates the poet's life within the master-narrative of his generation. We are told how he, like so many others, took up the Revolution as a cause. He, too, became disillusioned after the Terror and turned to the dubious comfort offered by Godwin. Finally, he then became a true political free-thinker, viewing radical and Tory alike skeptically but siding with England as the last outpost of a measure of freedom in Europe. Periodic asides in books IX and X specifically justify this succession of allegiances precisely because it was representative. The revolution in feeling he endured after Britain declared war on France in 1793 affected everyone: "Not in my single self alone I found, / But in the minds of all ingenuous youth, / Change and subversion from this hour" (X.231–3). He goes on to squarely blame the war for estranging not only himself, but an entire generation, from the objectives of the nation, taking "from the best youth in England their dear pride, / Their joy, in England" (X.277–8). The mental trauma *The Prelude* goes on to document also draws on a pattern of behavior derived from the experiences of others: Wordsworth's shock, as chronicled in his autobiography, accords with the experiences of friends like James Losh and John Tweddell, who with the collapse of their political hopes "suffered near breakdowns" (Johnston, *Hidden*, 465). Near the conclusion of book X, Wordsworth again insists that he has been

> tracing faithfully
> The workings of a youthful mind, beneath
> The breath of great events, its hopes no less
> Than universal.

> (X.939–42)

Indeed, the commonality of these experiences seems a large part of why they are included in the poem, since they are described as detours in the larger trajectory of the narrator's poetic development. He offers his hopes for England's failure in battle as a temporary falling away from a pre-ordained plan, asserting that his upbringing could not allow the pain of such intensely wrong-headed commitments to affect him permanently.[25] This biographical framework was not Wordsworth's idea, but a gift from Coleridge, who could hardly have imagined how personally useful it would become to his friend. Writing about the ill-fated *Recluse* in September 1799, Coleridge had urged his friend:

> I wish you would write a poem, in blank verse, addressed to those who, in consequence of the complete failure of the French Revolution, have thrown up all hopes of the amelioration of mankind, and are sinking into an almost epicurean selfishness, disguising the same under the soft titles of domestic attachment and contempt for visionary *philosophes*.

> (*Collected letters*, 527)

Johnston notes the serendipity of Coleridge's suggestion, which suddenly gave the aimless *Prelude* a task: "the 'tedious tale' (according to Wordsworth) of his life had been given a point and mission: it could save their entire generation" from political disillusion (*Hidden*, 681). It could also save a particularly truant young man from charges of his own kind of detachment and selfishness.

By situating Wordsworth's life within this framework, the 1805 *Prelude* makes the choice the poem of 1799 defers. The later work chooses intelligibility over ambivalence, subservience over rebellion. Early on, the possibility of a narrative more consistent with the political equivocation of the poet's earlier work arises; perhaps he should write of "How in tyrannic times, some unknown man, / Unheard of in the chronicles of kings, / Suffered in silence for the love of truth" (I.202–4). Instead, *The Prelude* ultimately takes a different road, choosing to locate the poet's history within the flattening context of a politically polarized culture. Rather than chart his development in ambiguous relation to cultural constraints, Wordsworth situates his autobiography within a consistent framework of clearly defined social norms, "in the very world which is the world / Of all of us, the place in which, in the end, / We find our happiness, or not at all" (X.725–7). An obvious rejoinder to this view of *The Prelude* as a political vindication is that its publication was a very long time in coming; going public in 1805 would seem to make far more sense than the posthumous publication that eventually took place. For Johnston, this delay testifies to the dangerous nature of the poem's truths in a society where Jacobinism remained a bugbear for decades: "Had (*The Prelude*) appeared in 1807, Wordsworth would have awakened to find himself *in*famous" (*Hidden*, 835). Johnston claims that the poem to Coleridge was in some sense never intended for public consumption – that it was the story for friends and family the poet could not tell the world. The difficulty with this theory, in terms of Johnston's own interpretation, is that for an "open" account it already conceals significant details such as the Annette Vallon story, details that those friends and family knew but that were not included in any version of the text – hence the need for Johnston's assiduous detective work. Wordsworth seems to have held the poem back from the public for many reasons, but although it lived in manuscript for decades, it was not just (or even primarily) an account for his intimate circle. In charting a rebellious youth, *The Prelude* is, instead, a tremendously risky and bold exercise in political self-fashioning. Wordsworth's own experiences suggested to him that not having been a Jacobin, or a Tory – not having been any kind of committed actor in the political drama of the age, in which everyone else, it seemed, had now taken a role – was perhaps the most dangerous, least comprehensible position of all. The conflict of sensations without name must, at last, be given a culturally intelligible label. The years of revision enabled by the endlessly deferred publication of the poem reflected the enormous importance of presenting the narrative he ultimately selected in precisely the correct way. The volatility of the poem's story in the context of nineteenth-century British society, even after he labored for decades to shape his experiences into an exculpatory narrative, was evidenced by the perception of Wordsworth after the 1850 publication as a largely unrepentant revolutionary. On its face, this reception vindicates Johnston's reading. The question is whether, by 1804, Wordsworth's culture could provide a man of his age and experiences with any denouement that would be more convincing.

Gene Ruoff suggests that adding *The Prelude's* book on France was the culmination of composition of several poems between 1802 and 1804. The poet's first turn away from the deeply personal and the idiosyncratic occurred in 1802, when he wrote and published Miltonic sonnets pronouncing authoritatively on the degraded state of both France and England. The Intimations Ode, completed in the spring of 1804, went on to justify the emphasis of these sonnets. Ruoff argues that the Ode's final revisions modify the entropic view of human development necessitated by the poem's myth of the pre-existent soul. The Ode's speaker finally sees his powers as diminishing but never exhausted, a view made possible by his enduring connection with human aspiration and activity. Wordsworth simultaneously finished the Ode and decided to expand *The Prelude* to include his experiences in France; for Ruoff, both decisions reflect a desire to tell "not an internal life story, a story of isolated mystical moments, but a life lived in social, historical time" (287). These artistic decisions fulfilled a line of thinking that had led Wordsworth to rent his own home in late 1799, marry Mary Hutchinson in 1802, and regard his poems – beginning with the 1800 *Lyrical Ballads* – as intellectual property that he could and should control.[26]

Its French books reflect the 1805 *Prelude's* heightened awareness that life cannot be lived in the interstices of cultural and moral classification. Earlier poems indicated that homelessness appealed to Wordsworth precisely because it seemed to offer such a life, to embody a potential criminality and political iconoclasm that resisted clear affiliation within prevailing notions or controversies. The end of the 1799 *Prelude* implies that such ambivalence toward the status quo is prone to misinterpretation as hostile opposition. The 1805 *Prelude* goes farther, asserting that homelessness is no more exempt from the restrictions of social context than any other mode of existence. It may even be more vulnerable than most, because observers especially will define the wanderer in terms of readily intelligible allegiances or convictions. The 1805 poem brings the insights of "The Thorn," where a community eventually casts a quasi-vagrant as nothing less than an infanticide, to an account of the poet's life and development.

Like part two of the poem's 1799 version, the early books of the 1805 *Prelude* respond to this tendency by sporadically trying to locate the young poet's physical and mental wanderings within a larger sphere of distinct, if poorly defined, purpose. The speaker's subsequent encounter with a blind beggar in book VII – "London" – crystallizes the dangers of a vagrancy whose relation to political opinions and widely accepted cultural values is unclear. After this realization, the poet increasingly portrays his own habits and life through a moral lens minimizing his attraction to the vagrant's distance from social norms. Counterintuitive though it may seem, his decision to portray himself as a revolutionary partisan is central to this project. In an extension of the campaign that began with "The Old Cumberland Beggar," the wanderers and homeless people that do appear late in the 1805 *Prelude* not only are purged of any subversive potential; they embody some of the most desirable qualities that enable the existing order of society to continue. The episode of the blind beggar demonstrates that if we do not perform this activity, if we do not shape actively society's perceptions of us, others will invariably come to their own conclusions, even if we claim that the vagrant are to some extent beyond judgment.

By 1804, when most of the 1805 *Prelude* was written, the situation in Britain virtually demanded the inclusion of some history of Wordsworth's political views. In authorizing all Wordsworth's professional and literary aspirations, *The Prelude*'s logic makes aesthetic self-justification inseparable from a progressive purification of the marginality that for so many years had drawn the poet to the homeless. In the terminology of the vagrancy laws, it was time to give an account of himself, an account more conclusive than the elusive poetic autobiography encoded in "Resolution and

Independence." This act would have seemed less imperative in the more temperate political climate of 1801 or even 1803. But renewed war with France, declared on 18 May 1803, led to growing state powers and rekindled popular fears. Addington reinstated the income tax, which had been discontinued during the brief peace; with its mutiplying schedules and new, professional tax collectors directly employed by the crown, the burgeoning Treasury office emblematized the war's ongoing extension of state bureaucracy. After again becoming prime minister in May 1804, Pitt reorganized the Treasury into six divisions, with an entire department exclusively dedicated to revenues and tax collection (Emsley, *British Society*, 106–7). Yet more than any legislation, the loyalist sentiment of 1803 to 1805 depended on the omnipresent threat of Napoleonic invasion. Cartoons and broadsides usually depicted Britain's defender as John Bull or a stalwart volunteer rather than the prime minister. As in 1797, foreigners and even British strangers were viewed suspiciously, especially near the coasts.[27]

To ensure popular loyalty to the war effort, an array of influential figures sprang into action. Pamphleteers tried to smooth over the fact that the poor could ill afford the militia substitutes that exempted the rich from military service, or the new taxes that were to pay for the long years of war ahead. *John Bull turned into a Galley Slave* put the best possible face on service in the English militia, arguing that it was surely preferable to being drafted into the French army. Clergymen preached against the French from their pulpits; cartoonists satirized Bonaparte's imperial hopes. Theater impresarios at the Theatre Royal, Covent Garden, and Haymarket had all staged that most stirring representation of French defeat, Shakespeare's *Henry V*, by the end of 1803 (115–18). When the war resumed, even dissenter William Frend, dismissed from his Cambridge fellowship in the early 1790s for opposing war with France, penned a pamphlet whose title alone communicates his ideological reversal: *Patriotism: or the love of our country*. Dedicated to the burgeoning volunteer corps, the tract appeared in May 1804. Those like Colonel Despard who chose the path of outright treason were arrested and quickly prosecuted; the same fate awaited anyone involved in the production of anti-war literature. The temper of the times coupled with these efforts effectively turned the country away from debating the merits of reform. One of the government's leading spies told his superiors in January 1804 that "'a complete triumph'" had been obtained over domestic treason, an opinion verified by a survey of extant materials (quoted in Hone, 137).

Wordsworth's final response to this situation emerges in the 1805 *Prelude*'s books VII–XIII, composed or assembled during Pitt's reascension to national leadership.[28] Yet even before homelessness is explicitly equated with support for solid conservative values (roughly in book VIII), the poem periodically portrays the freedom of vagrant life as encompassed by and subservient to higher purposes. The preamble of 1805 book I – lines 1–54 – probably dates from late 1799. Like part two of the 1799 *Prelude*, it repeatedly invokes vagrant states circumscribed by figures of stability. The poem's narrator begins by walking at will from a city with a heart not "scared at its own liberty" or afraid to take "a wandering cloud" for its guide (I.16, 18). Yet the reason for this – "I cannot miss my way" (19) – compromises our image of this excursion as free from constraint. By definition, a wanderer is someone who strays from an appointed path, who has no defined way to miss. Line 19 implies that the speaker really may be free only to discover some predetermined course of travel. The joy of rambling gives him no desire to prolong that state; instead, his first task is to "fix my habitation" (10).

The virtues of limited indirection become clear in composition perhaps dating from the poem's resumption in 1804.[29] This new material contains a litany of epic topics, none of which really engages the narrator's interest. He becomes fearful that unconfined liberty to choose a course of action may just result in "unprofitably traveling towards the grave" (I.270). In the end, he deliberately chooses a "theme / Of single and of determined bounds" (I.669–70), his life story, hoping it will "fix the wavering balance of my mind" (650). Adherence to a unified plan appears necessary for writing poetry, and the wavering mind in particular is not suited or ready to compose a great public epic of the type book I repeatedly invokes. The topics considered for poetry before the turn to autobiography at the end of book I are as often civic as philosophical, involving leaders from countries throughout Europe. To write the poem of a nation, one must first prove to be a member of it. In certain contexts, homelessness is not an advantage but a liability; it impedes rather than enables the development of purpose.

In describing his first year at Cambridge, the narrator adopts a somewhat different approach, trying to reconcile homelessness and a life of purpose. What looks like vagrancy, we are told, is really subservience to a higher goal. The poet justifies his disagreements with relatives about the course of his future by arguing that he was nature's "chosen son" (III.82) – properly viewed, willful disobedience to one entity is really only following a loftier call. The narrator goes on to assure us that his classmates' perceptions of him were clouded by the same misunderstanding. He describes his predilection for walking alone, "Oft did I leave / My comrades, and the crowd, buildings and groves, / And walked among the fields ... " (III.97–9), and his tendency to endow the natural world with sentience. Some called him mad, but he defensively argues that such behavior really demonstrated valuable access to a lost wisdom, as if the knowledge of the ancients "may in these tutored days no more be seen / With undisordered sight" (III.154–5). Periods when the poet admits that he strayed from a course of study or duty often are judged harshly in the early books. Moments of idle sociability, like getting tipsy in Milton's old rooms, constitute a "treasonable growth / Of indecisive judgments" that impairs his understanding of nature's teachings (III.214–15). In describing his desire to see the Alps and avoid his uncle in 1790, the speaker's tone becomes even more severe. He tells of an "over-love / Of freedom," which led him to turn "From regulations even of my own / As from restraints and bonds" (VI.43–4; 47–8). This resistance stemmed not from a sense of greater mission, he states flatly, but from "cowardice" (VI.43), even though it facilitated the visionary experience of crossing the Alps.

Good intentions and self-chastisement aside, however, the poem's early books question Wordsworth's oxymoronic claim to be a purposeful wanderer almost as frequently as they validate it. What scholars now assure themselves is the "dedication to poetry" in book IV, experienced while the narrator walks alone through fields at dawn, is not clearly a dedication to anything besides "blessedness" (IV.345).[30] Wordsworth the solitary, wandering (but secretly directed) student often gives way to Wordsworth the gregarious, aimless college freshman " ... if a throng was near / That way I leaned by nature, for my heart / Was social and loved idleness and joy" (III.234–6). By the end of book III the narrator still prefers to be misunderstood by his readers rather than define himself in terms of stock classifications. He easily assigns classmates to familiar college stereotypes: "loyal students faithful to their books; / Half-and-half idlers, hardy recusants, / And honest dunces" (III.62–4). The book later gives a more elaborate enunciation of the same viewpoint, reducing the entire campus to personifications such as Labour, Hope, Idleness, Shame, Submission, and the like.

However, the narrator himself deliberately stands aloof from such convenient categories, apparently seeing an exact portrait of himself in none of them and refusing to reduce himself to any one class. He concludes by describing himself still as a wanderer, studious at times yet a dilettante at heart, "roving as through a cabinet / Or wide museum" (III.652–3) wherein "A casual rarity is singled out / And has its brief perusal, then gives way / To others, all supplanted in their turn" (III.658–60).

In its early stages, then, the poem continues to grapple with difficulties in pronouncing definitively on the valence of homelessness: is it virtue or vice? Statements of each view have the effect of cancelling each other out. If the narrator imperfectly understands his own inclinations and what they mean, the situation is even more extreme for those around him. People as different as his Cambridge classmates and his Hawkshead neighbors appear at times to accept or understand him, yet at other moments seem deeply ignorant of or unsympathetic toward his nature. At the university he clearly has friends and a social life. Book III also implies, though, that the speaker's "truant eyes / Unruly, peep[ing] about for vagrant fruit" (III.529–30) are seen by some as freakish if not downright immoral, a feeling buttressed by the allusion in these lines to Eve's eating the apple in *Paradise Lost*. Book IV tells of his dancing until dawn at local gatherings, and of his enthusiastic round of greetings from residents when returning for his first summer vacation from Cambridge. The account of the latter event is typically ambivalent. Led about by Ann Tyson, with whom he had boarded while at Hawkshead,

> The face of every neighbor whom I met
> Was as a volume to me; some I hailed
> Far off, upon the road, or at their work –
> Unceremonious greetings, interchanged
> With half a length of a long field between.

(IV.58–62)

This is particularly problematic formulation, implying great intimacy while demonstrating great reserve. The traveler has returned "home" from college, but his familiarity with the people of Hawkshead seems little more than acquaintanceship. He greets them across the distances of sizable fields, and neither the speaker nor his "friends" seem interested in doing anything to shrink this gap. No one stops working to talk to the speaker, and he does not join them on their land. The presence of such physical distance also belies the claim that he reads each face with ease, since the description intimates that the faces in question are barely discernible. Later in this book, the speaker claims that during this time he felt an intensified affection for local people but acknowledges that "This chiefly" (IV.208) concerned one person, Tyson herself.

The uncertainty of the narrator's position, familiar with this community and its values, yet something of a stranger, is poignantly illustrated by his reunion with Tyson's dog. In his frequent walks with the dog before leaving for Cambridge, the speaker relied on the animal to warn him of approaching passers-by on the road.

> Punctual to such admonishment, I hushed
> My voice, composed my gait, and shaped myself
> To give and take a greeting that might save
> My name from piteous rumours, such as wait
> On men suspected to be crazed in brain.

> (IV.116–20)

The dog's warning gives the speaker time to stop talking to himself as he wanders so as to appear simply an average young person. He specifically seeks to avoid the gossip that stigmatizes Martha Ray or the "strolling bedlamites" he himself will defend much later in the poem (XII.158).[31] The narrator appears to his neighbors to be, as he calls them, an open volume whose contents are readable easily. But his vagrant habits and the truant imagination they reflect indicate a separation from the community and its standards. In the excerpt, he conceals his true self because communicating his ambiguous position is not possible. To others, he would seem to be merely an insane wanderer. Because poetic energies flow from an existence vagrant as well as purposeful – between acceptance and alienation, sanity and madness – relinquishing that vantage point is unthinkable. Walking along the road in this way the boy can be "busy with the toil of verse" (IV.102), while attending local parties that summer makes him feel enervated and dull.[32]

Lest we think that the speaker conclusively favors the world of the wanderer over that of the villager, however, book IV ends with the episode of the discharged soldier. This encounter, the longest one in the poem with a vagrant, begins as the speaker again walks a public road alone. The activity restores a mind worn out by more late-night socializing and leads to the visions we now expect to accompany the poet's travels: " ... what beauteous pictures now / Rose in harmonious imagery" (IV.392–3). A released soldier, now a vagrant sitting beside the roadside, destroys this claim and causes the narrator to react like the very villagers he himself fears. Like the narrator earlier in book IV, the soldier is talking to himself: "From his lips meanwhile / There issued murmuring sounds, as if of pain ... " (IV.421–2). However, he lacks the narrator's dog to warn him about observers. The figure's physical posture is ambiguous; he has traveled many miles but is now fixed, which discomfits the narrator. Propped up by a milestone, he is somewhere between sitting and standing; Geoffrey Hartman observes the soldier exists between life and death, fixity and movement (224–5). In the context of a nation at war, his position is culturally uncertain as well.

The Salisbury Plain poems demonstrate how discharged soldiers could import violence, crime, and civil unrest into the society to which they returned. Veterans who became vagrants might well be ending where they began, since throughout the eighteenth century the government had forced vagrants into military service when troops or sailors were needed (Webb, 367–9). In Wordsworth's poem, the soldier's very presence silently criticizes Britain's leaders; of all *The Prelude*'s wanderers, he is the one whose sickly condition and wanderings are direct products of government policy and military service. By 1799, Addington "expressed the general conviction when he asserted that the West Indies had destroyed the British army" during the 1790s campaigns to wrest France's colonies from its control (Duffy, 327). While his wasted state makes Wordsworth's soldier an unlikely figure of outright rebellion, the West Indies' notorious reputation as a repository of fatal, incurable diseases, most notably yellow fever and malaria, meant that regiments slated for service in the "tropic islands" (IV.446) had high rates of desertion before embarking and extremely poor morale. In the summer of 1797, some six months before Wordsworth's episode originally was composed, 37 Geo. III, c. 73 was enacted to try to curb the burgeoning desertion problem.[33] Once they reached the islands, desertion did soldiers little good, but the fear of disease coupled with the conviction that they would catch it brought entire regiments to a state of near-paralysis. Some responded with outright rebellion rather than such fatalism: the bloodiest naval mutiny of the period, aboard the frigate *Hermione* in 1797, occurred off the coast of Puerto Rico partially as a result of the miseries of the theater of engagement. If the outcome of the war was to depend on this range of military response – terror, malaise, or revolt – clearly the outlook was bleak.[34] By 1803–4, fighting in the colonies had assumed a new importance since they were the only theater in which the British continued to attack the French. Until the bad harvest of late 1804 necessitated action, Addington and then Pitt were content to wait for an invasion (Emsley, *British Society*, 99, 122). The "indifference" (IV.444, 476) of Wordsworth's soldier to his service, the fact that he tells of military involvement "Remembering the importance of his theme / But feeling it no longer" (IV.476–7), may not suggest the energy necessary for revolution. Set against the invasion scares of 1797–8 and 1803–5, this attitude does imply an apathy (shared by many serving in the Indies) to the nation's viability that might work to undermine the state or ignore any call to its defense. Is *The Prelude*'s discharged soldier a loyalist or a patriot? We cannot know, indeed he does not seem to know, for certain. The soldier's alienation from convention and public opinion is underlined by his profound insensibility to the narrator's parting admonition that he should "not linger in the public ways, / But ask for timely furtherance" (IV.490–1). He responds that he trusts to God and other travelers for sustenance, though his decrepit condition and inattention to the narrator insinuate a lack of interest in even these sources of aid. In the end, the soldier thanks the poet for his effort while rejecting the notion that he should actively seek intervention on his behalf.

The discharged soldier's indifference to the narrator's views parallels some of Wordsworth's own attitudes during the original episode's composition in Somerset. In 1804, when this episode is incorporated into *The Prelude*, Wordsworth looks a lot more like his narrator in more generally conforming to expectations. The narrator, although a young man of wandering habits, also carefully invokes his membership in a community. A final line added to the episode in 1804 explains that, after saying farewell to the soldier, the narrator "sought with quiet heart my distant home" (IV.504). That Wordsworth the citizen occupied such a middle ground as late as 1803–4 is illustrated by his own foray into the world of soldiering, his enrollment in the Grasmere Volunteers. He signed up on 3 October 1803, believing that the villagers "had turned out almost to a Man" (*Early Years*, 409). It is tempting to read this act as sealing a whole-hearted commitment to the war, much as his earlier gestures are believed to define Wordsworth the committed young radical.[35] This choice is not as patriotic as it may seem. Wordsworth's decision to volunteer was very much in keeping with his muted interest in *The Prelude*'s early books in occupying a marginal space as outcast even as he is a community member.

Readying the home defense forces had been a government priority since the spring of 1803, when another war came to seem inevitable. In March the militia was reestablished, and in the next few months Addington instituted a slew of new military groups which made all able-bodied males liable to state service. By the end of the summer, a man had to go through three ballots – for the militia, the supplementary militia, and the army of reserve – before he could be assured of an exemption from the military. These entities subjected recruits to military discipline and could compel service anywhere in the British Isles. By joining the local volunteers, which were civilian creations and not subject to strict supervision, one could evade all ballots and quite probably remain at home (Glover, 233). Volunteering had, in effect, ceased to be voluntary. In the fall of 1803, there were an "enormous number of offers of service" to the volunteers (Emsley, *British Society*, 102), and by December 1803 there were about 450 000 volunteers in Great Britain and Ireland. A volunteer's exemption from other forms of service had been in place since June 1803, but the multiplying number of ballots only led to mass enrollments in these groups in the fall – the same time Wordsworth joined the Grasmere unit.

Consequently, J. E. Cookson maintains that it is facile to see the explosion of so-called volunteering enthusiasm as a direct "outgrowth of counter-revolutionary loyalism" ("English Volunteer," 867). The government never was able to institute strict discipline in the volunteers; the corps often trained when they felt like it, which could be quite rarely. This may explain why, as Johnston observes, Wordsworth soon "withdrew from active participation in the drills," though the Grasmere contingent apparently enjoyed an atypically high reputation as a volunteer unit (*Hidden*, 806). In Wordsworth's letters, we hear nothing more of his involvement in the Grasmere Volunteers after the beginning of 1804. Many units were stubbornly disorganized and some even included people openly hostile to the state. In notoriously radical Sheffield, the lord lieutenant tried to embrace this resource by recruiting suspected thieves and poachers for the volunteers; his efforts to discipline such men into soldiers were fruitless. In the end, "the volunteers were written off ... as a force wrongly constituted, having bad social effects and (being) basically uncontrollable" (Cookson, "English Volunteer", 887). By 1806 officials were planning the movement's demise. This background gives an ironic tinge to Moorman's comment that "Fortunately for posterity, Wordsworth's military enthusiasm did not interrupt the main flow of his poetry ... " (603). A letter from Thomas Poole to Coleridge suggests surprise at the notion that Wordsworth would even go so far as to enroll in the volunteers (quoted in Moorman, 601–2). Wordsworth's decision to volunteer is far from unequivocal testimony to his convictions about the war effort. It should be seen against a complex matrix of social motivation affecting hundreds of thousands of other Britons. There were many other, stronger degrees of military commitment and perhaps no weaker sort of alignment with the government. Wordsworth lacked the apathy of his discharged soldier, a position increasingly difficult to occupy due to the political climate and military recruitment. Yet like his 1804 narrator, his precise affinity for the values of the nation was unclear.

The speaker's modulated detachment from the values and even the events of the world continues through book VI and much of VII. In each case, his peculiar sort of indifferent conforming has its roots in physical and mental wandering. On his return to Cambridge for a second year, "did I at nights frequent our groves / And tributary walks the last, and oft / The only one, who had been lingering there ... " (VI.81–3). His habits became more regular, and he applied himself with greater diligence to university courses. But by and large, his efforts in school remained "the rambling studies of a truant youth" (VI.111). The continental walking tour of 1790 introduces the narrator first-hand to the great changes taking place in France, whose importance he comes to understand through personal experiences that inspire memories: traveling with delegates coming home from the Fête de la Fédération, he and his companion Robert Jones are welcomed with the reverence accorded to Old Testament angels. The narrator vividly remembers his joy at the events in France, "standing then on the top of golden hours" (VI.353). Yet claims that, in this climate, to be young was very heaven are played off against book VI's concluding comments about a parallel revolution he witnessed in progress in Belgium:

> A stripling, scarcely of the household then
> Of social life, I looked upon these things

> As from a distance – heard, and saw, and felt,
> Was touched but with no intimate concern. ...

> (VI.693–6)

He ultimately remains disengaged from the continent's ongoing transformation.[36]

Book VII for the most part continues along the same track. He moves to London in the early 1790s to pitch "my vagrant tent, / A casual dweller and at large, among / The unfenced regions of society" (VII.60–2), identifying himself with the poorest laborers who often lived on unenclosed village wastes or common areas. The narrator plunges into the chaos of London life with the glee of the unconcerned tourist. "To have a house, / It was enough – what matter for a home?" (VII.76–7). Many aspects of city life shock him, such as the prostitute with her beautiful boy. It is a mistake, however, to see in these figures doubles for a narrator who does not fit into London's shadowy life. Like Mary of Buttermere, Wordsworth is a country youth newly exposed to the variety and trickery that city life breeds. But he is hardly the "artless (child) of the hills" (VII.325) he describes her to be; if book I is to be believed, from childhood he had been familiar with the pleasure of deceit and theft. He also bears little resemblance to the prostitute's child, "who walked with hair unsigned / Amid the fiery furnace" of London's small-time criminals (VII.398–9). The poem up until this point has argued that the poet's emerging greatness is due in part to *not* being "embalmed / By Nature" as he imagines this innocent boy to be (VII.400–1). This image conflates purity with a sort of life-in-death, while Wordsworth has chosen the vital world of gritty, changing experience

Consequently, memories of London's excitement and variety of stimuli continue to fascinate him in maturity. Even now, "some portion of that motley imagery, / A vivid pleasure of my youth" are "Among the lonely places that I love, / A frequent daydream for my riper mind" (VII.150–1, 152–3). The theatricals at Sadler's Wells, particularly absorbing to him, reinforce his awareness of his mental powers: "with what flashes ... the mind / Turned this way, that way sportive and alert / And watchful ..." (VII.270–2). The narrator hesitates in pursuing descriptions of such events, feeling they are too low to deserve his attention here, yet when he thinks of higher themes he feels "the imaginative power / Languish within [him]" (VII.499–500).

The treatment of London life and the vagrant narrator who is drawn to it is transformed by the poet's subsequent encounter with a blind beggar standing in a London street. Three beggars have been mentioned so far in book VII: "the scavenger that begs with hat in hand" (164), "A traveling cripple" who walks with his arms (219), and a man in a sailor's uniform "beside a range / Of written characters" that tell his story to onlookers (221–2). None affect the narrator like the man he later sees. Why does this beggar make a stronger impression than even the discharged soldier or than the other, equally destitute beggars seen in London?[37] The narrator begins by remembering the feeling that made the city unique for him, that in the street "The face of everyone / That passes by me is a mystery" (VII.597–8). He has felt this before in lines 171–5 when seeing beggars earlier. What makes this feeling significant later in the book is its location in an unusual context.

> … all the ballast of familiar life –
> The present, and the past, hope, fear, all stays,
> All laws of acting, thinking, speaking man –
> Went from me, neither knowing me, nor known.
> And once, far travelled in such mood, beyond
> The reach of common indications, lost
> Amid the moving pageant, 'twas my chance
> Abruptly to be smitten with the view
> Of a blind beggar, who, with upright face,
> Stood propped against a wall, upon his chest
> Wearing a written paper, to explain
> The story of the man, and who he was.
> My mind did at this spectacle turn round
> As with the might of waters, and it seemed
> To me that in this label was a type
> Or emblem of the utmost that we know
> Both of ourselves and of the universe,
> And on the shape of this unmoving man,
> His fixed face and sightless eyes, I looked
> As if admonished from another world.
>
> (601–23)

Like the narrator in the early books, the beggar occupies a marginal position. Though he may have a home, the law would hold him a vagrant simply for going through the streets to beg, a livelihood his poverty and his handicap would make it exceedingly difficult to forgo. Stationary yet vagrant, the blind beggar is most closely allied in Wordsworth's corpus with the quasi-vagrants of *Lyrical Ballads* who may or may not have a residence but who exist at the social periphery of a community. Something about this man, however, prevents Wordsworth from encountering him even in the abortive fashion described in "The Thorn" between the sea captain and Martha Ray. Part of the episode's point is that this is what cannot *be* encountered, that what we see here is not an individual but an icon. Wordsworth experiences not communication but revelation.

If nothing else, the beggar's position initially goes hand in hand with *The Prelude*'s implicit hope: the activities and lifestyle of vagrancy confer a certain freedom from established social strictures and conventions. All this changes when the narrator considers the significance of the sign the beggar wears. As J. Douglas Kneale has observed, since this beggar is blind he cannot "read his own history," implying that "the self must be given its identity partly through the interpretive efforts of others" (94).[38] Kneale's analysis does not go quite far enough, for the further implication is that unlike the pauper-sailor earlier in book VII, who also has a written paper beside him, someone else also has *written* the blind beggar's paper for him. This is a question not only of self-knowledge but of self-definition. The blind beggar cannot be sure what his sign says, or if it tells the truth about his past. He has depended on others to write it, and he must rely on others to read it aloud to him, much as he also relies on them for sustenance. This imperfect system, prone to misunderstandings and inaccuracy, is the only way he can apprehend his story, through the filter of other people, with their judgments and prejudices. The vagrant's life is as bounded by social interpretation and convention as language itself, including the language of the label that defines him for the world. The effect of his handicap underscores this fact: he is a vagrant dependent on sighted helpers to navigate the city streets. As long as he remains alone, he also remains stationary.

The opening of book VII reinforces the importance of a socially mediated label like that pinned on the blind beggar. For the community of Hawkshead, perhaps the most amazing aspect of life in London is that people live "Even next-door neighbors, as we say, / yet still / Strangers, and knowing not each other's names"

(VII.119–20). The existence of the blind beggar's label, however, implies that the fears of Hawkshead residents are exaggerated. Even in London, the center of carnivalesque riot, the inhabitants devise labels or names for the stranger whose name may be unknown, much as someone wrote the blind man's story for him.[39] This is not to say, of course, that the label will be necessarily accurate or one the individual in question would have chosen for himself, but the process itself appears hard to stop. This interpretation would allow us to see the beggar's extreme immobility and passivity – he is "propped against a wall," has a "fixed face," and is an "unmoving man" – as emblematic of a person's helplessness in the face of such social tendencies. No condition, not even vagrancy, can place us beyond "All laws of acting, thinking, speaking man," as the narrator at the episode's beginning believes. If we refuse to define ourselves by reference to conventional social guideposts, the world will do it for us. Declining to resolve who we are, which explains much of the appeal homelessness has for Wordsworth, is in fact making a kind of decision. If we try to tell our next-door neighbor we have no name, he is likely to call us by one of his own creation. The narrator's experience of this moment originates in his long walk through the city's maze, guided only by a sightseer's indirection. For the blind beggar, of course, sightseeing is out of the question, and repeated links between the beggar's condition, his label and fixity override the narrative's previous identification of vagrancy with social mobility and creative empowerment. The poet is "admonished" (the same term he used earlier in describing how Ann Tyson's dog would warn him to conceal his mutterings from passers-by) for assuming earlier that any connection necessarily existed between these things. The beggar's label leads to such wide-ranging conclusions since it is nothing less than an "emblem of the utmost that we know," supplanting the earlier claim that the sublime Alps of the walking tour are the true bearers of transcendent knowledge.[40]

The sight of the blind beggar reshapes the tone of *The Prelude*'s narration. From here until its end, the speaker often pauses for sharp value judgments on remembered events, and even his younger self becomes the repository of entrenched, clearly defined opinions. Later the speaker asserts that "I did not judge, / I never thought of judging" (XI.237–8), but in book VII judgment promptly descends on London. The description of Bartholomew Fair which closes book VII condemns all that earlier has been seen as confusing and interesting, identifying the city not with creative exhilaration but with deformity. The fair's crowds and attractions put "The whole creative powers of man asleep" (VII.655); the presence of "All-out-of-the-way, far-fetched, perverted things" makes it a "parliament of monsters" (VII.688, 692). The tents and booths "Are vomiting" women, men and children (VII.694). The poet's playful mind, intrigued by the melodramas of popular theater, has suddenly become repulsed by the sideshows and acrobats. Now it is the city, not the poet, that has "no law, no meaning, no end" (705), and what before seemed liberating, chaotic anonymity is now actually "Oppression" (706). This new tone, dependent on a conventional moral vocabulary hostile to ambiguity, carries over into the book's conclusion. Here, the narrator suddenly displays an extended anxiety about the decorum of describing such a scene. He is eager to circumscribe his "freedom" and "perfect openness of mind" in choosing subject matter through "just restraint" and "real modesty" (VII.731–4).

The remainder of *The Prelude* serves to modify, if not completely alter, many earlier statements about the character of the narrator and the homeless life to which he is drawn. Book VIII begins this enterprise, identifying wandering life with hard work, self-denial, and an attachment to a definable area of land. The type for this figure is the shepherd. He may theoretically exemplify "Man free, man working for himself, with choice / Of time, and place, and object" (VIII.152–3); however, the poem's concrete examples of this freedom are defined strictly.[41] The matron's tale, of a young boy who almost dies searching for his father's lost sheep, shows that the shepherd's liberty is little more than the necessity of maintaining his flock. The image of the shepherd's "rolling hut, his home" (VIII.336) may seem the perfect image of vagrant freedom, but its function is only to keep the herder close to his flock at lambing time.

This new figure of wandering authority now is placed as a monitory presence at a scene of possible transgression narrated in book I. When we first see the boy stealing raven's eggs, his isolation and physical danger underscore the morally questionable nature of his act. In an abrupt turnaround, book VIII informs us that the narrator recalls seeing a shepherd at such moments, standing over him like a power "under God, / Presiding" (394–5). God is not the genius who typically supervises the important events of Wordsworth's youth, and inserting such a presence here drains any murky illegality from the act of egg stealing. By claiming God oversaw this moment, the poet guarantees that such an act is really virtuous rather than potentially wrong. Our image of the poet's childhood undergoes rehabilitation as even the content of nature's teaching changes. For the first time, he states that nature taught him a love of social integration, being even from youth "a gracious guide to lead me forth / Beyond the bosom of my family, / My friends and youthful playmates" (VIII.72–4). Perhaps most significantly, book VIII dismisses earlier writings dealing with vagrancy and its manifestations – and only ones dealing with vagrancy – as childhood drivel. For the poet of late 1804 it is inappropriate to focus on marginal homeless people. Characters at the heart of Wordsworth's earlier productions like "The Thorn" now are considered the playthings of fancy, an example of the "tragic super-tragic" (VIII.532). The strength of suffering like Martha Ray's is written off as exaggeration. For if the younger Wordsworth heard one mention of a woman going to visit a grave,

> The fact was caught at greedily, and there
> She was a visitant the whole year through,
> Wetting the turf with never ending tears,
> And all the storms of heaven must beat on her.

> (VIII.538–41)

"The Thorn" is lumped together with the account of the female beggar in *An Evening Walk*, as both are rejected as juvenilia.[42]

By the time he reviews his Cambridge days in book VIII, this new narrator bears little relation to the irresponsible figure who stayed out late in book III. Shaped by observing the serious responsibilities of industrious laborers, he "began to deem myself / A moral agent, judging between good / And evil" (VIII.667–9). He claims that during college he became obsessed with "acting well" (VIII.675), and even felt "guilt and wretchedness" over his behavior (658). This review of books I–VII is in a sense a second beginning for *The Prelude*, inaugurating a review of key events and glossing earlier material with a new eye for moral evaluation and social convention. In book VIII, the 1790 alpine tour, bred of a desire to avoid work, is virtually ignored. Only the simile of the cave describing imagination's awakening, originally composed for the conclusion to the Simplon Pass episode in VI, remains (Reed, *Thirteen-Book Prelude*, 21). Its context is now London, not the Alps, and the delinquent force motivating the 1790 trip is absent from the passage. Perhaps the greatest change comes in the presentation of London itself, all the more startling since it totally reverses the conclusion of the previous book, itself a reversal of still earlier material. Among the city's crowds the poet now affirms he felt

> the unity of man,
> One spirit over ignorance and vice
> Predominant, in good and evil hearts
> One sense for moral judgments. ...

> (VIII.827–30)

As the editors of the Norton edition comment, this view "comes as a surprise" after book VII (310n). In VIII, moral deformity is supplanted by assertions that the city's residents know what is right and act accordingly. The end of book VII and book VIII, however, share the key goal of resolving the city's opacity into moral clarity. The theatricals Wordsworth enjoys are outside the city, in Sadler's Wells; their peripheral situation, physically and ideologically, allows them play within existing prescriptions. After the sight of the blind beggar, the narrator posits the shrinkage of that play to virtually nothing. Book VIII then recoups the experience as a positive one by coating the events of VII in a moral patina, identifying London with culturally ratified acts of virtue and justice.

The image of the indigent vagrant also undergoes drastic rehabilitation after book VII. The homeless now are seen as unfortunate but good people unfairly labeled as degenerates. The disturbing indifference of the discharged soldier is replaced with a vision of the open road that is almost homey.[43] In telling of his emotional recovery from the French Revolution's failure in the late 1790s, the narrator speaks of the men he currently meets in his local rambles, "where if we meet a face / We almost meet a friend, on naked moors / With long, long ways before ... " (XII.141–3). The distance between him and the soldier, or even between him and his Hawkshead neighbors, has shrunk as his community now extends both near and far. The synecdoche of this passage, sliding "almost" inevitably from a face to a friend, is in keeping with the poem's new dedication to resolving interpretive signs into emblems of good or evil. The public road in book XII is touted as a way "to things unknown and without bound" (152), but this view is belied by the very ordinariness of the people the narrator meets there. Despite their uncouth appearance and manners, they are nothing less than archetypes for humanity. In them he sees "with most delight the passions of mankind, / There saw into the depth of human souls – / Souls that appear to have no depth at all to vulgar eyes" (XII.166–8). In the language of the encounter with the blind beggar, the narrator removes an old label from these people to replace it with one more to his liking. There can be no indeterminacy about the nature of the homeless, so now their exile is imposed from without, unreflective of a choice to stand aloof from a culture that limits and constraints. The poor vagrant's story is "a tale of honour" replete with "loftiest promises of good and fair" (XII.183, 184). As for the narrator, he acknowledges his own continued weakness for wandering far afield but maintains that he now prefers walking with a beloved woman, "living in some place, / Deep vale, or anywhere the home of both, / From which it would be misery to stir … " (XII. 132–4). The magnetic force of home's comforts makes travel beyond the horizon of domestic influence seem unlikely and almost unbearable. He can see the nobility of unfortunate wanderers, but he has become a settled man. The newly recognized importance of context in vagrant life also has crucial implications for autobiography. By deciding to include books IX and X, Wordsworth places a label on his own chest – the consolation being that at least it is partially of his making. His own life in these books loses his reservations about commitment and fellowship, and becomes bound up with the great story that for many defined the experiences of his generation. In locating his life amid these events Wordsworth intends to make himself intelligible to his culture. It therefore prepares him to write the great national and philosophical epics that he defers in book I.[44]

The story of Vaudracour and Julia offers a paradigm for how the revolutionary books flatten or distort any personal ambivalence about politics into the master-narrative of All British Youth. As with his own story, Wordsworth offers us this digression on the understanding that, although it may be drawn from "obscurity" (551), it is "not in its spirit singular" (553): the narrative is representative of the experiences of many. In an aside to the ongoing import of somatic mobility through due process, the story is presented as an example of the crippling effects of *lettres de cachet* in French culture. Even if all other hopes fail, Wordsworth the young patriot hopes, surely this will change in France. Yet it seems that what separates

Vaudracour and Julia is not French tyranny but their own con-
fused responses to it. From the outset, Vaudracour wants to be "in
honorable wedlock with his love" (X.601) but is "inwardly pre-
pared to turn aside / From law and custom" (X.602–3). Even this
isn't quite right, however, for he repeatedly seeks his father's bless-
ing for his marriage to a woman of a lower class. In the end, he
brings his child to his father's house, but after being refused
entrance he despondently accepts lodging in an isolated family res-
idence where he ineptly kills his own child. During the course of
his feud with his father, Vaudracour is imprisoned twice by *lettres
de cachet*, but each time he is released by powerful friends affected
by his condition. Johnston has persuasively described
Vaudracour's inconsistent reponses in terms of a larger ambiva-
lence about patriarchal authority; he is burdened with a father
"whom he dreams of reforming by sympathy but fears to rebel
against by force."[45] The thrust of this comment can easily be
extended to describe the actions of Julia. She, too, transgresses
custom by having an illegitimate child, but she refuses to disobey
her parents, who will not grant her permission to marry until
Vaudracour's father approves. In the end, she submits to giving up
her child and going into a convent. In a story where parental
authority is so clearly conflated with state tyranny, it does little
good to separate them. But the real tragedy of Vaudracour isn't
that his imbecile mind can't finally hear "the voice of freedom" that
sounds through France; it's that he wouldn't have heard it even
with his mind intact (X.931). Vaudracour and Julia were never truly
revolutionaries.

The story itself, standing in for Wordsworth's liaison with
Annette Vallon, tells us a great deal about how Wordsworth could
change facts to fit personal need.[46] Wordsworth did not marry
Vallon when he could have, and she raised Caroline alone.
Vaudracour is separated from Julia, and their child mysteriously
dies. Vaudracour and Julia's story also suggests how the rest of *The
Prelude* might distort other obligations than those of lover to mis-
tress. The story's frame works to minimize an awareness of the
conflicts that alone can explain some of the characters' behavior.
The real culprit here, we are told, is the *lettre de cachet*, not
Vaudracour's uncertainty. The narrator at points seems to have
some knowledge of these conflicts, but declines to flesh them out or
offer them as rationales for behavior. The narrator says of
Vaudracour during his second imprisonment:

> ... my memory could add
> Much how the youth, and in short space of time,
> Was traversed from without – much, too, of thoughts
> By which he was employed in solitude
> Under privation and restraint, and what
> Through dark and shapeless fear of things to come,
> And what through strong compunction for the past,
> He suffered, breaking down in heart and mind.

(IX.744–51)

This passage tells us enough to know that Vaudracour's imbecile mind is some time in the making. The language is deliberately vague, hinting at deep conflicts, regrets and fears yet maddeningly withholding their content. A similar sense of unexplained complexity surfaces when Vaudracour reproaches Julia after the birth of their son: "how much thine eyes / Have cost me!" (IX.818–19). This suggestion of blame is never elaborated on, and Vaudracour descends into insanity before he can explain it to us. The narrator refuses to enlighten us as to his own motivations just as he refuses to disclose or illuminate Vaudracour's. Perhaps most annoying of all, the narrator absolves himself from any responsibility for the narrative by saying he is just repeating a well-known tale as it was told to him. At the outset, he will only "without choice of circumstance, submissively / Relate what I have heard" (IX.644–5). He refuses to take responsibility for the ending's tragedy for the same reason: "The tale I follow to its last recess / Of suffering and of peace, I know not which / Theirs be the blame who caused the woe, not mine" (IX.909–11). Behind this narrative veil, alternately of reserve and of ignorance, hide the real feelings that would give depth and credibility to the characters of Vaudracour and Julia. Such information is suppressed in favor of the surface of their tragedy, whose story recalls the readily intelligible plot line of the original star-crossed lovers, Romeo and Juliet (as an allusion at line 642 suggests; Norton edn, 344n.).

These strange digressions and narrative eddies might appear to be debris left over by incompetent storytelling, but they provide a useful model of what goes on elsewhere in *The Prelude*'s discussion of Wordsworth's residence in France, book X. Parts of Wordsworth's account of his experiences during the French Revolution read a lot like the story of Vaudracour and Julia. Much as the narrator of their story separates himself from the outcome of the very story he tells, the poet explains his interest in France by referring to a generational imperative. Further, the uppermost level of narrative in books IX and X often conflicts with biographical information or submerged feelings that occasionally disrupt the textual surface. The contours of the surface narrative in the French books are easy to recite: the journey to Orléans; the poet's friendship with Michael Beaupuy; his decision to take up the revolution as a cause; his return to England and alienation from his countrymen; his adherence to Godwinism and final recovery from that malady. But there are undercurrents, ill-explained or even unmentioned in the poem, that make us question this trajectory. Why during his stay in Orléans does the poet stay and keep company with royalist officers, though he himself becomes a patriot? Why, during his serious talks about politics with Beaupuy, does he find himself daydreaming about medieval romances?[47] Why, when *The Prelude* claims he becomes a patriot in France, does he involve himself with Annette Vallon just as her own attitude toward the revolution is beginning its transformation from support to loathing? Why, if his belief in Godwin's ideas proves so debilitating, does he ultimately shake off depression with such ease?

Book X is replete with passages whose small inconsistencies and outright contradictions ripple the smooth textual surface the last half of the poem purports to present. In a representative example, the reversals mount to virtual incoherence during the poem's characterization of Wordsworth's mindset during his return to Paris in 1792. He alternately claims that the September massacres appeared to him an isolated event – "but these were past" (X.34), and he was as far from anticipating the Terror "as angels are from guilt" (X.127) – and then admits that he really had little sense of the significance of the actions about him, since they were "a volume whose contents he knows / Are memorable but from him locked up, / Being written in a tongue he cannot read" (X.51–3). To an extent, such confessions may reflect the genuine and inevitable bewilderment of anyone living through those volatile, violent times. The turns of Wordsworth's rhetoric also serve a more practical function, establishing a pattern of ideological investment only to call into question the depth of that commitment and so to exonerate him from its effects. Such equivocations align Wordsworth with other British and French republicans while arguing that he really did not understand what he said he believed in. His ensuing night-time fears in

Paris and the allusions to *Macbeth* do little to clear this up; awaiting some new signal preparatory to more revolutionary bloodletting, he like the usurper finds he cannot sleep. His claims in the next lines of a deeper serenity – the "comments of a calmer mind" (X.78) – cast him in the role of Duncan rather than Macbeth, but this identification is immediately thrown into doubt since his calmness is one "from which / I could not gather full security" (X.79–80). At the level of narrative, Wordsworth tries to arbitrate these conflicts (like the horse, who learns his "manage" [X.70] by projecting them onto the Girondins with whom he theoretically was allied. Louvet's heroic denunciation of Robespierre is futile because his allies in the National Convention shrink from supporting him. Like Wordsworth's own revolutionary trajectory (as the poem has it) from passion to doubt, the Girondins' apostasy is justified through reference to a group mentality further legitimated by its being common knowledge. "'Tis well known," Wordsworth begins,

> What was the issue of that charge, and how
> Louvet was left alone without support
> Of his irresolute friends; but these are things
> Of which I speak only as they were storm
> Or sunshine to my individual mind,
> No further.

> (X.101–6)

His demurral at the end argues that if anything he was even less sure of Louvet than the conventioneers whose cowardice or uncertainty prevented them from backing his vehement resistance to tyrannic authority. This interpretation gains strength from ensuing lines implying that for all their differences, Robespierre and Louvet were united through an equally misguided extremist zeal.

> The indecision on their part whose aim
> Seemed best, and the straightforward path of those
> Who in attack or in defense alike
> Were strong through their impiety – greatly I
> Was agitated.

> (X.113–17)

The identities of those caught in between the attackers and defenders is not spelled out, but we can hazard a guess as to at least one of their names. So tentative is Wordsworth at this juncture, however, that he will not even commit to being a party of the indecisive; their aims "seemed best," but this formulation does not inspire confidence that their beliefs might have proved less damaging than those of anyone else. The concluding lines do not grant the young Wordsworth any stronger political affiliation than agitation, fearing that in such an atmosphere any choice between leaders, parties and ideologies could easily turn out to be the wrong one. In a moment tantamount to seeing Vaudracour in his jail cell, we have had a glimpse into the shifting currents underlying Wordsworth's "dedication" to France and republicanism.

In similar fashion, when he haltingly tries to explain why he returned to England in 1792 rather than stay and work for French advancement, Wordsworth's reasoning divulges a complex matrix of opposing motives and inclinations. He asserts that he was tempted to continue the fight for political stability in France, remembering "How much the destiny of man had still / Hung upon single persons," and that he, as a "spirit faithful to itself," might be effective (X.137–8). Yet, at the time he excused himself, thinking how since antiquity "tyrannic power is weak," and that the radical elements could never take their ideas as far as they might like (X.167). He then adds that he still believes (despite the demise of so many opposing Robespierre in the Terror) that "the virtue of one paramount mind / Would have abashed those impious crests" (X.179–80). Then, he tells us the real reason for his return was a desperate need for money. Finally, he concludes that it's probably just as well, since "I doubtless should have made a common cause / With some who perished ..." (X.194–5). In the incoherent logic of these lines, the value of individual action against the state is affirmed, then rendered unnecessary, then affirmed again, then ignored as a motive for personal action, and finally dismissed.

Even the trauma of the war, which Wordsworth blames for a generation's breakdown, turns out not to be a particular surprise to him: "Nor had I doubted that this day would come" (X.245). This didn't, he quickly affirms, prevent it from hitting him as hard as anyone else, but again, his metaphors point to a more convoluted state of affairs. Initially, he naturalizes the image of patriotism by comparing the loyal subject to a leaf on a tree, contending that for himself, he wished for no "happier fortune than to wither there"

(X.256). This claim doesn't sit particularly well, apparently, for he then gives up on a systematic attempt to describe his political loyalties, admitting that to hear of dead Britons on the battlefields of Europe "was a grief – / Grief call it not, 'twas anything but that – / A conflict of sensations without name" (X.263–5). In a renewed struggle to convey those sensations, he resorts to another metaphor, probably based on an actual event in Robert Jones' church, where he heard prayers for British victories and sat alone "like an uninvited guest / Whom no one owned" (X.272–3). Several aspects of this comparison merit comment, the most obvious being Wordsworth's risible claim that in the early 1790s he loved the church as an emblem of rural community; his letters from those years, documenting his failure to stomach a clerical career, reveal a different attitude altogether. Additionally, here the replacement of the tree with the band of churchgoers as a trope for national loyalty makes Wordsworth's relationship to that loyalty a much more contingent affair. The language of this second metaphor makes Wordsworth not a leaf blown off the tree, but an "uninvited guest / Whom no one owned" and who "sate silent, shall I add, / Fed on the day of vengeance yet to come!"(X.272–4). The passive image of the tree metaphor, which allowed Wordsworth to image himself a leaf "cut off / And tossed about in whirlwinds" (X.257–8), competes with the idea of the guest who essentially has disinvited himself through his treacherous sentiments.

These sorts of tensions bubble over in the 1805 *Prelude's* book X only to be subordinated in the poem's concluding arc to the generational master-narrative established earlier. Misguided involvement in revolution gives way to disenchantment with it and then to a new appreciation of British values enabling a reawakening of the poet's sources of creative imagination. If not for its artistic merits and the peculiarities of its deferred publication, we might almost call the 1805 *Prelude* the most ambitious propaganda pamphlet that emerged from Britain's return to war in 1803; it aims not to win over the converted, but to document and legitimize a process of reversal by which the most radical hearts have returned to Britain after knowing barbarism abroad and political error at home. He plays up rather than elides those youthful sympathies in a task that, if it succeeded, would be an even bigger victory than suppression for a government leadership convinced of treachery – a full, signed confession followed by a humiliating penance, a life-long knowledge of chastisement, and a resolution to sin no more. In keeping with this objective, the conclusion of *The Prelude* is careful to emphasize that the imaginative faculty, along with the vagrancy with which it has been so long identified, now partakes of the values and limitations of the society within which it operates. The way in which the first spot of time is incorporated into book XI of the 1805 *Prelude* provides a representative manifestation of this tendency. The 1799 version of this scene establishes it as an antidote to the pressures of social and familial life, a position initially endorsed by the 1805 passage. The spots of time that follow lift the narrator up when he feels oppressed "By false opinion and contentious thought" or by "trivial occupations" (XI.260, 262). New in the 1805 version is the sense that such memories establish how we control the status of objects about us. The power of such scenes mostly grows out of moments which demonstrate "that the mind / Is lord and master, and that outward sense / Is but the obedient servant of her will" (XI.270–2).

This introduction of a definitive hierarchy contradicts much of what comes before in the 1799 *Prelude* and Wordsworth's earlier writings, which oppose imagination/nature, subject/object, the written word/the spoken word, but refuse to privilege consistently one pole of each opposition over another. Like "Tintern Abbey," the book II passage on the infant babe, for example, states that the human mind works "in alliance" with what it beholds. This will change in the concluding books, just as the balance between subservience to the natural world and subversion of it transforms into a purer allegiance with the human mind, now lord and master. By the same token the wandering vagrant, long interesting to Wordsworth as a symbol for straddling oppositions, now acknowledges that culture and nation are lord and master.

In its 1799 incarnation, the gibbet in the first spot of time intimates that the boy's wandering from his guide may lead to more serious violations of convention. However, while the green burial ridge of 1799 and its moldering gibbet suggest crime and its judgment, their gradual erasure from the landscape implies even unequivocal wrongdoing eventually may be forgotten. The body is slowly being assimilated into the earth; the gibbet is being reclaimed through decay for nature. Community judgments seem potentially mutable, even when they concern convicted murderers. Where the pronouncements of justice are changeable, a space opens for the ambivalence about authority that Wordsworth locates in the homeless. In the 1805 version, the child again becomes separated from James, stumbles down into a hollow, and sees the gibbet moldering. Revisions go on to supplant possible guilt and punishment with certain and unforgiving retribution. This substitution is effected by replacing the green ridge of turf present in the original poem with text.

> ... on the turf
> Hard by, soon after that fell deed was wrought,
> Some unknown hand had carved the murderer's name.
> The monumental writing was engraven
> In times long past, and still from year to year
> By superstition of the neighborhood
> The grass is cleared away; and to this hour
> The letters are all fresh and visible.

(XI.291–8)

Villagers purposefully work together to keep the memory of the criminal and his end alive. This "supervision," akin to the entrenched suspicions about Martha Ray in "The Thorn," infuses community rulings about marginal figures in *The Prelude* with a new resilience. The monumental writing also recalls the lettering on the blind beggar's chest. There are obvious differences between the murderer and the beggar as criminals: one has committed a clear atrocity, the other is technically violating the law but might well escape arrest. The lettering near the gibbet shows that society treats these men in related ways. Both, we might say, are now blind and immobile, and both now are defined by socially mediated labels because both have relinquished the right to define themselves by virtue of their status in society (the beggar) or their behavior (the killer). Like the vagrant poor and perhaps even the lost little boy, the murderer exists at the margins of society because of his acts, and this robs him of the power to write his own story. His life has become the raw material out of which neighbors can spin gossip and children ghost stories. The murderer's label might seem exempt from this interpretation since we know it to be his own name – it is not, as may be true of the beggar, one having little to do with "who he really is." Yet the murderer's neighbors have used the man's name against him, to perpetuate the memory of a crime that otherwise might be forgotten or perhaps even forgiven. The name is now less his than the appropriated property of a community using it to perpetuate an awareness of the murder and its punishment.[48]

In a revised ending to this scene, the adult poet self-consciously distances himself from the ambiguous position occupied by the younger self who lost his way and found a memory that endured for years. He remembers that subsequently he has walked near the site of the gibbet, not alone but with his "two dear ones" (XI.316), Dorothy Wordsworth and Mary Hutchinson. Thoughts of impending marriage and a stable household come to envelop what was once a moment of reckless identification with "A man, the murderer of his wife" (1799: 1.309). That he killed his wife is also excised when this passage is imported into the 1805 poem, appropriately so since it is strangely out of keeping with the scene of domestic happiness that now closes the first spot of time. The potential criminality of homeless wandering is contained by later memories of domestic stability and human connection. More than that, we are asked to believe in a continuum between those two experiences, a continuity that accrues the energy but not the content of the original crime to Wordsworth's relationship with his wife and sister: "so feeling comes in aid / Of feeling, and diversity of strength / Attends us, if but once we have been strong" (XI.325–7).

For all this affirmation of the poet's undiminished and ongoing creative talents, it bears noting that this domestic idyll is followed immediately by fears that Wordsworth's imaginative powers are weakening.

> The days gone by
> Come back upon me from the dawn almost
> Of life; the hiding places of my power
> Seem open, I approach, and then they close;
> I see by glimpses now, when age comes on
> May scarcely see at all …
>
> (XI.333–8)

The dynamic of companionship called up by invoking his wife and sister, both living with him at Grasmere, leads to a view of change not as growth but as loss. This rubric forces the poet to view mobility very differently than in his early verse. From *An Evening Walk*, where the motion of playing schoolboys obscured their relation to the churchyard dead, to the wretched yet reflective homeless people of "Salisbury Plain," to the fearful but determined wanderer of "Tintern Abbey," Wordsworth's characters on the move typically have inhabited a cultural space resisting ossification or manipulation. When movement through time only sensitizes us to what we are losing rather than what we might gain, as it begins to do in the 1805 *Prelude*, the poet combats motion with a kind of psychic embalming: "… I would enshrine the spirit of the past / For future restoration" (XI.341–2).[49] The process pathetically portends the very psychic paralysis and stagnation previously staved off by the mobility of vagrancy. This change in attitude, and the codification of the poet's imminent conservatism which it presages, is a marker for modernity's notorious dissatisfaction with Wordsworth's later poetry.

In the 1805 *Prelude*, the creative imagination's ultimate affiliation with community rather than homelessness completes the poet's journey to maturity. The first community we are told he chooses is that of Godwinian rationalism, which seems to offer definitive criteria for the establishment of true precepts and the public good. Tellingly, in the poem's narrative he finally rejects Godwin because his philosophy does not offer any greater moral certainty than the life of homelessness itself:

> … demanding proof,
> And seeking it is every thing, I lost
> All feeling of conviction, and, in fine,
> Sick, wearied out with contrarieties,
> Yielded up moral questions in despair. …
>
>   (X.896–900)

In the last two books of his epic, Wordsworth explains how, with the help of what Thomas McFarland has called the significant group,[50] he recovers from this now painful sense of uncertainty. Interactions with relatives and friends at last allow the articulation of firm unclouded moral judgments. The poet still figures himself as a kind of political independent, who is skeptical of public men regardless of their avowed position: he sees "Ambition, folly, madness, in the men / Who thrust themselves upon this passive world / As rulers" (XII.71–3). His essential orthodoxy emerges in his affirmation that moral valences are distinguishable, and that preserving these distinctions is critical to our peace of mind. Living in fellowship with his own community, "clearer far / My sense of what was excellent and right …" (XII.62–3). These shared moral values, so far from the ambiguities of earlier books, are crucial to *The Prelude's* conclusion because they verify Wordsworth and Coleridge's fitness to usher in a new era of human power and consciousness. Only the poet's tempered sense of good and evil enables him to condemn with such certainty the mental habits that "substitute a universe of death, / The falsest of all worlds, in place of that / Which is divine and true" (XIII.141–3).

This statement comes at the end of the poem's final episode, the ascent of Snowdon, which indicates how the carefully the narrator now manages the introduction of vagrancy into his text. In what is meant to be the crowning metaphor for the imagination's interactions with the external world, at night the narrator sees from the mountain top a horizon dominated by shooting mists. They seem to draw their fantastic energy from an opening in the cloud cover: " ... in that breach, / Through which the homeless voice of waters rose ... had Nature lodged / The soul, the imagination of the whole" (XIII.62–5). The human imagination creates images of transcendent truth from the raw material of the senses, we later are told, just as here nature appears to manipulate the energy emanating from the chasm to create the cloudy wilderness. This imaginative capacity "alone is genuine liberty" (XIII.122). This equation of imagination with the freedom of homelessness instructively delineates the boundaries of vagrant liberty at this point in *The Prelude*. To the extent that we do accept Wordsworth's metaphor, these homeless waters, like the human vagrants of book XII, depart from the poet's earlier depiction of homelessness. The power which the voice from the chasm embodies does not complicate the narrator's relation to society or its values, but provides the basis for definitive "truth in moral judgments" (XIII.118). Theresa Kelley argues that the ascent of Snowdon shows how forces that resist definition and articulation, such as the sublime, can be contained: "On Snowdon the uncreated and the unknown are lodged at last, fixed in the speaker's discourse as 'perfect' images, that is to say, as vehicles perfectly matched to their tenor" (130).[51] In the language of my own project, the ascent of Snowdon seeks to "fix" or stabilize figures of vagrant independence. Homelessness now is situated on a clearly understandable and socially sanctioned grid of possibilities; whoever possesses imaginative liberty still requires friendship and love "to complete the man, / Perfect him, made imperfect in himself" (XIII.202–3). Rather than interrogating the rigidity of cultural classification by demonstrating how permeable the membranes between deviance and morality, crime and legality, are, homelessness works to shore up the boundaries dividing these concepts into distinguishable opposites.

The Prelude concludes with tributes to the poet's own friends and loves – Dorothy Wordsworth, Raisley Calvert, and Coleridge – who have believed in him or will verify that his autobiography confirms his creative powers. Indeed, this fellowship is finally what assures *The Prelude's* author of its artistic value. Culture and community defined the socially marginal blind beggar of London and the murderer of the spots of time with little necessary reference to who they perceived themselves to be. By finally situating himself among a circle of supporters, the poet may sacrifice the vitality of his vagrant past but he also escapes possible victimization by a hostile society. Memories of a wandering childhood alienated from much of human society endowed the adult author with the creative force to write his autobiographical masterpiece. Ironically, only a close-knit domestic community, only a friend like Coleridge, could fulfill the mature Wordsworth's intense need for his poem to receive meaningful, external validation. His confidence in the loyalty of his closest friend enables him to assert that in the end, whatever *The Prelude's* limitations, "To thee the work shall justify itself" (XIII.410). Like Dorothy in "Tintern Abbey," Coleridge finally is the poem's ideal audience because in a sense he is Wordsworth, a fellow poet and literary collaborator whose poems had been published alongside Wordsworth's own, just as the two men walk side by side through the Somerset landscape in the concluding lines of *The Prelude.*

In 1813, Wordsworth made a decision that serves as a useful milestone of the distance he traveled after the end of the 1790s. The poet needed money. He was trying to support an extended family that included his wife, children, sister, and sister-in-law. To escape the view of the graveyard where two of his children were buried, he also had just moved from the Rectory in Grasmere to Rydal Mount, a large home that took considerable money to furnish. Desperate for funds, he applied to Lord Lonsdale, the heir to his old enemy James Lowther, who gave him a job as regional Distributor of Stamps, responsible for taxes on paper used for legal transactions. In accepting and by all accounts conscientiously carrying out the duties of this position, Wordsworth became part of the new system of revenue collection initiated by Pitt in the early 1800s to finance the French war. In 1819, Lowther's patronage helped Wordsworth to another title with particular resonance for judging the poor and homeless: justice of the peace. The demands of domestic life, imagined through the eyes of women and men in his early poems, had become the poet's own, leading him to relinquish personal and political independence for financial security. On the basis of Lonsdale's favors, Wordsworth would campaign for his interest in future elections and gain the reputation among his literary successors as a "Tory hireling" (Gill, *Wordsworth*, 296). His new source of income helped Wordsworth to the peace and quiet he needed to complete and publish *The Excursion*, a poem whose conclusions reinforce the distance between the 1790s and 1810s for Wordsworth as a man and a writer and for Britain as a nation. Consolidating the themes concluding the 1805 *Prelude, The Excursion* presents a Wanderer whose homelessness provides practical and ideological support for community values and national stability. He leads the narrator and dejected Solitary not to an understanding of the vagrant's marginality, but to an Anglican pastor who salves spiritual dejection with epitaphic platitudes and vespers held outdoors. Read in this way, *The Excursion* along with *The Prelude* may suggest a reason for Wordsworth's lifelong failure to complete, or even envision more than the outlines of, the Recluse project. His own life would become increasingly dominated by public roles in the worlds of literature and politics, realms whose expectations *The Prelude* finally argues cannot be escaped or denied. Perhaps *The Prelude* and the years Wordsworth spent revising it provided the poet with a welcome distraction from the philosophical writing of *The Recluse*, writing for which he seems to have been dispositionally unsuited. Composing *The Prelude* may have meant the end of *The Recluse* in other ways as well. After an autobiography so pervasively bearing the imprint of public and political pressures, Wordsworth would have been as hard-pressed to theorize about the virtues of seclusion as he ultimately became to document the marginal gains of the homeless.

Notes

INTRODUCTION: HOMELESSNESS YESTERDAY AND TODAY –
REPRESSION OR RELIEF?

1. William Carroll documents how, in the Tudor–Stuart period, master-
less men were widely believed to be seditionaries and "ready mater-
ial for riot and insurrection" (39). Beier finds evidence to support this
perception, tying vagrants' discontents to larger institutional chal-
lenges: the homeless "broke with official conventions of family, econ-
omic, religious and political life, some even venturing down the
dangerous paths of organized crime and rebellion" (*Masterless Men*,
xix). The history of homelessness in America brings this line of
thought into the recent past: Joel Blau connects the historical bias
against American tramps to "other manifestations of political disorder
such as the Paris Commune, the 1877 railroad strike, and the growth
of a labor movement" (34–5). Similarly, David Snow and Leon
Anderson note that during the early twentieth century, radical
unions, including the International Workers of the World, actively
recruited hobos (14).

2. David Simpson gestures toward the opposing poles from which the
homeless were viewed when he comments that the "vagrant, or
beggar, is either a person who does not aspire to, and perhaps threat-
ens property … or he is a person who has been dispossessed, or who
has tried and failed to acquire the substance necessary to gain a set-
tlement in a particular parish" (*Historical Imagination*, 161). Donald
Reiman similarly contends that giving beggars charity never feels
"quite right" because we suspect both that our help is insufficient and
that we have been manipulated by "fraudulent beggars" ("Beggars",
74). Robin Jervis points to the instability not just of perceptions of the
homeless, but of the rationales behind proposals designed to address
their situation; during the eighteenth century, the workhouse as an
institution of relief is both attacked and defended on humanitarian
grounds ("Wordsworth," 202).

3. Marginals differ from liminal figures, who briefly escape governance
by social convention through special, sacred rituals. Unlike margin-
als, liminars can be associated with values widely accepted but
imperfectly realized in society – for example, they can embody or
divine the nature of "pure" justice, untainted by quotidian concerns
and biases. In Turner's model, the liminar's unclear status often is
resolved through his or her elevation to a higher social position (233,
241). The notion of liminality has become a powerful tool for scholars
interested in border states. In literary studies, Gary Harrison views
Wordsworth's vagrants as liminal figures who remind his narrators of
the instability of economic prosperity and reprimand them for a lack

of perseverance under duress. Robin Jervis similarly identifies the freedom sought by politically radical walkers with Turner's liminars, though his generalized treatment of a wide range of pedestrian acts overlooks the inherent criminality of vagrancy during the period (see *Romantic Writing*). In sociology, David Snow and Leon Anderson also invoke Turner's idea of liminality in depicting homeless "straddlers," people in a transitional state between accepting their condition and seeking to get off the street (52).

4. Quoted in Johnston, *Hidden* 499.
5. For an examination of Wordsworth and vagrancy emphasizing political and economic theories of liberalism rather than the daily workings of vagrancy law or the immediate political climate, see Celeste Langan's *Romantic Vagrancy*. Langan argues that affiliations between the wanderer's movements, the circulation of capital, and the ideals of representative democracy identify Wordsworth's vagrants with both economic and political freedom. In this reading, the negotiations constituting the character of the vagrant and the modern subject result from competing liberal discourses, rather than from specific conflicts characteristic of perceptions of homelessness.

    Andrea Henderson's work on the changing nature of subjectivity in the Romantic period usefully augments Langan's argument. In *Romantic Identities*, Henderson describes how exchange value in the eighteenth century becomes a destabilizing model for personal identity, essentially transplanting the mechanics of capitalist circulation into the realm of psychological modeling. Insofar as Wordsworth's homeless suffer both physical and mental dislocation, they do recall the circulation of capital that Langan and Henderson explore. However, I see the homeless less as emblems of capitalism than as casualties of it, with their circulation challenging the nature of capitalist economics even as their wanderings may mimic its workings.

6. For the connection between vagrancy and the emergence of a wage-based economy, see Williams, *Country and the City* (84); Beier, *Problem of the Poor* (30); Chambliss (70); Foote (615).
7. For example, "all persons going about as patent-gatherers, or gatherers of alms, under false pretenses of loss by fire, or other casualty, or going about as collectors for prisons, gaols, or hospitals, all fencers and bearwards, all common players of interludes... all persons pretending to be gypsies, of wandering in the habit or form of Egyptians, or pretending to having skill in physiognomy, palmestry, or like crafty science, or pretending to tell fortunes... or playing or betting at any unlawful games or plays ..." (quoted in Ribton-Turner, 199–200). The list goes on.
8. Duplicates of all passes and examinations were to be included in the rolls of the country quarter sessions. The best introduction to parish documentation, including that relevant to vagrancy and poor law, remains W. E. Tate's, *The Parish Chest*; see especially 188–239. Tate also provides summaries of key eighteenth-century vagrancy statutes, 210–11. W. B. Stephens' *Sources for English Local History* provides another useful overview of local records pertaining to the poor laws.

9. J. R. Poynter explains that "... the aim of relief was always closely related to the desire to restrain, since rulers feared vagabonds before they pitied the indigent, and the poor law was often confused in practice with the Vagrancy Laws and their harsh provisions for vagabonds of different degrees of roguery" (2).

10. The 1662 Act of Settlement "authorized justices to return to his previous parish within forty days anyone moving into a new parish and renting a house with an annual value of less than £10" (Himmelfarb, 25). This law remained unmodified until 1795, when Parliament allowed removals only of those actually chargeable – unless the person in question was a pregnant woman. For extended discussion of settlement law, see Taylor, 8–25 and Poynter, 3–7. The laboring poor usually acquired settlements through birth, marriage, or possession of a small piece of land. While the law of settlement had influential critics, most notably Adam Smith whose *The Wealth of Nations* called it "an evident violation of natural liberty and justice" (141), removals continued throughout the century.

11. For Christian's position at Cambridge, see Johnston, *Hidden*, 114.

12. For a particularly scathing portrait of the such arbitrary power, see William Godwin's novel *Caleb Williams*.

13. Olejniczak finds that during the 1780s, the English incarcerated one vagrant in 2170 arrested, where the French sent one in 1860 to the *dépôts de mendicité* ("English"). The French system of apprehending and punishing the homeless is discussed in greater detail in chapter 1.

14. In his landmark article "Property, Authority, and the Criminal Law," Douglas Hay provides a useful context for the discretionary nature of enforcement regarding Georgian vagrancy law. Hay reconciles England's savage eighteenth-century penal code with the country's decentralized, weak policing forces by emphasizing the enormous discretionary powers this arrangement gave to magistrates. Prosecution and conviction could be last resorts in this system, even if guilt was clear, and the condemned could and often did have capital sentences commuted. Conversely, authorities could employ the law in all its ferocity to make examples of offenders in times of crisis. Such careful manipulations of the law served to perpetuate British society's paternalistic character. Hay is concerned with violent crime and crimes against property, but a similar dynamic appears to have governed administration of vagrancy law.

    For another critique of the Webbs' findings that focuses on methodology, particularly with regard to their volume on the effects of the New Poor Law passed in 1834, see Alan Kidd's "Historians or polemicists? How the Webbs wrote their history of the English poor laws."

15. Blau summarizes the kinds of laws aimed at the homeless, 3–4. In New York, where police already are authorized to arrest subway panhandlers, the latest round of legislation has prohibited begging within 10 feet of any automatic teller machine; see the *New York Times*, 27 June 1996, A1.

On homelessness as an indictment of American society, cf. Christopher Jencks: "At a political level, the spread of homelessness suggests that something has gone fundamentally wrong with America's economic or social institutions" (v). See also Blau, 111, and Liebow, 230, though he notes that the homeless women he himself studied usually gave a "mid-level" cause for their homelessness – unemployment or divorce, for example – rather blaming "the system" (214).

16. Brendan O'Flaherty, surveying cities in the US and abroad, contends that police react generally with tolerance toward the homeless. He states that, like Georgian constables, the police only enforce laws aimed at the homeless if they perceive enforcement as furthering the broader goal of keeping the peace. For similar findings see Snow and Anderson (98–100). The police in Toth's account of the tunnel people are more ambivalent, alternately menacing and supportive (59–67). This assessment rings true in light of my own (admittedly anecdotal) experiences living in New York City from 1987 to 1997. While the officers I observed could be tolerant, it was by no means the case that, as O'Flaherty claims, a homeless person "may act bizarrely, offend property owners, or render the space unusable by others, but the police will not intervene" (269). I often witnessed homeless people who were sleeping on public benches, for example, being roused by police and told to move on, and during his first term in office Mayor Rudolph Guiliani targeted the homeless as threats to the city's "quality of life," a view fueling initiatives such as his campaign against the "squeegee men" who demanded tips for washing car windows at intersections.

17. In addition, see Rossi, chapter 3. Jencks discusses the controversy over Rossi's estimates and the earlier, 1984 tally by the Department of Housing and Urban Development in chapters 1–2. Jencks points out that even Martha Burt's respected quantitative study *Over the Edge*, based on a 1987 survey, "does not tell us much about those who avoid shelters, soup kitchens, and the company of other homeless individuals. I doubt that such people are numerous, but I can see no way of proving this" (12).

18. Toth also remarks that most of the people she spoke with did not want her to use their real names in her book (5–6).

19. Liebow's Appendix C, "How Many Homeless?" is a particularly succinct summation of these problems.

20. See also Balmori and Morton's *Transitory Gardens, Uprooted Lives*, a written and photographic record of the temporary gardens devised by squatters and the homeless in Manhattan.

21. They note that some of these activities nevertheless require the hard work sanctioned by conventional American values: "…to scavenge involves no less toil and sweat than most kinds of manual labor" (169).

22. Roe's extended argument for Wordsworth's youthful radicalism is *Wordsworth and Coleridge: The Radical Years*.

23. In addition to Roe and Johnston, other historicist critics, including Jerome McGann, Marjorie Levinson, David Simpson and Alan Liu, have assumed that poetic displacements resulted from Wordsworth's

debilitating disappointment over the collapse of domestic reform and the souring of the French Revolution.

24. In his discussions of Wordsworth's proposals for *The Philanthropist*, Mark Schoenfield approaches my view when he argues that "…one specific problem for Wordsworth was how to express a moderate republican view without being co-opted by, or shoved into, the violence of one side or the other" (79). Wordsworth's dedication (if we define this as a systematic and committed pursuit of a goal) to even "moderate republicanism" is unclear if we scrutinize the record.

CHAPTER 1   UNSETTLING POWERS IN THE EARLY LANDSCAPES

1. All quotations come from James Averill's edition of the poem's 1793 reading text.

2. Langan also notes a pun here, but for her it signifies a logic of cancellation rather than expansion. As one who, in the course of the poem, is "evacuated of his positive contents," the speaker's evening of differences recalls the liberal guarantee of obscurity to the individual (22).

3. Quotes from the 1794 revisions come from the reading text in Averill's edition of *An Evening Walk*. See pp. 129–30 on the editorial procedure for compiling this version of the poem.

4. Johnston explains that a sizar "was a reduced free status," the lowest of the seven categories of student at Cambridge (*Hidden*, 119). The title did not necessarily carry a stigma; Newton and Wordsworth's own very successful uncle William Cookson had been sizars, but students so classified were expected to work hard and distinguish themselves, two tasks that Wordsworth rapidly lost interest in once arriving at the university.

5. Mayo and Glen (33–56) both note the popularity of such poems and morals in the literary magazines. However, Langhorne's *The Country Justice* (1775), to which *An Evening Walk* is often compared, actually highlights Wordsworth's departures from expectations. Langhorne's description of a vagrant who dies giving birth is an occasion for affirming certain values and class distinctions. The woman dies on the road, having been ejected from the nearby village during her labor by a heartless parish officer. Langhorne's dead vagrant is supposed to spur the country justice into combat with "the shuffling farmer" (27), whose "low-born pride" can only be checked by the "honest rage" (49) of the JP; see Lonsdale's *Oxford Book of Eighteenth Century Verse*. In *An Evening Walk*, Wordsworth declines to moralize after his sketch of the vagrant mother and does not proclaim himself a member of a supervisory elite.

6. Harrison employs Cowper as a foil to the Wordsworth of "Resolution and Independence" by showing how the latter's mature works eschew Cowper's distance in favor of close encounters with the poor

that humanize them and interrogate middle-class economic stability; see pp. 65–71, 117–38.

7.   Quotations from *The Task* are taken from Cowper's *Poetical Works*, ed. H.S. Milford. Anne Wallace points out that engaging in such walks was not, by the early to mid-nineteenth century, mutually exclusive with the social position of a gentleman. As methods of cheap transportation such as the railway flourished, walking became optional for many laborers: "… as walking became a matter of choice, it became a possible positive choice: since the common person need not travel by walking, so walking travelers need not necessarily be poor" (62).

8.   Liu's *Wordsworth* discusses this subject extensively (61–137).

9.   Like Eric Birdsall in his introduction to *Descriptive Sketches*, Johnston maintains that Wordsworth reversed his opinion of a curacy out of a desire to marry Annette Vallon (*Hidden*, 333).

10.   The letter closes with another reversal. Wordsworth encourages Mathews to remember that he lives in a "free country, where every road is open, where talents and industry are more liberally rewarded than amongst any other nation …" (77). Literary opportunities in England once more are associated with the boundless freedom of the open road.

11.   Wallace contends that for Wordsworth the opposition between walking and cultivation was in fact a false dichotomy. In readings of "Salisbury Plain," "The Old Cumberland Beggar," and especially *The Excursion*, she argues that walking replaces the vanishing rural occupations of small farmers. By continuing to use ancient rights of way, which often crossed newly enclosed lands and commons, walkers reclaim those lands for public use and supplant the role of labor in the Virgilian Georgic (114–30). Wallace's thoughtful study generally conflates the gentleman walker and the destitute vagrant, though they may walk for very different reasons and with different goals. This means that her theory works well for poems like *The Excursion* but is less successfully applied to "Salisbury Plain," where the journey is aimless and destitution so complete that appropriation of wealth or enactment of nation-building via walking is arguable.

12.   Privacy in the middle-class home became important as dwellings lost their medieval, public character and were differentiated into rooms with private or social functions. These changes were accompanied by less frequent intrusions by business associates, friends, and servants. Certain times were set aside for socializing, and even next-door neighbors arranged visits through notes. "It was impolite to drop in uninvited, even on your close friends" (Rybczynski, 108). Mark Girouard traces the related shift from an emphasis on sociability to an appreciation of seclusion as a mode of aesthetic appreciation particularly suited to picturesque nature. For example, paintings of country homes, he demonstrates, illuminate this change. Until mid-century, such structures usually are shown with a house party. Afterward, they appear in solitude, with only a laborer or proprietor in the foreground.

Philippe Ariès associates these notions of privacy with a feeling that childhood was a unique and positive period in an individual's life. This contributed to the fact that, by Wordsworth's time, upper- and middle-class children were often cared for by a small number of adults. This pattern suggests that "sociability and the concept of the family were incompatible" (Ariès, 407). L. J. Jordanova confirms Ariès' conclusions, particularly among middle-class boys (47). Although Wordsworth's own experiences deviate from this pattern in some respects, it provides a useful heuristic for his class.

13. Continuing to explore Wordsworth's early professionalism, Pfau argues that the juxtaposition of the swan and beggar set pieces avoids political or social commentary in *An Evening Walk* because the woman is purely "an aesthetic casualty" (103). Her imaginary status in this reading is an emblem of the mediation that situates professional production within capitalism's transmutation of labor and material into circulating wealth (101–5).

14. All quotations are from the 1793 version of *Descriptive Sketches*, edited by Eric Birdsall. Prose citations refer to page numbers in the Cornell volume.

15. In a related observation, Wallace contrasts eighteenth-century ideas of travel emphasizing destination with poems, including Wordsworth's, that use the activity of walking to suggest the importance of observation and process in travel (17–66).

16. Following Raymond Williams in *Marxism and Literature* (55–71), when I speak of ideology in Wordsworth I refer to the practices that produce meanings for specific groups. For the role of ideology in state apparatuses, such as the family or religious institutions, cf. Althusser's discussions of ideological delusion. Terry Eagleton's *Ideology* reminds us of the two typical uses of "ideology" by Marxist theorists: one camp "has been preoccupied with ideas of true and false cognition, with ideology as illusion … whereas an alternative tradition of thought has been less epistemological than sociological, concerned more with the function of ideas within social life than with their reality or unreality" (3). Like the Marxist tradition itself, Wordsworth's early work straddles this division. Perhaps most clearly in *Descriptive Sketches*, he anticipates Althusser's argument that "ideology represents the imaginary relationship of individuals to their conditions of existence" (153). Yet the poet invariably considers this phenomenon by examining the impact of ideological deception on the minds and material conditions of ordinary people.

17. See chapters 3 and 4 of Hufton's *The Poor of Eighteenth-Century France 1750–1789*.

18. For example, magistrates usually required evidence that the vagrant had not worked for the past six months before convicting (Hufton, 228).

19. Schwartz presents the aristocracy's view of the Fear (245–6).

20. For the Comité's report, see Adams (249). The ongoing distrust of the homeless reflected the interests of landed proprietors leading the early revolutionary government. Cobban explains the desire of

France's new leaders to preserve the wealth embodied in their estates: "... if we can pass any general verdict on social developments at this time, it would be that they consolidated the claims of property against the propertyless and of the richer, on all levels, against the poorer" (161). Doyle agrees, noting that the word property recurs "obsessively" throughout the Declaration of the Rights of Man and the Citizen (208). To the extent that Wordsworth is critical of this perspective, he appears to have been less sympathetic to the early, moderate republicans than is now generally thought.

21.   Providing food and shelter to the poor traveler, a customary boon granted by farmers, became increasingly rare as fear of itinerants grew during the eighteenth century. Vagrants, in turn, might reinforce their demands for such assistance with threats, and the memory of such encounters fueled the panic during the Great Fear. Wordsworth's inclusion of customary hospitality in *Descriptive Sketches* suggests how at certain moments the revolutionary atmosphere could suspend, rather than exacerbate, historical bias against the unknown itinerant. In a letter from the poet's first trip to France in 1790, he indicates to his sister a direct relation between kindness to strangers and political upheaval, partly attributing the "politeness diffused thro the lowest ranks" of French society to the country's being "mad with joy, in consequence of the revolution" (*Early Years*, 36).

22.   Robin Jervis' discussion of *Descriptive Sketches* also captures the ambiguity of the speaker's response here, noting "the contradiction between the traveller's self-consciousness as a transitory observer of foreign people and places, and his/her desire to make meaningful contact" with the foreign other (*Romantic* 99).

23.   While Wordsworth in *Descriptive Sketches* is focusing on peasants rather than the gentry, his portraits of families consistently make mention of the kind of privacy and intimacy grounding the ideal of the Georgian home.

24.   Johnston's scenario requires Wordsworth to fail in gaining Blois since if he did, either he didn't marry Vallon after all, or he became a bigamist in marrying Mary Hutchinson some ten years later.

25.   Johnston explains this seeming incongruity, theorizing that the decision not to publish the letter reflects on the prudence of Joseph Johnson rather than on Wordsworth himself. He also gives a new reason for the letter's inflammatory rhetoric, however, that has nothing to do with any political convictions Wordsworth may have possessed, namely his uncles' "self-righteous retraction" of their offer of a curacy when they learned of his behavior in France (*Hidden*, 333–4).

Perhaps the most interesting part of Johnston's speculation over the 1793 trip concerns his point that to make such a journey, Wordsworth would have had to be an expert political faker, familiar with the different factions and able to impersonate the zeal of a royalist and a revolutionary with equal skill as he crossed battle lines. "From a royalist fifth columnist, Wordsworth would have had to transmute himself into a fellow-traveling international revolutionary sympathizer. ... A royalist white cockade in one pocket and a revolutionary tricolor in the other would have been handy travel aids" (381). This image conveys an ideological flexibility very much akin to the one I associate with the early Wordsworth.

26. Wordsworth also adds a mention of the indigent who have houses – the "cottage poor" – in the 1794 version's conclusion (774). The speaker acknowledges that their homes are a blessing to the poor who possess them, providing contentment and protection. As the inhabitants prepare for sleep, "those peaceful precincts own / A charm at any other time unknown" (777–8). He adds that for the weary laborers inside these dwellings, night and sleep are the "best friends of Poverty" (788). But thoughts of death come into peculiar contact with praise of home life. The speaker compares the sleep of the cottaged poor to the eternal rest of the dead residents of a nearby ruined abbey. If the Grasmere boys' wild movements downplayed their connection to the corpses in their graves, this final description of the housed poor underscores such a link, especially since we are told that these poor families will sleep *better* than their (long-dead) monastic predecessors. This closing observation, occurring as evening is passing into night, carries an eerie residue of possibility: are the cottaged poor different from dead monks to whom they have been compared? Will they wake up in the morning? We assume so, but there is an uncomfortable sense of finality in this equation that comes so close to the end of the poem itself.

27. James Chandler notes that this passage parallels the opening of *The Social Contract* (282n.). For an analysis linking vagrancy in Rousseau's later writings with digressive literary forms that anticipate Wordsworth, see Langan, chapter 1. Rousseau describes primitive humanity's existence as idyllic because it is free from knowledge of agriculture and metallurgy as well as social conventions, such as private property, that accompany such knowledge. Wordsworth idealizes not the original state of nature *per se* but rather early ideas of nationalism that grew out of it. This view is similar to Rousseau's in the "Discourse on the Origins and Foundations of Inequality among Men" that the earliest society's blend of natural freedoms and simple relations "must have been the happiest and most enduring epoch" (39).

28. On 10 August 1792, probably a few months after Wordsworth wrote the Swiss passages for *Descriptive Sketches*, the Louvre, guarded by Swiss mercenaries hired to protect Louis XVI, was stormed by an armed mob slaughtering counter-revolutionaries. In the ensuing massacre, the Swiss were literally hacked to pieces by the crowd and many of the remains mutilated (Schama, 615). When it dismissed all Swiss mercenaries in French service in September 1792, the National Convention significantly refused to pay the discharged soldiers the compensation due them under their contracts (Luck, 277), essentially a refusal to abide the notion of legitimate military service detached from national mission.

29.   While allied armies threatened Swiss borders throughout 1792, the
       confederation struggled to remain neutral in the continental fray.
       This was partly the result of internal divisions: French-speaking
       cantons tended to be sympathetic toward the early changes in
       France, while the German-speaking areas viewed the early republic
       with suspicion if not alarm. And while the revolution excited
       Swiss intellectuals, it terrified the ruling classes, who "sensed a
       clear danger of a conflagration on their own soil in which order
       would be destroyed" (Thürer, 80). These leaders were akin to the
       Geneva burghers who had made anathema the doctrines of
       Rousseau.
30.   Luck documents the Swiss' flight to France (273); for examples of
       repression in the cantons, see Thürer (67–8).
31.   Since the fifteenth century, French kings had contracted for the ser-
       vices of Swiss mercenaries. The practice ironically originated after a
       1444 battle between the Swiss and the French, one of the last in the
       great Swiss battles for liberation, in which the Swiss fought to the last
       man rather than surrender (Thürer, 39).
          Wordsworth's footnote also recalls prior conflicts emphasizing the
       mercenary's most unpleasant position – the prospect of fighting
       against his own countrymen. This had happened during the War of
       the Spanish Succession in the 1709 Battle of Malplaquet when,
       fighting for the opposed forces of France and Holland, Swiss merce-
       naries killed each other. By the eighteenth century, the medieval her-
       itage of an independent citizenry repelling invaders had degenerated
       into paid self-slaughter to defend foreign despotisms (72).
32.   Janet Thomson's *Mercenaries, Pirates, and Sovereigns* describes some of
       the considerations in this process (86–9).
33.   See, for example, Sheats, *Making* (59–74); Roe, *Radical Years* (68–9);
       Birdsall's introduction to *Descriptive Sketches*; and Jervis, *Romantic* (97).
       Izenberg alone observes that the concluding lines imply that "cankers
       of mortality and guilt lie like an unassimilable, potentially fatal source
       of infection, at the center of political hope" (176).
34.   On Wordsworth's financial problems in 1792 and particularly in early
       1793, when his uncles withdrew their offer of a curacy, see Gill,
       Wordsworth (68–9).
35.   From Wordsworth's translation of this ode, lines 3 and 6–12, in
       Averill, *An Evening Walk* (135).

CHAPTER 2   SALISBURY PLAIN AND THE RECUPERATION
OF FREEDOM

1.   The dominant view of the Salisbury Plain poems identifies them as
       the high-water mark of Wordsworth's radical sympathies. Johnston's
       The Hidden Wordsworth and Roe's *Wordsworth and Coleridge: The
       Radical Years*, discussed below, are the most forceful arguments in
       favor of Wordsworth's youthful radicalism; for other comparisons

between Wordsworth, Godwin, and other radical authors see Enid Welsford's *Salisbury Plain*, Stephen Gill's "'Adventures on Salisbury Plain' and Wordsworth's Poetry of Protest 1795–97," and Gill's subsequent biography of Wordsworth. Tracing Burke's influence on Wordsworth's early poetry, James Chandler nonetheless views "Salisbury Plain" as the product of Wordsworth's "most fervently radical period" and calls the opening three stanzas "a paraphrase" of Rousseau's second *Discourse* (130–1).

2. The exact dates of composition for "Salisbury Plain" are uncertain. Wordsworth's letters claim that it was composed in the late summer of 1793, but the oldest manuscript extant probably dates from the Windy Brow period between April and May 1794 (Gill's "Preface," *Salisbury Plain Poems*, 5–7). The difference between these two dates, given changes in England and France during these years, may have great significance. My argument is of necessity based on the Windy Brow manuscript, DC MS 10, printed in the Cornell Wordsworth volume. Although much of this verse may date from earlier in the decade, Wordsworth included such material in the fair copy presumably because he believed it relevant to British conditions in mid-1794.

3. Of course, not all trades or social classes suffered. High corn prices made agriculture lucrative, and metallurgy thrived on government military contracts. But the war's disruption of trade created massive unemployment among wage-laborers, particularly in the industrial centers in the Midlands and the North (Porter, 312–13). Citing prosecution statistics, Beattie documents the resulting crime wave, particularly the rise in property crime (233, 237).

4. The proclamation's immediate target was Part 2 of Paine's *The Rights of Man;* the government's methods in obtaining the manuscript and then suppressing its publication testify to the efficacy of the growing spying network (Emsley, "Repression," 805).

5. For the prosecution's attempts to define sedition, see Emsley ("An Aspect," 156). Albert Goodwin gives a detailed account of these trials (343–58). Not everyone charged in the early 1790s was so fortunate. The infamous Scottish treason trials of 1793 had led to sentences of transportation for Maurice Margarot, Thomas Fysshe Palmer, Thomas Muir, and William Skirving.

6. Many associated physical mobility among the poor with revolutionary chaos. In *The History of the Poor* (1793–4), Justice of the Peace Thomas Ruggles argued along with Adam Smith for reform of the settlement laws. But Ruggles tellingly acknowledged the current sentiment against his view:

> … is it not just that every individual should enjoy as much freedom, as is consistent with the freedom of the whole? But it may be possibly replied that … this is not the time; see what the cry of liberty, and the call for freedom, have done upon the continent; the answer is obvious; the cases are widely different; the one is a temporary anarchy arising from the abolition of all government;

the other would be a recovery from a restraint inimical to the interests of labour and industry...

(x)

7. In a related initiative, 35 Geo. III, c.34 (enacted April 1795) would enable magistrates to enlist able-bodied, male vagrants and vagabonds in the navy. The statute's intent may have been less to swell troop enrollments than to control a volatile group when social disorder could be disastrous. London magistrate Patrick Colquhoun had proposed the law to high-ranking officials in January 1794 primarily to rid "'society of a vast number of idle, dissolute and abandoned characters which the law cannot reach at present though they live chiefly by the commission of crimes ...'" (quoted in Emsley, *British Society*, 52).

8. For more on the Alien Office created by the Alien Act, see footnote 34 below. I discuss the Middlesex Justice Bill in greater detail in Chapter 4.

9. John Rieder also points out the legal tone of the poem when he states that in "Salisbury Plain" the narrative voice seems to exhibit the characters "as evidence in a brief against the state" (327).

10. In the famous Scottish trials of 1793, lawyer Thomas Muir, founder of the Whig Friends of the People in Edinburgh, was convicted of treason and transported in part "because someone, against his recommendation, took a copy of Paine's works with uncut pages from the pocket of his greatcoat lying on a chair..." (Liu, "Trying," 68). According to Emsley, the term "seditious words" was designed to cover a variety of offenses, from criticizing impressment gangs to wishing the king executed ("An Aspect").

11. In a chapter on the Salisbury Plain poems, "All Track Quite Lost," David Collings argues that the plain itself is an ambiguous space. By showing how war destabilizes systems of signification as well as categories like life and death, deviation and direction, these poems document a process of cultural dismemberment. Although Collings' Lacanian analysis is more concerned with psychoanalytic aspects of this problem, he suggests how even the concept of the nation state is problematized. The entity which should divide humanity from savagery incorporates nature's most violent and destructive qualities (18–49). Robin Jervis speaks more generally about how the poem's setting vexes distinctions between past and present but leads to "no final resolution of the accumulated tension" (*Romantic* 104).

12. For Moss' "The Beggar" see his *Poems*; for "Pray Remember the Poor," see Smart's *Collected Poems*; for Blake's "Human Abstract," see the Princeton edition of *Songs of Innocence and Experience*.

13. "ASP" indicates material from the second version of this poem, "Adventures on Salisbury Plain."

14. My notion of an examination mode draws on Foucault's description of the practice as a humble modality of modern discipline. Foucault's examination "combines the techniques of an observing hierarchy and those of a normalizing judgment. It is a normalizing gaze, a sur-

veillance that makes it possible to qualify, to classify and to punish" (*D & P*, 184).

Foucault speaks of a type of examination dominant in nineteenth-century Europe. The key role of examination in the administration of the British vagrancy laws makes them important precursors to a more comprehensive system of social regulation. Beier points out in *Masterless Men* that the legal examination originated in England in 1383 as a practice specifically aimed at policing "new and exceptional crimes ... thought to threaten the state and social order, such as treason, witchcraft and vagabondage." The development of examination procedure and documentation marked a significant "extension of state authority" (12). The horizontality of Salisbury Plain tropes Wordsworth's protest against what Foucault calls the verticality of examination.

15. Chandler maintains that in "Salisbury Plain," "compassion alone is not enough because it generates too ephemeral a perception of existing evils to insure that abiding reforms are made" (136), and that "Reasoned inquiry alone is capable of exposing error to the light it cannot bear ..." (137). The ephemeral nature of the encounter should not be confused with an ephemeral effect in the participants. Further, Chandler assumes that the poem recognizes the option of "abiding reform" through other means. In "Salisbury Plain," such a notion is in serious doubt by the end. Pity may or may not be adequate, but it seems to be the best one can do.

16. Paul Kelley and Chandler (see this chapter's note 1) document the passage's echoes of Rousseau's "Discourse on the Origins of Inequality."

17. Celeste Langan assesses this difference in terms of the legal concept of neighborage, which plaintiffs in the eighteenth and nineteenth centuries tried to argue guaranteed the right to wander over another's lands. Langan contends that "The female vagrant" and *Lyrical Ballads* work to preserve this right by relocating it within the practices of reading and publishing under copyright (77–82, 127–37).

18. Although supposedly an educated friend and valued counselor, the Georgian wife was still expected to be a compliant, subservient helpmate. Women had virtually no independent legal rights; rape was punished as an offense against male ownership rather than female identity, and husbands, lovers, and fathers were free to beat their wives and daughters (McLynn, 102–3).

L. J. Jordanova observes that even when women took positions on public matters, they were unrecognized as active members of society. Burke and Rousseau agreed on the limited scope of a woman's social role.

Although women were active in popular protests in the early modern period, and participated in bread riots and counter-revolutionary demonstrations during the French revolution, political theorists of the eighteenth century [including Rousseau and French republicans] uniformly accorded women a passive role in public life, which they were allowed to affect through their family responsibilities, rather than directly as full citizens.

(49–50)

19. Anne Mellor remarks on how Wollstonecraft's support for egalitarian marriage worked to undermine a male-centered social, political, and cosmic order – the very consequences Burke feared (38). The independent woman in Wollstonecraft's model of marriage became a public creature tangibly shaping her political environment. Husbands who could be "content with rational fellowship instead of slavish obedience" would find their wives "more affectionate sisters, more faithful wives, more reasonable mothers – in a word, better citizens" (Wollstonecraft, 263).

20. Stone (233) and Jordanova (47) also comment on the feelings of isolation and uselessness endured by middle-class Georgian women.

21. Wordsworth indicates familiarity with Godwin and *Political Justice*, even before their meeting in 1795, in his letter to William Mathews of 17 February 1794 (Roe, *Radical Years*, 176–7). This letter suggests that he had read Godwin's treatise before making the fair copy of "Salisbury Plain" at Windy Brow.

22. Quotations from the original 1793 text are reconstructed via Priestley's editorial apparatus. Quotations derived from two separate volumes are cited by a plus (+) sign between the volumes involved.

23. This sort of direct extremism is more obviously characteristic of Thomas Paine, the most widely read of all the radical pamphleteers, than of Godwin. A sample from the second part of *The Rights of Man*, however, indicates significant rhetorical similarities between Paine and Godwin: "If systems of government can be introduced, less expencive, and more productive of general happiness, than those which have existed, all attempts to oppose their progress will in the end be fruitless. Reason, like time, will make its own way, and prejudice will fall in a combat with interest" (161).

24. Skepticism about radical philosophy also comes to the fore in *The Borderers*, written after "Adventures on Salisbury Plain." Rivers, an amoral rationalist who convinces a man that it is his duty to become a murderer, is a recognizable parody of the principled radical. Yet in a manner consistent with Wordsworth's earlier poetry, rejecting one ideology does not mean embracing another. Gill remarks, "it is striking that in the play, although Rivers condemns himself, no other structure of values emerges at all strongly" (*Wordsworth*, 114–15). The character Mortimer, overwhelmed by guilt over his complicity in murder, significantly becomes a vagrant. He neither submits to law nor adopts Rivers' radicalism.

25. John Williams comes to much the same conclusion about "Adventures on Salisbury Plain": "the radical philosophy of Paine which sought to sweep away all social ills through the application of rational political principles is denied as a policy as morally damaging as that of contemporary reactionary politicians" (77).

26. In "Citizen Wordsworth," Roe gives a useful account of the histories and names of the members of Frend's gathering (27–8); his comment about Dyer appears on p. 27.

27. A letter to Mathews, dated 17 February 1794, also suggests that Wordsworth was uncertain where his political allegiances really lay and what his role should be. He indicates his knowledge of *Political Justice* in a strange way: he asks Mathews, "What remarks do you make on the Portuguese?" Godwin mentions the Portuguese when discussing the duties of an enlightened reformer in a despotic state. If one were living in repressive Portugal, for example, is there a duty to disseminate the doctrines of liberty despite the obvious personal costs? Godwin advises that the would-be reformer publish from a more liberal, foreign clime; truth would triumph if advocated from outside Portugal itself. Remaining in Portugal and concealing one's views is the most odious option. In a statement consistent with his reasons for hating monarchy, Godwin writes that "Conscious disguise" makes us "solitary, morose, and misanthropical" (3: 303); a sincere person can "never ... give way to the affair of the day" (3: 305). If Wordsworth shared Godwin's hatred of censorship, his own public silence on radical issues signified not insincerity but uncertainty.

28. Another letter to Mathews similarly supports the men acquitted of treason in 1794, yet questions their ideas. Horne Tooke, for example, is said to be motivated by "a wish to vex powerful individuals, [rather] than to be an instrument of public good" (24 December 1794 and 7 January 1795; *Early Years*, 137). Ultimately, Wordsworth countenances compromise, supporting the reformers "so long as they are temperate" (137).

29. The earliest surviving draft of this second poem is DC MS 16, which probably dates from mid-1799. Gill believes that some stanzas, at least, date from 1797 or 1798. He adds, "Although such evidence suggests that the 1795 poem is now lost to us, there is no doubt that substantially, if not in every detail, it has survived in the poem MS 2, *Adventures on Salisbury Plain*" ("Preface," *Salisbury Plain Poems*, 12). This is the version I draw on here.

30. Albert Goodwin notes the widespread belief that the 1794 acquittals "had narrowly averted a general proscription of all who had promoted reform associations or who had expressed pro-French sympathies" (361).

31. A key cause of civil unrest since May of 1795 had been skyrocketing grain prices due to the short harvest of 1794 (Thompson, *English Working Class*, 65–6). For a detailed account of the 1795 famine, see Wells' *Wretched Faces*.

32. Cf. V. A. C. Gatrell: "... the crowd's function was to bear witness to the might of the law and the wickedness of crime and to internalize those things" (90–1). Foucault goes so far as to say that an execution in secret "would scarcely have had any meaning" (*D & P*, 58).

33. The eighteenth-century perception of Britain as a free land was very much bound up with the lack of the "trappings of a police state"

(Christie, 175). The small standing army had restricted powers, and the government lacked France's centralized bureaucracy. Emsley's work on the often haphazard nature of prosecutions for sedition argues for the British state's inefficiencies: the small size of the Home Office staff, among other things, meant that enforcing many statutes was generally "a hit and miss affair" ("Repression," 822; cf. Eastwood, 149).

34. Roger Wells' revisionist reading of repression in the 1790s argues that the official policing network has been seriously underestimated because of an emphasis on Home Office papers. Wells spotlights the Alien Office, which was established in January 1793 to intercept French agents, their English comrades, and anyone else threatening Hanoverian security. "Quite simply the Fountain Head of the British secret service" (*Insurrection*, 30), the Alien Office was part of a "systematic collection of intelligence on a scale hitherto unappreciated…" (42). Cf. Elizabeth Sparrow's "The Alien Office, 1792–1806."

The practice of poor law authorities during this time offers an example of how systematic surveillance was in use by officials far beyond the Home Office *per se*. In the 1790s, poor law and charity claimants increasingly were subjected to a thorough investigation into their private affairs to determine their needs. Minute inquiry was more characteristic of rural areas than larger cities, but in Manchester, officials visited every appellant in his/her home and made a daily report on them, "a remarkable bureaucratic exercise for the eighteenth century" (Wells, *Wretched Faces*, 303).

35. Even during the mid-1780s, constitutional guarantees like Habeas Corpus remained untouched. It had been suspended during the American War, but was reinstated in 1783 despite the crime wave (Emsley, "Repression," 808).

36. The panic of the 1780s attained such heights partly because of "the violent character of so much of the crime being reported…" (Beattie, 223). During the 1790s, objections to the military might still turn violent: in August 1794, there were five days of rioting in London over the army's practice of employing contractors, or "crimps," who were believed to kidnap men for service. In scale and duration, these disturbances were the largest in London since the Gordon riots. Yet soldiers did not join in the protests, regulars restraining the rioters performed admirably, and the riots were less against the government itself than against independent recruiters it employed. See Stevenson's "The London 'Crimp' Riots of 1794."

37. For a full account of these events see Peter Linebaugh's "The Tyburn Riot Against the Surgeons."

38. Although Gary Harrison acknowledges their goodness, he believes that Wordsworth ultimately does not approve of the thieves. Instead, their conduct is an example of Godwin's warning about the reprisals to which long-term oppression of the poor will expose the rich. "That the female vagrant rejects the gypsy life only places Wordsworth's radicalism within the limits of Godwin's, Paine's, and later Shelley's…" (104).

39.   Rieder's comments shed more light on the poet's feelings about gibbeting later in life. In *An Unpublished Tour* – composed 1811–12 – Wordsworth condemns the practice even for those he now readily labels traitors, "should times unfortunately breed such offenders" (*Prose*, 2 : 334). He goes on:

>   Whom can the ignominy of this exposure deter from wickedness? Surely not those from whose hand the most inhuman cruelties are to be apprehended! There is no place which a hardened villain would prefer for the perpetration of a murder to the foot of a gibbet, if it lay within his choice.
>
>   (334)

40.   Gatrell seeks to correct assessments by investigators like Foucault and McLynn, who perceive a powerful element of subversion among execution-day crowds. Execution days provided an excuse for work stoppages, all-day stays at the tavern, pickpocketing, and fights.

CHAPTER 3   LIFE DURING WARTIME IN *LYRICAL BALLADS*

1.   Discussions of poems from the 1798 and 1800 *Lyrical Ballads* are based on the texts in *Lyrical Ballads, and Other Poems, 1797–1800*, eds Butler and Green.
2.   This treatment of repetitive movement reflects a new concern in Wordsworth's corpus: the problems a sojourner faces in finding a home. Kenneth Johnston comments on how in the 1798 *Lyrical Ballads* "the great danger is mental breakdown, caused by apparent rejection from English society itself" (*Hidden*, 726).
       The 1798 *Lyrical Ballads* includes representations of more conventional sorts of homelessness, such as "The Female Vagrant" and "The Complaint of a forsaken Indian Woman." But "The Thorn," "The Idiot Boy," and "The last of the Flock," among others, consider not vagrants *per se* but people on the move whose motives and desires are incomprehensible or mysterious. The mentality of these individuals can be inscrutable enough for them to be considered mentally incompetent or insane.
3.   Cf. Lipking, whose argument I discuss in greater detail in a moment: "… since neither the protection nor the inhibition of the law applies to [abandoned women] any longer, they constitute a potential threat to a well-ordered society" (xvii).
4.   Lipking applies this theory to a wide range of cultures. He argues that Irish ballads about a lover's desertion are implied critiques of English subjugation, and that ancient Chinese love poems comment on dynastic concerns. He summarizes, poetry about "abandonment … cannot be set apart from politics" (11).
5.   In addition to "The Thorn," see "The Mad Mother," "Ruth," and "The Female Vagrant." "The Complaint of a forsaken Indian

Woman" also can be read in this context. For speculation on the identification in Wordsworth between female abandonment and male acts of violence, a connection absent in "The Thorn," see Anne Rylestone's "Violence and the Abandoned Woman in Wordsworth's Poetry."

6. Alan Liu and Marjorie Levinson, for example, have passed over the poem in their efforts to give historical resonance to Wordsworth's work. Gary Harrison and David Simpson's interest in the eighteenth-century's discourses on poverty has not led them to focus on the "The Thorn."

7. Historically, such pain was magnified by the abandoned woman's disgrace before her community. Even if she was not pregnant, if a betrothed woman who had had sex with her fiancé was deserted by him, then "the honour of both was ruined in the eyes of the community: the man was then a liar, and the woman unchaste" (Stone, 398).

8. Cf. *Madness and Civilization*, where Michel Foucault suggests the affinities between madness and vagrancy by defining insanity as "the mobility of reason," adding that it acts as "an ironic sign that misplaces the guideposts between the real and the chimerical" (37). It is her ability to confuse or render irrelevant basic interpretive categories that makes Martha Ray fascinating to her neighbors.

9. Such lines led to Robert Southey's remark in the *Critical Review* (1798) that "'he who impersonates tiresome loquacity, becomes tiresome himself'" (quoted in Campbell, 84), a view later endorsed by Coleridge. Paul Hamilton states that these "naive lines … brought Wordsworth more critical vituperation than any others he wrote" (57). In the only serious reading of these lines I have uncovered, Paul Sheats argues that they satirize the class snobbery of eighteenth-century readers intent on separating "high" poetic diction from "low" conversational prose (92–100). To this extent, Martha Ray's transgressions of interpretive categories are reinforced by the poem's broader violations of aesthetic decorum.

10. Susan Wolfson, by contrast, endows the narrator with greater awareness of his shortcomings, arguing that he "underscores the impossibility of ever constructing a believable chain of causation through observation" ("Language", 31–4). In a related analysis, Alan Bewell contends that the narrator's interpretive difficulties stem from his contradictory desire to provide both a scientific account for Martha's behavior that relies on empirical examination and a supernatural explanation developed through storytelling and gossip (168).

11. Stuart law punishing bastardy explicitly linked rising illegitimacy rates with a culture of sexual permissiveness fostered by vagrant life; cf. 7 Jas. I, c. 4 and Hoffer and Hull (13). Beier validates this equation of homelessness with irregular sexual activity: early modern vagrants met sexual partners "by coincidence and circumstance. Their relationships were evanescent ones, and this made them dangerous in the eyes of those who ruled" (*Masterless Men*, 68).

12. Tudor measures against bastardy were designed to shame the unwed poor into supporting their own children. 18 Elizabeth I, c. 3, threat-

ened unwed mothers (and fathers if caught) with whipping and incarceration if their bastards required financial assistance from the parish. Rather than face such punishment, many poor women chose concealment of pregnancy followed by infanticide (Hoffer and Hull, 13–17). Cf. Stone (325).

13. According to 21 Jas. I, c. 27, if a mother "'endeavour privately either by drowning or secret burying thereof, or any other way, either by herself or the procuring of others, so to conceal the death thereof, as that it may not come to light, whether [the child] be born alive or not, but be concealed, in every such case the mother so offending shall suffer death …'" (quoted in Malcolmson, 197).

14. The social isolation attendant upon unwed motherhood might still be intense, but mostly for women who, unlike Martha Ray, had no obvious parish of settlement. Parish overseers eager to avoid supporting the child often ran unwed women out of town while they were in labor (Bouch and Jones, 295–6).

    As this practice suggests, the parish in which an unwed woman did give birth "became exclusively preoccupied with the economic problem of transferring the maintenance costs of a bastard child from the poor rate of the parish to the father, or failing that to some other body" (Stone, 400). By the eighteenth century, it was common for the midwife and a local woman to question an unwed mother during labor, refusing to help her unless she gave them the father's name and related information. The Midwife's Oath of 1726 made this standard procedure.

15. Malcolmson finds that between 1730 and 1774, although almost all women in Old Bailey trials for infanticide were guilty of concealment, 46 of the 61 tried were acquitted (197). Cf. Hoffer and Hull (65), McLynn (114). Some very flimsy defenses, for example the exhibition at the trial of linen ostensibly made in joyful anticipation of a child, often were sufficient to exact an acquittal. Other legal strategies included claiming that the child was stillborn or was killed "accidentally" while the mother tried to cut the umbilical cord herself and missed (Malcolmson, 198–9; Beattie, 120–1).

    Georgians became less interested in a woman's guilt or innocence than in the sensational particulars of infanticide cases. "Newspapers were particularly prone to dwell on the lurid details…; the discoveries of mutilated bodies, the corpses in the Thames, the remains which were turned up by dogs and swine" (Malcolmson, 189–90). To encourage sales, publishers featured coverage of infanticide trials in their advertisements for pamphlets on seventeenth- and eighteenth-century court proceedings (Hoffer and Hull, xviii).

16. Many types of legal prosecution show how vagrants were victimized when times were hard. Evidence from the Stuart period bears out that the homeless were far more likely to be indicted for theft and found guilty than local people. M. J. Ingram observes that, during the reigns of Elizabeth I and James I, "the reverse side of the coin of neighborliness was … xenophobia towards the wandering poor…" (133). Early modern fears of vagrants and witches illustrate how

"ideas of neighborly tolerance come under stress" during periods of economic and social upheaval (134).

17.   Also like infanticide law, treason statutes had lain largely unused for decades. In the years between the Jacobite rebellion of 1745 and the 1790s, treason prosecutions mostly were aimed at coiners rather than the clearly political targets of the Jacobite and Jacobin eras (McLynn, 322).

18.   Financial panic soon followed. After news of the landing in Wales, a run on the banks forced the substitution of paper money for gold – the creation, in effect, of a kind of bastard currency – due to bullion shortages. This supposedly temporary measure remained in effect until 1821 (Emsley, *British Society*, 57).

19.   Government propaganda reached an apex in the *Anti-Jacobin Review*. First published in November 1797, it regularly featured prominent ministerial contributors who explained why Britain fought.

      Albert Goodwin provides the date of Habeas Corpus' suspension (367); for the long prison terms that resulted, see Emsley's *British Society* (68). The suspension would be reaffirmed on 20 May 1799, 20 February 1800, 31 December 1800, and 18 April 1801 (Albert Goodwin, 368n.). Elliott gives a detailed account of the radical organizations' plans in early 1798 (165–88).

20.   Local and provincial support of conservative initiatives had been in evidence since the Church-and-King mobs of the early 1790s. But before 1797, enthusiasm for loyalist associations and action had been on the wane in many areas since 1794 (Wells, "English," 208).

21.   Many historians of the period, including David Eastwood, Ian Christie, and Clive Emsley, maintain that 1797–8 witnessed a genuine upsurge in patriotic feeling. As Roy Porter puts it, "Under invasion threat, patriotism was more popular than Paine" (352).

22.   The issue of invasion was a secondary factor in the defection of many peace supporters. War in the name of self-defense was seen very differently from British aggression against France earlier in the decade.

      Additionally, the government's success in averting revolution in the 1790s partly resulted from the careful use of local pressure on anti-war figures, who were often dissenting local businessmen or professionals. David Eastwood shows how the government consciously encouraged and directed unofficial harassment of its enemies. Voluntary acts by regional loyalists supplemented the state's power in crucial ways without opening the crown up to accusations that, like France, England was developing a military and spying bureaucracy.

23.   A person indicted by ex-officio information "was not necessarily informed of the charges against him and he might have to pay to find this out. There was no compulsion for the Attorney General to bring the accused to trial; he could leave the threat hanging over the accused's head and, in the event of the accused being unable to offer bail, he could technically be held in prison without trial. Furthermore, even if acquitted, it was impossible to recover court

costs" (Emsley, "An Aspect," 168). Emsley summarizes the Wakefield case.

24. Pitt capitalized on the new mood by launching several new programs, including a series of taxes to fund the war effort. All these initiatives, though, required extensive grassroots support.

   Wakefield's January trial was timed to coincide with Pitt's solicitation of voluntary donations to the government war chest. The guilty verdict helped Pitt present donations as every subject's duty, and support for his plan in small communities led to the suppression of anti-war and anti-government sympathizers (Cookson, *Friends*, 168). Emsley credits "the prevailing loyalist climate," as much as official pressure, with the diminishing numbers of reformist publications in 1798 (*British Society*, 70).

25. Mark Reed estimates that stanzas 1 and 2 of the poem were completed by 19 March 1798, and that the rest probably were finished by May (*Early*, 32).

26. Johnson had published *An Evening Walk* and *Descriptive Sketches* in 1793. The poet's last-minute desire to have Johnson, rather than Joseph Cottle, print the 1798 *Lyrical Ballads* suggests that Wordsworth still kept up with the London publisher (Gill, *Wordsworth*, 150).

27. For Coleridge's account of this series of events, see his *Biographia Literaria* (193–7). The earliest critical investigation of this situation is A. J. Eaglestone's "Wordsworth, Coleridge and the Spy," while Roe's *Wordsworth and Coleridge: The Radical Years* gives the best account of the entire episode (248–62). Johnston is intrigued by the mention in Walsh's correspondence of Wordsworth as a name "known" to Richard Ford, Bow Street magistrate and spying liaison, and alternately suggests that either this shows Wordsworth had been spied on before, perhaps in 1795, or that he was himself now in the employ of the secret service (*Hidden*, 527–36).

28. Walsh emerges from this incident looking considerably fairer than the local people involved in his inquiries. One of his letters to the Home Office recounts Mogg's suspicions but discounts most of them, concluding dryly that "Mr. Mogg is by no means the most intelligent Man in the World" (quoted in Roe, *Radical Years*, 250). Walsh's posture coupled with the Home Office's inaction buttresses "The Thorn's" argument that private citizens can be more tyrannical than government authorities.

29. Coleridge's letter to Thelwall is dated 21 August 1797. Thelwall himself had good reason to know the power of local coercion. In 1796, his lectures at Yarmouth and other towns were disrupted by militia officers disguised as servicemen and clergymen who had planted themselves in the audience. He subsequently wrote that "'the petty tyranny of provincial persecution'" was more damaging than government repression (quoted in Albert Goodwin, 405).

30. Like his counterpart, Tricky is a huntsman of sorts, though his preferred prey are spies and traitors. The thanks the narrator gets for helping Simon Lee unearth a stump seem hypocritical in light of Tricky's role in turning local opinion against the poet and his sister.

The fact that the poem is set in South Wales, rather than Somerset, further argues for situating the lyric alongside the botched invasion, which took place in the same region.

Simpson identifies Simon Lee's hunting with the feudal obligations he believes the poem eulogizes. He notes Tricky's role in starting the rumors but does not go beyond saying that "Exchanges between the Wordsworths and the Trickys must have been somewhat tense and embarrassed" (*Historical Imagination,* 150).

31. This note appears in Butler and Green's edition of *Lyrical Ballads.*

32. Pamela Woof notes the Wordsworths' use of telescopes to make observations of the moon while at Alfoxden (132).

33. In an alternative reading, William Howard argues that the listener's questions undermine the speaker's claim to objectivity and demonstrate a sympathetic desire to discover Martha's real story (233). This theory, however, demands that we see the narrator as a figure acting alone, when his account persistently situates his speculations within a larger communal pattern. Howard also fails to explain the auditor's fascination with what is clearly gossip, an interest that would be curbed by a sincere desire to learn the truth about Martha Ray.

34. Geoffrey Jackson extends responsibility for this pattern to readers who uncritically accept the narrator's account when first reading the poem (94).

35. Celeste Langan explains Martha's redundancies as a failure of language, rather than the community; her solitary sentence ("Woe is me") produces "out of linguistic impoverishment a 'beggar's cant' that substitutes repetition for an extensive vocabulary or a narrative rationale" (73–4). Insofar as one's expressive options are products of social life, the failure of language to convey Martha's condition is another way to figure the interpretive shortcomings of her neighbors.

36. Roe acknowledges "the oppressive political climate in Britain was … a factor that encouraged Wordsworth to go into exile abroad," but he emphasizes the Wakefield trial and Johnson's imprisonment rather than the Alfoxden difficulties ("Revising the Revolution," 97). E. P. Thompson suggests Wordsworth and Coleridge really left Britain to avoid being drafted into a Somerset corps raising troops to defend the coastline ("Disenchantment," 168).

37. The critical quotation used by Brett and Jones appears in Kenneth MacLean's *Agrarian Age.* Part of the passage, which MacLean intends for "The Old Cumberland Beggar," reads, "Wordsworth saw the regular appearances of the beggar on his rounds as a reminder of acts of kindness… His round thus served to keep all the human sympathies alive…" (61). MacLean's statement appears in Brett and Jones' note to "Old Man Travelling" (295).

38. Reed argues that "the full conception of the OCB, as an overtly exhortatory poem in its present form," came into being between 25 January and 5 March 1798 (*Early,* 342). Lines later designated as "Old Man Travelling" probably were composed in late 1796 and early 1797.

39. Charles Burney, reading for the *Monthly Review,* clearly felt that "Old Man Travelling" criticized the government's policies. As a result, the magazine's 1799 review of *Lyrical Ballads* recommended that the poem's ending be changed":... the termination seems pointed against the war; from which, however, we are now no more able to separate ourselves, than Hercules was to free himself from the shirt of Nessus. The old traveller's son might have died by disease" (Reiman, *Romantics,* 716).

40. The assignment of such qualities has been another cause of critical confusion. Historically, the Cumberland beggar rather than the traveling father has been identified with independence. Cf. Cleanth Brooks (378), Harold Bloom (173–8), and more recently Mark Koch (24–5).

41. The ongoing import of such acts becomes clear in the Fenwick note. Wordsworth objected to the new poor law of 1834 specifically because it would eliminate this sort of outrelief. Unlike Burke, Wordsworth maintained that government outrelief was essential because it allowed almsgivers to feel they were bestowing charity voluntarily. A law obliging the poor to choose between starvation and the workhouse would "force" people to give alms rather than encourage them to do so out of good will (Curtis, 56).

42. As I noted in Chapter 2, Wordsworth was not the first to argue so; Harrison notes that belief in the socially useful role of almsgiving was a Georgian commonplace. For example, Thomas Alcock promoted the social virtues of voluntary giving decades before, although he viewed such benefits as a reason for cutting all public assistance. His *Observations on the Defects of the Poor Laws* (1752) argued that in a nation where a pauper's only aid was the voluntary handout, "the People live in natural Love and Dependence, and the several ranks of Kings and Subjects, Masters and Servants, Parents and Children, High and Low, Rich and Poor, are attached to each other by the reciprocal good offices of Kindness and Gratitude ..." (quoted in Poynter, 13–14). Voluntary giving strengthened the entire British social hierarchy. For other readings of the beggar as community builder, see Anne Wallace (147–8), Michael Friedman (135), and Raymond Williams, *Country and the City* (130).

43. For example, James Chandler sees the poem as a Burkean validation of habit that renders state relief unnecessary (62–92), while David Simpson interprets the poem as a condemnation of Jeremy Bentham's workhouse scheme in *Pauper Management Improved* (1797). He concludes, though, that the poem occupies "a complex and even confused position" in relation to the poor relief debate, sympathizing with both conservative and more liberal views (*Historical Imagination,* 167). Gary Harrison agrees, situating Wordsworth's conservatism in the work as a response to Bentham that draws on late eighteenth-century paternalism toward the poor (157–62). Mark Koch draws very similar conclusions. Robin Jervis gestures toward the complex of concerns at issue here beside the debate on the poor laws, but is interested in the poem chiefly for its arguments about charity (201–2).

Other influences on the poem's composition probably included Pitt's hotly debated poor law bill of 1796, with its "strange muddling of a new system of workhouses with a new profusion of outrelief" (Poynter, 65), and Thomas Malthus's morose mediation on the inevitability of scarcity, his *Essay on the Principle of Population* (1798).

44.   Tensions over food pricing ran high throughout the decade, but the bad harvests of 1799 and 1800 produced an especially black mood among the poor. Citing a popular rhyme from these years:

> Peace
> and Large Bread
> or
> a King without a head,

Emsley explains that ever-increasing taxes, inflation and yet more impressment made this period of dearth even more devastating than that of 1794–5 (*British Society*, 87). London saw three days of bread riots in September 1800, in which protesters coupled demands for managed food pricing with calls for a new government (Hone, 93).

45.   Brooks and Bloom also have seen the beggar's freedom as a kind of compensation for his hard life, though these critics have not focused on the limited nature of that independence. Edward Bostetter rather fixes on "The Old Cumberland Beggar" as disturbing evidence of Wordsworth's insensitivity toward the poor (55). Koch comes closest to my view when he states that "Freedom, however harsh and destitute, is a more humane existence than confinement in the factory/prison" (25).

In a related vein, Mary Jacobus argues that "the poem's attack on institutionalization implies an essentially humane respect for the individual" (*Tradition*, 182).

46.   Wordsworth's aversion to domestication is also notable in his refusal to contrast the unpleasantness of the workhouse with the joys of family life. Such images were common in contemporary poems such as Crabbe's "The Village," but as David Simpson points out, the individuals of "The Old Cumberland Beggar" can seem as isolated as the pauper they help (41).

47.   "Andrew Jones," another volume II addition to *Lyrical Ballads* in 1800, suggests just how fragile such customs can be. When a horseman less conscientious than that of "The Old Cumberland Beggar" throws to the ground some coins for a crippled vagrant, the title character has no reservations about claiming the money himself: "Quoth Andrew, 'Under half-a-crown, / What a man finds is all his own, / And so, my Friend, good day to you'" (28–30). Through this depiction of miserliness "Andrew Jones" also shows why official outrelief is necessary, while a workhouse system is not.

48.   The balance Wordsworth struggles to achieve did not always seem harmonious to his readers. In one much-quoted criticism of the poem, Charles Lamb commented that "… the instructions conveyed [in the poem] are too direct and like a lecture: they don't slide into

the mind of the reader, while he is imagining no such matter. An intelligent reader finds a sort of insult in being told, I will teach you how to think upon this subject" (*Selected Letters,* 51). As Lamb's rebellion against readerly coaching implies, Wordsworth allows his homeless protagonist and the villagers more autonomy than he does his readers or the maligned statesmen. The poem's exhortatory form is in keeping with the author's increasing interest in resolving or downplaying the kind of ambiguities that in the hands of statesmen or hostile locals can be turned against the vagrant.

49. In a representative assessment, Helen Darbishire's *Poet Wordsworth* maintains that "Tintern Abbey" is the first "full expression" of Wordsworth's genius (59–60). Patrick Campbell chronicles the historical progression of the poem's critical enshrinement (76–84).

50. Like the political activists of the 1790s, contestants in this dispute have been separated by a generational divide. Historicist treatments include James Chandler's *Wordsworth's Second Nature,* Marjorie Levinson's *Wordsworth's Great Period Poems,* and Kenneth Johnston's "The Politics of Tintern Abbey." For critiques of these interpretations, particularly Levinson's, see M. H. Abrams' "On Political Readings of *Lyrical Ballads,*" Helen Vendler's "'Tintern Abbey': Two Assaults," and Thomas McFarland's *William Wordsworth.*

51. Laura Quinney makes a related, if more general, point in linking the poem's discontinuous self to the motif of disappointment in eighteenth-century poetry. She observes that the weighty unintelligibility the poem complains under "describes a certain species of disappointment: the doubt of continuity, the dread of things happening to no particular purpose and experience proceeding without any kind of accumulation" (144).

52. In this regard, my analysis agrees with Regina Hewitt who sees "Tintern Abbey" as evidence of a new awareness of "the value of the country in promoting community" (79), confirming Wordsworth's shift since 1793 to a more sociological mode of poetic investigation.

53. Wordsworth's notes to these poems appear on the cited page numbers in Butler and Green's edition of *Lyrical Ballads.*

54. Most of the reforming organizations of the 1790s were based in London and events there, such as the 1795 bread riot that reportedly led to an assassination attempt on George III, prompted many of Pitt's measures. Once made law, repressive statutes were enforced most effectively against reformers living in the capital or its environs.

In addition, Wordsworth's identification of the city with cultural oppression accords with official hostility in London toward vagrants, the poet's chosen emblem of marginality. Throughout the eighteenth century, official antagonism toward the homeless had stemmed from the elites' desire to restrain the growth of the metropolis, especially its poor sections. Raymond Williams observes that the ruling classes sought economic benefits from practices like enclosure without taking responsibility for the dispossession and migration to cities that such practices created. "Poor people and vagrants, the casualties of a changing rural economy… were the explicit objects of exclusion from the developing city" (*Country and the City*, 145). Nicholas Rogers details eighteenth-century reforms in London policing of vagrancy that would be emulated by authorities elsewhere.

55. Wordsworth's use of this trope parallels his conflation in *The Prelude* of "inspiration" with actual physical perceptions of wind and of breathing. Cf. M. H. Abrams' "The Correspondent Breeze."

56. Initially, Wordsworth traveled with Hawkshead schoolfellow William Calvert, with whom he spent about a month on the Isle of Wight. Their subsequent tour of the mainland was interrupted by a carriage accident, after which the two men separated, Calvert continuing on horseback and Wordsworth walking on foot across Salisbury Plain and into northern Wales. How long he stayed there and where he went next are unknown; by December, he was back in Whitehaven (Gill, *Wordsworth*, 74–8). Johnston questions how much of this trip even occurred, suggesting instead that Wordsworth used the tour as a cover story to conceal a secret return to France (see *Hidden*, chapter 15).

57. This notion of memory has been previously associated more with *The Prelude* than "Tintern Abbey." For example, Karl Kroeber identifies Wordsworth's changeable memory as a fundamental component of his autobiographical aesthetic, since the spots of time "are narrative incidents, not epiphanies, and Wordsworth's memories of them follow historical sequence, undergoing modifications in time. This perhaps accounts for the reality which his personal reminiscences convey. We believe in Wordsworth's memories because he does not claim that they are unchanging; they, too, are vital" (*Romantic*, 22). Margery Sabin explicitly connects the pliancy of memory in *The Prelude* to the poem's larger arguments for philosophical and aesthetic liberty: "… the crucial point for Wordsworth is that memory does not confine the mind to the already finished round of emotional experience" (93). Sabin goes on the suggest that the flexibility of Wordsworth's memory distinguishes him from Rousseau, who prides himself on faithfully reproducing scenes from the past.

58. Mark Foster goes farther, arguing that the association of Dorothy with a home reflects Wordsworth's desire "to invest his intuitions with some of the substance of real property" (80).

59. For example, see John Barrell's "The uses of Dorothy" in *Poetry, language and politics* (137–67), Margaret Homans' *Bearing the Word* (120), and Marlon Ross' *The Masculine Contours of Desire* (109–10). While I largely agree with such criticisms of Wordsworth's initial presentation of his sister, this presentation changes in ways that are more empowering for her as the poem concludes.

60. It is interestingly when he views Dorothy, rather than the landscape, that the speaker comes closest to the late eighteenth-century interest in consuming beautiful objects. Many tourists could afford to visit the Wye, North Wales, and the Lake District because they profited from scientific and industrial advances helpful to farming and husbandry. The motives for picturesque appreciation grew out of "an improving agriculture and from trade" (Williams, *Country and the City*, 128), just

as the speaker here appreciates his sister because she embodies what he has had to lose to acquire abundant recompense.

61. Michael Vander Weele notes a literary tradition at work in this image as well, identifying in the architectural imagery of memory a line of allusion stretching back to Augustine's *Confessions*. He adds that the traditional figuration of memory as a home, palace, or cloister "is neither passive nor neutral. The images of memory do not only reflect the world but also act upon it" (17).

CHAPTER 4   SUSPICIOUS LIVES: DELINQUENCY IN THE 1802 POEMS

1. Sir Francis Burdett's 1802 Middlesex campaign for Parliament illustrates the changed tactics of reformers. Avoiding mention of France, Burdett championed individual rights he argued were guaranteed by the British constitution, which allowed the people peacefully to replace a tyrannical administration. Although opponents called him a Jacobin, Burdett won in 1802 and in 1803, when charges of fraud led to a second election for the same seat. His victory showed how the days of radical plans for protest and even insurrection were giving way to "legitimate" (i.e. legal, parliamentary) means for changing the government (Hone, 145).

2. David Philips calls the 1792 law "a significant break" with the past, considerably expanding the scope of earlier efforts at professional policing such as the Bow Street Runners. He attributes its surprisingly smooth passage through Parliament to "the atmosphere of fear and repression generated in England in reaction to the French Revolution and the spread of 'Jacobin' ideas among the English lower orders" (169).

3. Philips notes that although the 1792 bill was to have expired at the end of three years, "most people were well aware that the Act was more than a temporary experiment. It represented a decision by an important section of the governing class that the old system of unpaid JP and parish constable would no longer serve the purpose of keeping the peace in the metropolis. And as other towns grew, with the growth of industry and commerce, and experienced similar problems to London's, so the principle would be extended to them" (171).

4. Colquhoun uses the term police in the older sense of the general maintenance of community and order as well as in the more modern sense of a body of paid government enforcers of the law.

5. The shift from reaction to prevention in nineteenth-century policing also explains what Foucault has called the garrulity of criminological discourse, a repetitious character stemming from the new desire to transform an individual, as well as punish a crime (*Power/Knowledge*, 47).

6. "Alice Fell" would be written on 12 and 13 March 1802, and "Beggars" would follow immediately thereafter on 13 and 14 March; see Curtis's edition of the 1807 *Poems* (113, 120).

7.   For example, Harrison explains the man's pride at the woman's begging through a nostalgia for a time when charity strengthened the bonds between rich and poor (150).

8.   For a view of Alice's grief as a refuge from, rather than a call to, imagination, see Geoffrey Hartman (143).

9.   This image becomes even more sinister in a later revision, which identifies the cloak with those "Upon a murderer's gibbet hung" (MS 42, p. 121). The metaphoric death of the scarecrow simile is supplanted by the literal one of the hanged killer, and the scarecrow's role of frightening away destructive birds becomes the murderer's doom in serving as an example of the dangers of violent criminality.

10.   David Simpson claims that the speaker's desire to rectify the source of Alice's grief, the loss of her cloak, argues for the importance of giving necessities like food and clothing for the indigent, whether or not they fit middle-class criteria for the "deserving" poor. Thus, Alice's exact relation to Durham and other "real circumstances of the child's life" become irrelevant to his act of kindness (*Historical Imagination*, 178).

11.   Bialostosky also argues that the speaker's final claim is conjecture (*Making Tales*, 139); for an opposing view, see Simpson, *Historical Imagination* (223n.).

12.   Sarah Goodwin also links Alice's enigmatic grief to incipient crime, specifically the most common female offense of prostitution. Regarding the excessive character of Alice's anguish, Goodwin comments that "it expresses what cannot be explained away. Poverty, here, is not a simple problem to be solved by cash. Instead, it represents a state of mind – one that the poet feels himself at times to have shared" (167). For Goodwin, the burdens of Alice's poverty express Wordsworth's anxieties over the prospects of his illegitimate 10-year-old daughter, Caroline, whose French mother had been able to contact him again as a result of the Peace of Amiens.

13.   The innkeeper, of course, might well be one of those officials, a petty constable for example, but the speaker does not identify him as such.

14.   I am using the second version of "Beggars" in Curtis' edition on p. 113. Derived from DC MS. 41, this text seems closest to the original 1802 version of the poem.

15.   For Dorothy Wordsworth's account, see entry for 10 June 1800, *Journals* (47).

16.   Robin Jervis points out that the Wordsworths always asked for beggars' stories before relieving them with bread or alms, making the vagrant's narrative into a kind of commodity. In her anecdote about the beggar boys, "What Dorothy seems not to like ... on the evidence of this passage, is *lies* from mendicant children, since this smacks of dishonest 'trading'" (Jervis, "Wordsworth", 206). While Jervis does not address the fact that the speaker of "Beggars" seems immune to such considerations, he does argue that William converts Dorothy's bad trade into a good one by making the story into a poem.

17.   Simpson finds in the poem a nostalgia for a prelapsarian world in which judgment itself is in abeyance (*Historical Imagination*, 176–7).

I am making a somewhat different point, arguing that the poem simultaneously wants to argue for the ability to judge and for the power to apply that ability only sporadically.

18. Where I emphasize the speaker's psychology, Frosch explains the poem's lack of resolution through its debt to Dorothy Wordsworth's fact-based journals. As a genre, the journals' treatment of encounters with vagrants adheres more closely to the protocols of traditional vagrant examination, as opposed to the new notion of "suspected" criminals pioneered by the Middlesex Justice Bill. Dorothy's oft-noted emphasis on quotidian details and respect for description of materials in and of itself works in opposition to the new, broader objectives outlined for magistrates and constables. In composing "Beggars," a poem he originally had trouble finishing because he "could not escape" Dorothy's journal account, William "recoiled by behaving humbly, by being faithful to the text, by demonstrating his love for nature that he did need and did not want to offend" (Frosch, 629).

19. To some extent, this line of argument has been anticipated by critics who see the "Resolution and Independence" as an expression of Wordsworth's insecurities about entering the literary marketplace, for example see Kurt Heinzelman, *The Economics of the Imagination* (212–15), and Charles Rzepka, "A Gift that Complicates Employ: Poetry and Poverty in 'Resolution and Independence.'" Extending on such concerns, Gary Harrison articulates the most persuasive materialist reading of the poem to date. Harrison identifies the leech-gatherer with the double heritage of the minstrel as honorable pauper and liminal vagabond. This liminality in turn endows the old man with moral authority to inculcate the virtues of hard work and independence even as his hardships justify the giving of charity. In Harrison's view, Wordsworth concludes by appropriating for himself this same "dubious freedom" (138).

20. The original old man, in fact, was on his way to buy some religious texts to sell; gathering leeches was only one of the activities by which he earned money. See Dorothy Wordsworth's account of the original encounter on 3 October 1800 in her *Journals* (63).

21. Gene Ruoff calls attention to the connection between the "torturous indirection" of the similes and their origins in the poet's disturbed mind, adding that "Language loses its transparency in an extended simile of this sort, as the strenuous attempt to convey the importance and meaning of the old man ends up calling attention primarily to the actions of the poet's mind" (152). It is precisely such transparency, in both observation and the language used to describe it, that is assumed by professional models of law enforcement. The speaker's difficulties consequently challenge the legitimacy of those models.

22. Schoenfield's detailed study goes on to show how Wordsworth, despite his obvious distaste for legal professionalism in this instance, was in fact deeply influenced by his father's and brother's profession, selectively employing legal metaphors and themes even as he distanced himself from the lawyer's practice. For example, Schoenfield, like Goldberg, finds the preface to *Lyrical Ballads* to be a professional

manifesto that reflects the law's authority to define the literary mar-
ketplace as well as the author's cultural prestige and economic rights.
Specifically, he argues that the preface defines the relation between
reader and writer as a kind of legal contract whose provisions
exclude the critics, most of whom, Schoenfield points out, were
themselves lawyers (120–35). The preface's disdain for "specialized
language" in favor of the language of men seems to eschew profes-
sionalism. Yet since the reader can only access that quotidian
language through "the mediated experience of Wordsworth,"
Schoenfield argues, this is only partly true (75).

23.   By the end of the eighteenth century, the word leech had already
      begun to mean "one 'who sticks' to another for the purpose of
      getting gain out of him"; the OED locates the first instance of this
      usage in Cowper's *The Task* (1784).

24.   Cheryl Wanko remarks that the speaker's entire pose of depending
      on others for his subsistence is leech-like, as is his seeking out the old
      man not to relieve the vagrant's distress but to seek help himself:
      "Even though leeches are scarce, the Leech-gatherer has managed to
      find one" (60).

25.   Clifford Siskin, in contrast, argues that the leech-gatherer's eloquent
      speech, narrow skills and ability "to stick to what he does and
      knows" make the old man "the embodiment of his speciality" (36). In
      concluding by internalizing the leech-gatherer as a model of literary
      professionalization, Wordsworth's speaker can stave off fears of
      poetic madness. For my view of the old man as the antithesis of a
      professional, see above.

CHAPTER 5   ERRANT THOUGHTS AND SOCIAL CRIMES IN *THE PRELUDE*

1.   All quotations from the 1805 *Prelude* are taken from Mark Reed's
      edition, Cornell University Press.

2.   For the dating of MS.JJ, see *The Prelude 1799, 1805, 1850*, p. 485; cf.
      The Prelude, 1798–1799, ed. Stephen Parrish, pp. 3, 8–9. Quotation of
      MS.JJ comes from Parrish's reading text, pp. 123–30.

3.   In another view of MS.JJ's opening, Paul Magnuson argues that the
      poet "invokes childhood to be tempered, to be steadied" (187), a
      notion Magnuson traces to Coleridge's "Frost at Midnight."

4.   Roe takes this view about as far as it can go. Deciphering the
      passage's echoes of *Macbeth*, he emphasizes the child's guilt above all,
      and what he perceives as its anticipation of the poet's guilt over the
      excesses of the French Revolution (*Politics* 152).

5.   Susan Wolfson identifies this physical ambiguity with rhetorical qual-
      ities: "The boy hangs, ambiguously sustained or threatened by the
      winds of this suddenly alien border world, even as Wordsworth's
      poetry ambiguously suspends the *whats* of the last three lines
      between awed exclamation and troubled inquiry" (*Questioning*

Presence, 158). For Paul de Man, "The Boy of Winander," also composed at Goslar, displays similar tensions. The lyrics's use of the word "hang," in particular, shows how spatial and rhetorical ambiguities reflect the precarious situation of the human mind, "above an earth, the stability of which it cannot participate in, and beneath a heaven that has rejected it" (54).

6. In the final version of the 1799 *Prelude*, part one, only the card-playing scene is set indoors. This scene probably was drafted in late November or December 1799. The scarcity of portraits of domestic life continues into part two, where not a single distinct memory concerns his life at Cockermouth or the Hawkshead home where Wordsworth boarded.

7. The Wordsworths left Hamburg for Goslar only to exchange fraud for intense isolation. Wordsworth could not afford lodging with a family he and Dorothy could learn German from, and their command of the language was never sure. In a letter to Coleridge, Wordsworth connected such solitude with the introspection characteristic of MS.JJ – "As I have had no books, I have been obliged to write in self-defence" (*Early Years*, 236).

    The Wordsworths' cultural dislocation was extreme. Symptomatically, the much-awaited conversation with the poet Klopstock, which had to take place in French, revealed gaping differences in taste between English and German. This disassociation from German values, language, and customs continued throughout the visit (Moorman, 411–15). By February 1799, Dorothy was still unable to decipher consistently the behavior around her. She writes of

    > the extreme folly of people who draw conclusions respecting national character from the narrow limits of common observation. We have been much with German hosts and hostesses and notwithstanding the supposed identifying tendency of national manners ... these persons appeared in every respects as if made in contrast to each other.
    >
    > (Quoted in Moorman, 431)

    The detachment and wandering in MS.JJ accords with this experience. The "social" scenes of part one, involving ice-skating and card-playing, were only added near the end of the 1799 poem's composition, when the poet and his sister had arranged to rent Dove Cottage in Grasmere.

8. For example, 23 Geo. III, c. 88 (1782–3) stipulates that "'divers ill-disposed Persons' found in possession of the tools of the house-breaking trade are to be arrested as vagabonds." Even if such implements were lacking, any suspicious-looking loiterer found about a person's grounds or home was liable to arrest (quoted in Ribton-Turner, 209). The lengthy list of spaces, from houses to enclosed gardens, protected under this act shows a desire to safeguard an entire domestic sphere that vagrancy and housebreaking were perceived to threaten.

9. The statute asserts that "idle and disorderly Persons frequently assemble ... to support and assist each other in the Destruction of Game in the Night, and are, if interrupted, guilty of great Violence ... and to the Encouragement of Idleness and Immorality: and such Practices are found by Experience to lead to the Commission of Crimes and Felonies" (*Collection of the Public General Statutes*, 421). The act authorized the punishment of two or more people as vagabonds who are found in "any Forest, Chase, Park, Wood, Plantation, Paddock, Field, Meadow, or other open or inclosed Ground, in the Night ... having any Gun, Net, (or) Engine" to kill game (421–2).

10. The poacher's tools were traditionally not guns, effective in killing but also in drawing unwanted attention, but rather nets and snares. "The simple wire snare, pegged in the ground one night, (was) easily checked for hares or rabbits on later evenings" (Hay, "poaching," 194).

11. Like the vagrancy acts, the game laws may have been partly intended to force the poor into exclusive dependence on a wage-based economy for survival, McLynn has argued (217). This theory remains controversial; for a summary of its problems, see Joanna Innes and John Styles, "The Crime Wave."

    Douglas Hay offers a view of poaching's attractions that goes beyond economics. Like their betters, the Georgian poor may have hunted in part for simple enjoyment. "The excitement of snaring hares, eluding keepers and shooting deer were very real pleasures ... the cottagers took pride in their exploits. Although it was risking a £10 fine (and therefore a year in gaol, for few could pay it), some men kept hidden in their cottages the heads and antlers of the deer they had felled, trophies of the chase. The convictions of those caught are the only direct evidence the historian has of a rich sporting tradition of thousands of working men on Cannock during a whole century" ("Poaching," 201–2). Cf. Munsche (5–6, 63).

12. For summaries of these diverse responses, see McLynn (210), Munsche (118–19).

13. Virtual pitched battles between deer-stealers and gamekeepers in the crown forest of Windsor focused Walpole's attention on poaching. Official anxiety over armed "blacks" also owed much to ministerial panic over the discovery of Jacobite conspiracies in 1722. These involved plans for an uprising and the assassination of the king. "These plots broke surface in May and June 1722 and the next twelve months saw an unrelenting pressure upon Papists and Nonjurors; the harassment of any oppositional press; the suspension of habeas corpus; new fines and new oaths of loyalty aimed primarily at Catholics ..." (Thompson, *Whigs*, 67–8).

    Government agents infiltrated gangs of "blacks" to discover if they were, in fact, disguised Jacobites; see Styles, "Criminal Records," and Cruickshanks and Erskine-Hill. In times of national upheaval groups like the "blacks," acting in a contested social space which some considered criminal and others just, drew the government's suspicions with a magnetic force. Walpole's spies arrested several Windsor poachers, allaying the government's anxiety by reclassifying men engaged in poaching activities as traitors. Its unpopularity meant that the Black Act was enforced in the eighteenth century only when "the national interest was brought into the picture, as when Walpole (dubbed) the Blacks Jacobites" (McLynn, 209).

14. Eighteenth-century game laws concerned mostly birds, who since they flew across property lines were not technically owned by the person on whose land they were found. Deer, in contrast, by the early eighteenth century increasingly were raised and lived in fenced parks. They were considered the property of the park's owner. The Black Act was so severe because the man illegally killing deer on another's land was a thief; killing a partridge in the same manner, by contrast, was a breach of privilege.

15. Munsche notes the passage of this legislation, as does Simon Schama. The assembly's action was spurred by game riots throughout northern France during March 1789. Angry peasants killed the birds, hares, and deer that were destroying their crops but traditionally could be hunted only by the aristocracy. Like the Georgians, Schama sees in the disturbances a sign for the future course of the revolution: "The game riots announced a movement from verbal complaint to violent action" (323).

16. For the likely dates of composition for the sports of time, see Parrish's introduction to the Cornell edition of the 1799 poem (20–1); remaining quotations from the 1799 *Prelude* come from Parrish's final reading text from the poem, based on MSS.U and V.

17. David Ellis comments on the paralyzed passivity of the speaker at various points in this episode, despite later claims transforming it into a source of aesthetic energy (126–7).

18. In a psychoanalytic reading of this episode, Richard Onorato also identifies James as a father figure, but he reads the loss of Wordsworth's mother (here, the girl with the pitcher) as the central subtext of the passage. Onorato assigns no symbolic value to the gibbet, arguing that "a large piece of moldering farm equipment that was strange to the child might have frightened him as much" (213).

David Collings offers a more complex but related interpretation in chapter 5 of *Wordsworthian Errancies*. He extends the 1799 *Prelude's* criminal interest in departing from the proper path to a departure from literary expectations about autobiography. In Wordsworth's struggle to reconcile deviance with a poem about artistic vocation, departures from proper development become evidence of the writer's unique poetic abilities. By featuring a wife-murderer, a double for Othello, the first spot of time shows the cost of patriarchy's symbolic order, particularly as it is encoded in traditional, male-centered narratives. These "violate the maternal body" or in larger terms show how "culture … violates nature" (143).

19. The incident probably refers to the death of James Jackson, schoolmaster at a nearby village, who drowned while bathing in Esthwaite Water on 18 June 1779 (Norton edn., 8n.).

20. Gayatri Chakravorty Spivak notes that the scene also incorporates elements of the Oedipus story. Onorato acknowledges that this episode suggests that the bond between father and son, "however beautiful described, was a burdensome fixation Wordsworth unconsciously wished to break" (254).
21. The previous suspension was in December 1798, where the Commons vote was an overwhelming 96 to 6 (the Foxites had ceased to attend Parliament by this time) (Hone, 123).
22. The disjunction between Wordsworth's genius and his rustic subjects would be criticized by reviewers from Francis Jeffrey to Lord Byron. Hazlitt also censures Wordsworth for his "unaccountable mixture of seeming simplicity and real abstruseness" (132).
23. Theoretically, the ability to make such superfine distinctions is the hallmark of the boy's development into a poet-philosopher. As he matures, the child develops

> ... silent inobtrusive sympathies,
> And gentle agitations of the mind
> From manifold distinctions, difference
> Perceived in things where to the common eye
> No difference is, and hence, from the same source,
> Sublimer joy.

$$(2.346-51)$$

The 1799 *Prelude* persistently shows how difficult it is to articulate such distinctions.

24. Jonathan Wordsworth's "The Five-Book *Prelude* of Early Spring 1804" describes this poem and how it "was abandoned very suddenly ca. 10 March 1804" (1).
25. Of his initial passion on Britain's declaration of war in 1793, the narrator states, "All else was progress on the self-same path," but "this, a stride at once / Into another region" (X.238; 240–1). By the next book, however, he takes his recovery from revolutionary passion for granted:

> I had felt
> Too forcibly, too early in my life,
> Visitings of imaginative power
> For this too last: I shook the habit off. ...

$$(XI.253)$$

26. For Wordsworth's views on the makeup and marketing of the second edition of *Lyrical Ballads*, which did not spare Coleridge's feelings, see Gill (*Wordsworth*, 185–7) and Johnston (*Hidden*, 741–3). Kurt Heinzelman describes how the Wordsworths, especially after William's marriage, viewed Dove Cottage as their own domestic space. Unlike at Alfoxden or Racedown, the family made improve-

ments in the grounds and sought to create there a household in the Georgic tradition, which focused on creative labor shared by both sexes ("Cult," 52–60).

27. Ann Hone reminds us that "Any assessment of the changed tempo and tone of the years 1803–5 must take into account the nature of the war which was resumed with France in May 1803. It was a patriotic war. The need to defend Britain and to contain the 'Corsican Tyrant' were national preoccupations" (138). Emsley relates how a gentleman traveling through Wales in 1803 barely escaped arrest by officials believing he was Napoleon, and how informers advised the Home Office of "men travelling and even sketching, probably quite innocently, on the coasts" (*British Society*, 113).

28. After the early March decision to expand the poem into 13 books, the 1805 IV and V were finished by 18 March. By April, the poet was working on 1805 VI (J. Wordsworth, "Five-Book *Prelude*," 24). Pitt became prime minister again in May 1804, but support for his return to power had been building in Parliament since war was declared almost a year before (Owen, 267). It is a suggestive coincidence that Wordsworth decided to "introduce politics to the poem for the first time" (J. Wordsworth, 24) in March, when it was increasingly apparent that Pitt would return to leadership. Late March to mid-June 1804 perhaps saw composition of 1805 books VII (including the blind beggar) through X, as well as XII (Reed, *Middle*, 13–14).

   Books XI–XIII, mostly put together in late 1804 and the spring of 1805, incorporate previously composed material, e.g. the spots of time, the ascent of Snowdon, but frequently alter the original import of such episodes either by adding new lines or changing a scene's context.

29. John Alban Finch establishes the date of the preamble (1–9). In "The Five-Book *Prelude*," Jonathan Wordsworth argues that the post-preamble 1805 I.551–27 likely dates from January 1804 ("Five," 8n.); however, Reed believes the lines could have been composed any time from mid-April 1801 to the spring of 1804 (*Thirteen-Book Prelude*, 8–10).

30. The Norton editors acknowledge this difficulty, but say that there is a "very strong implication" that the dedication is to poetry (142n.).

31. Wordsworth's dislike of gossip in all its forms is well illustrated by a poem composed sometime between 1802 and 1804, "Personal Talk." Responding to those who claim that stories about friends and neighbors, or "fits of sprightly malice do but bribe / The languid mind into activity" (17–18), the speaker argues that great literature performs the same function without questionable moral effects. For the poem's text, see Curtis' edition of *Poem, in Two Volumes*.

32. The role of movement in such vitality is reinforced in book V, where schoolboys play near the boy of Winander's grave. In an image out of *An Evening Walk*, the village church is "forgetful of this boy" as well as the other graves nearby (V.426). She hears instead "the gladsome sounds / That, from the rural school

ascending, play / Beneath her and about her" (V.429–31). This energy is allied with a pointed mixture of moral imperfections and virtues. The boys are

> not too wise,
> Too learned, or too good, but wanton, fresh,
> And bandied up and down by love and hate;
> Fierce, moody, patient, venturous, modest, shy. ...

(V.436–9)

Similarly, for the poet, "forgers of lawless tales" (V.548), writers about daring bandits and thieves, are essential to the education of a creative soul.

33. This dating of the discharged soldier episode comes from Beth Darlington's "Two Early Texts: 'A Night Piece' and 'The Discharged Soldier'" (425). For legislation on the desertion problem, see Lambert's *House of Commons Sessional papers of the Eighteenth Century*, vol. 103 (139–60).

34. Michael Duffy lucidly explains British objectives in the West Indian campaigns of the 1790s, as well as the impact of the climate and contagions on Europeans who had no immunity, were frequently malnourished, and were not overly concerned with hygiene (327–49).

35. While acknowledging complexity in the motives behind Wordsworth's enlistment, Liu affirms that it would be interpreted as clearly patriotic (*Wordsworth*, 23, 432, 632n.). Moorman and Johnston also explain this gesture through patriotism. Both biographers bring Wordsworth's 1803 invasion sonnets into their argument for Wordsworth's loyalism, but even here the evidence is mixed. The published sonnet "Anticipation. October 1803" imagines a foiled French invasion with exhilaration. Yet the unpublished "Lines on the Expected Invasion 1803" confers respectability on those hesitant to fight out of "no discreditable fear," "Uncertain what to choose and how to steer" (10, 12). In a letter of 9 October 1803, Dorothy Wordsworth adumbrates her brother's decision to enlist by referring not to his love of England but his hatred of imperial France (*Early Years*, 403).

36. Robin Jervis senses the poem's continuing deferral of resolution when he argues for its formal privileging of sequence over synthesis, a choice he attributes to Book VI's origins in the walking tour (*Romantic* 122).

37. Roe's inability to answer this question weakens his argument that the beggar's extraordinary impact is a tacit "acknowledgment [of] the ineffectuality of [Wordsworth's] own revolutionary idealism in looking for an end to such poverty" ("Revising," 91–2).

38. William Galperin supplements this view by suggesting this encounter disturbs the poet's cherished notion that his gifts and vocation entitle him to a transcendental exemption from such limitations. Involvement in the spectacle of London cures the narrator, even if only temporarily, of his own narcissism (124–7).

39. For a related reading, see David Simpson, who calls Wordsworth's London a "semiotic inferno" where "the linguistic metaphor [is] used to suggest exhaustion and overdetermination, the absence of meaning through the very oversupply of possible meanings" (*Irony*, 64).

40. Geraldine Friedman, by contrast, sees the social and representational frame the beggar is situated within as helpfully stabilizing, rather than oppressive, to Wordsworth. Seeing in the sightless beggar the one who cannot be seduced by the semiotic chaos of the city, Friedman argues that the vagrant represents the possibility of representation cleansed of the deforming, theatrical potential that Burke identifies with the French Revolution (44 –63).

   Burke's description of the French Revolution in 1790 certainly resembles Wordsworth's assessment of London after recalling the blind beggar: "Every thing seems out of nature in this strange chaos of levity and ferocity … . In viewing this monstrous tragi-comic scene, the most opposite passions necessarily succeed, and sometimes mix with each other in the mind; alternate contempt and indignation; alternate laughter and tears; alternate scorn and horror" (92–3).

41. The importance of Lake District subsistence life for the poet is discussed at length by Michael Friedman in *The Making of a Tory Humanist*.

42. Wordsworth's attitude in *The Prelude* toward "The Thorn" is complicated by his mention of it again in the closing lines of book XIII. Again, he seems to invoke the poem to mock "her who sate / In misery near the miserable thorn" (XIII.402–3). Yet, it is one of the only two Wordsworth poems from the Alfoxden days invoked to remind Coleridge of "All which then we were" (XIII.405), indicating it represented a kind of apex of their collaborative influence upon one another.

43. Theresa Kelley convincingly explains this process by reference to a general tendency in *The Prelude* to encase images or experiences of the sublime within a socializing, normative notion of the beautiful. Like the discharged soldier, Kelley argues, the vagrants of book XII both "evoke fear and awe, responses traditionally allied to the sublime" (127). As she points out, though, in book XII such fear can be contained simply by talking to and being friendly with the homeless. Kelley's idea of the Wordsworthian sublime as a mode that consistently evades easy classification or accurate linguistic representation complements my interest in *The Prelude*.

44. John Hodgson makes much the same point, though he does not see the revolutionary experience of *The Prelude* as the construct that I do. Experiences of the French Revolution facilitate Wordsworth's "poetic self-definition" and permeate scenes lacking overt political content, such as the poet's horseback ride on the Levens sands (Hodgson, 59). The poem "absorbs the French Revolution into the poetry of Wordsworth's private history only to represent that revolution everywhere" (62–3).

45. See Johnston's *Wordsworth and the Recluse* (180).

46. Spivak extends the reasoning of the many critics who have related the episode to Wordsworths's liaison with Annette Vallon. Spivak suggests that the poet's acknowledgment of paternity and mental disorder is managed by being thrust upon Vaudracour. Coleridge then becomes the poet's new alter ego, and Dorothy Wordsworth a mediating agent to an empowering androgyny. By ultimately shutting out both Annette Vallon (Julia) and Dorothy, Wordsworth allies himself with what Spivak identifies as the political and sexual program of the Romantic canon. See Richard Freadman and Seumas Miller for a critique of Spivak's assumptions and method.

47. James Heffernan perceptively explains this juxtaposition by casting Beaupuy as the perfect mediator, in Wordsworth's eyes, between past and present, chivalry and revolutionary fervor. Heffernan notes how here again the narrative smooths over problems that undermine belief in the poem's official story. For all his high aims, Beaupuy ultimately comes across as an ineffective dreamer. In his encounter with the hungry girl leading a cow along the roadside, a damsel in distress in the terms of romance, this latter-day knight can only comment on her condition to a third person. His words "have no practical effect on the starving girl, who gets absolutely nothing, not even a word of sympathy, from the benevolent Beaupuy" (53).

48. Burke describes English liberty, circumscribed by obligations to the past, in similar terms. The nation's freedom "has a pedigree and illustrating ancestors. It has its bearings and its ensigns armorial. It has its gallery of portraits; its monumental inscriptions; its record, evidences, and titles" (121).

49. "Home at Grasmere" tangles with this problem at length, juggling a desire to be a part of a community with fears about the way such involvement affects creativity. The narrator embraces his chosen retreat after years of wandering "Alone and devious" (6), and deifies the community as

> A termination and a last retreat,
> A Centre, come from whereso'er you will,
> A Whole without dependence or defect,
> Made for itself and happy in itself,
> Perfect Contentment, Unity entire.

> (147–51)

This same contentedness threatens to end not just vagrant life but the energy it produces. The poet now exists "Without desire in full complacency," and "entertained as in a placid sleep" (306, 308) a complacent morbidity hardly conducive to writing the *Recluse*, which "Home at Grasmere" was to begin. The poem only employs a vocabulary of creativity and desire when the narrator distances himself from the village he chooses as his home. For example, see his identification with wandering animals like migratory birds and his affirmation that

"Possessions have I that are solely mine, / Something within which yet is shared by none" (686–7). These citations come from the Cornell Wordsworth edition of "Home at Grasmere," MS.D, in the Cornell edition edited by Beth Darlington.

50. McFarland has said of the poet at Alfoxden and after that he was "impelled toward but at the same time retreating from both isolation and community" (*Romanticism*, 152). The result was Wordsworth's psychological investment in a "significant group," including his sister and brother John, Mary and Sara Hutchinson, and Coleridge, which was small in number but strong in attachment. Affiliation with the group "was by its very fact a turning away from undifferentiated social concern" (152).

51. Although his assumptions are almost the reverse of Theresa Kelley's, David Ellis suggests other considerations making the ascent a confusing model for imaginative independence. It is described to us by someone "whose own imagination (*as the representation defines it*) is virtually in abeyance" (Ellis, 147). That is, the cloudscape is described in a straightforward manner, as it actually appeared visually, and presumably as it was viewed by Wordsworth's companions on that night. The passage is comparatively free of the imaginative language that dominates an episode like the Simplon Pass in book VI. The notion that such power alone is true liberty is called into question by the fact that the narrator, before such a prospect, is an essentially passive spectator.

Bibliography

Abrams, M. H. "The Correspondent Breeze: A Romantic Metaphor." *English Romantic Poets: Modern Essays in Criticism*. Ed. M. H. Abrams. London: Oxford UP, 1960, 37–54.

—— "On Political Readings of *Lyrical Ballads.*" *Romantic Revolutions: Criticism and Theory*. Eds Kenneth R. Johnston et al. Bloomington: Indiana UP, 1990, 320–49.

Adams, Thomas McStay. *Bureaucrats and Beggars: French Social Policy in the Age of Enlightenment*. New York: Oxford UP, 1990.

Althusser, Louis. "Ideology and Ideological State Apparatuses (Notes towards an Investigation)." *Lenin and Philosophy and Other Essays*. Trans. Ben Brewster. London: New Left, 1971, 123–73.

Ariès, Philippe. *Centuries of Childhood: A Social History of Family Life*. Trans. Robert Baldick. New York: Vintage, 1962.

Averill, James. *Wordsworth and the Poetry of Human Suffering*. Ithaca, NY: Cornell UP, 1980.

Balmori, Diana and Margaret Morton. *Transitory Gardens, Uprooted Lives*. New Haven, CT: Yale UP, 1993.

Barrell, John. *Poetry, Language, and Politics*. Manchester: Manchester UP, 1988.

Beattie, J. M. *Crime and the Courts in England 1660–1800*. Oxford: Clarendon, 1986.

Beier, A. L. *Masterless Men: The Vagrancy Problem in England 1560–1640*. New York: Methuen, 1985.

—— *The Problem of the Poor in Tudor and Early Stuart England*. New York: Methuen, 1983.

Bewell, Alan. *Wordsworth and the Enlightenment: Nature, Man and Society in the Experimental Poetry*. New Haven, CT: Yale UP, 1989.

Bialostosky, Don H. *Making Tales: The Poetics of Wordsworth's Narrative Experiments*. Chicago: U of Chicago P, 1984.

—— *Wordsworth, dialogics, and the practice of criticism*. Cambridge: Cambridge UP, 1992.

Blackstone, William. *Commentaries on the Laws of England*, 1765, 4 vols. Birmingham, AL: Legal Classics Library, 1983.

Blake, William. *Songs of Innocence and Experience*. Ed. Andrew Lincoln. Blake's Illuminated Books 2. Princeton, NJ: William Blake Trust/ Princeton UP, 1991.

Blau, Joel. *The Visible Poor: Homelessness in the United States*. New York: Oxford UP, 1992.

Bloom, Harold. *The Visionary Company: A Reading of English Romantic Poetry*. New York: Doubleday, 1961.

Bostetter, Edward. *The Romantic Ventriloquists: Wordsworth, Coleridge, Keats, Shelley, Byron*. Seattle: U of Washington P, 1975.

Bouch, C. M. L. and G. P. Jones. *A Short Economic and Social History of the Lake Counties, 1500–1800*. Manchester: Manchester UP, 1961.

Brooks, Cleanth. "Wordsworth and Human Suffering: Notes on Two Early Poems." *From Sensibility to Romanticism: Essays Presented to Frederick A. Pottle*. Eds Frederick W. Hilles and Harold Bloom. New York: Oxford UP, 1965, 373–87.

Burke, Edmund. *Reflections on the Revolution in France*, 1790. Ed. Conor Cruise O'Brien. Harmondsworth: Penguin, 1987.

Burn, Richard. *The History of the Poor Laws: with Observations*. London, 1764.

Burt, Martha R. *Over the Edge: the Growth of Homelessness in the 1980s*. New York: Russell Sage Foundation, 1992.

Campbell, Patrick. *The Lyrical Ballads of Wordsworth and Coleridge: Critical Perspectives*. London: Macmillan, 1991.

Carroll, William C. "'The Nursery of Beggary': Enclosure, Vagrancy, and Sedition in the Tudor-Stuart Period." *Enclosure Acts: Sexuality, Property and Culture in Early Modern England*. Ed. Richard Burt and John Michael Archer. Ithaca: Cornell UP, 1994. 34–47.

Chambliss, William J. "A Sociological Analysis of the Law of Vagrancy." *Social Problems* 12 (1964): 67–77.

Chandler, James. *Wordsworth's Second Nature: A Study of the Poetry and Politics*. Chicago: U of Chicago P, 1984.

Christian, Edward. *Charges delivered to grand juries in the Isle of Ely, upon libels, vagrants, criminal law, religion, rebellious assemblies, &c*. London, 1819.

—— *A Treatise on the Game Laws*. London, 1817.

Christie, Ian. "Conservatism and Stability in British Society." *Philp*, 169–87.

Cobban, Alfred. *The Social Interpretation of the French Revolution*. Cambridge: Cambridge UP, 1964.

Coleridge, Samuel Taylor. *Biographia Literaria*. Eds James Engall and W. Jackson Bate. Princeton, NJ: Princeton UP, 1983.

—— *Collected Letters of Samuel Taylor Coleridge*. Ed. Earl Leslie Griggs. Vol. 1. Oxford: Clarendon, 1956.

—— *The Notebooks of Samuel Taylor Coleridge*. Ed. Kathleen Coburn. Vol. 1, 1794–1804. New York: Pantheon, 1957.

A Collection of the Public General Statutes, passed in the Thirty-ninth and Fortieth Years of the Reign of his Majesty King George III. London, 1800.

Collings, David. *Wordsworthian Errancies: The Poetics of Cultural Dismemberment*. Baltimore, MD: Johns Hopkins UP, 1994.

Colquhoun, Patrick. *A Treatise on Indigence*. London, 1806.

Cookson, J. E. "The English Volunteer Movement of the French Wars, 1793–1815: Some Contexts." *The Historical Journal* 32.4 (1989): 867–91.

—— *The Friends of Peace: Anti-War Liberalism in England, 1793–1815*. New York: Cambridge UP, 1982.

Cowper, William. *Poetical Works*. Ed. H. S. Milford. 4th edn rev. by Norma Russell. New York: Oxford UP, 1967.

Cruickshanks, Eveline and Howard Erskine-Hill. "The Waltham Black Act and Jacobitism." *Journal of British Studies* 24 (July 1985): 358–65.

Curtis, Jared, ed. *The Fenwick Notes of William Wordsworth*. London: Bristol Classic, 1993.

Darbishire, Helen. *The Poet Wordsworth*. Oxford: Clarendon, 1966.

Darlington, Beth. "Two Early Texts: 'A Night Piece' and 'The Discharged Soldier.'" *Bicentenary Wordsworth Studies*. Ed. Jonathan Wordsworth. Ithaca, NY: Cornell UP, 1970, 425–48.

De Man, Paul. "Wordsworth and Hölderlin." *The Rhetoric of Romanticism*. New York: Columbia UP, 1984. 47–65.

DeSelincourt, Ernest, ed. *The Letters of William and Dorothy Wordworth*. Vol. 1: *The Early Years 1787–1805*, 2nd edn rev. Chester L. Shaver. Oxford: Clarendon, 1967.

Doyle, William. *Origins of the French Revolution*, 2nd edn. Oxford: UP, 1988.

Duffy, Michael. *Soldiers, Sugar, and Seapower: The British Expeditions to the West Indies and the War with Revolutionary France*. Oxford: Clarendon, 1987.

Eaglestone, A. J. "Wordsworth, Coleridge and the Spy." *Coleridge: Studies by Several Hands on the Hundredth Anniversary of his Death*. Eds E. Blunden and E. L. Griggs. London: Constable, 1934, 73–87.

Eagleton, Terry. *Ideology: An Introduction*. New York: Verso, 1991.

Eastwood, David. "Patriotism and the English state in the 1790s." Philp, 146–68.

Elliott, Marianne. *Partners in Revolution: The United Irishmen and France*. New Haven, CT: Yale UP, 1982.

Ellis, David. *Wordsworth, Freud and the Spots of Time: Interpretation in The Prelude*. New York: Cambridge UP, 1985.

Emsley, Clive. "An Aspect of Pitt's 'Terror': Prosecutions for Sedition During the 1790s." *Social History* 6 (1981): 155–84.

—— *British Society and the French Wars 1793–1815*. London: Macmillan, 1979.

—— *Crime and Society in England, 1750–1900*, 2nd edn. London: Longman, 1996.

—— "Repression, 'terror' and the rule of law in England during the decade of the French Revolution." *English Historical Review* 100.C (October 1985): 801–25.

Essick, Robert N. "Wordsworth and Leech-Lore." *The Wordsworth Circle* 12 (1981): 100–2.

Finch, John Alban. "Wordsworth's Two-Handed Engine." *Bicentenary Wordsworth Studies*. Ed. Jonathan Wordsworth. Ithaca, NY: Cornell UP, 1970, 1–13.

Foote, Caleb. "Vagrancy Type Law and Its Administration." *University of Pennsylvania Law Review* 104 (1956): 615–27.

Foster, Mark. "'Tintern Abbey' and Wordsworth's Scene of Writing." *Studies in Romanticism* 25 (1986): 75–95.

Foucault, Michel. *Discipline and Punish: The Birth of the Prison*, 1975. Trans. Alan Sheridan. New York: Vintage, 1979.

—— *Madness and Civilization: A History of Insanity in the Age of Reason*, 1965. Trans. Richard Howard. New York: Vintage, 1988.

—— *Power/Knowledge: Selected Interviews and other Writings, 1972–1977*. Ed. Colin Gordon. Trans. Colin Gordon et al. New York: Pantheon, 1980.

Freadman, Richard and Seumas Miller. "Deconstruction and Critical Practice: Gayatri Spivak on *The Prelude*." *On Literary Theory and Philosophy: A Cross-Disciplinary Encounter*. Eds Richard Freadman and Lloyd Reinhardt. London: Macmillan, 1991, 16–40.

Frend, William. *Peace and Union*, 1793. Oxford: Woodstock, 1991.

Friedman, Geraldine. *The Insistence of History: Revolution in Burke, Wordsworth, Keats, and Baudelaire*. Stanford, CA: Stanford UP, 1996.

Friedman, Michael H. *The Making of a Tory Humanist: William Wordsworth and the Idea of Community*. New York: Columbia UP, 1979.

Frosch, Thomas R. "Wordsworth's 'Beggars' and a Brief Instance of Writer's Block." *Studies in Romanticism* 21 (1982): 619–36.

Galperin, William H. *The Return of the Visible in British Romanticism*. Baltimore, MD: Johns Hopkins UP, 1993.

Garside, Peter. "Picturesque figure and landscape: Meg Merrilies and the gypsies." *The Politics of the Picturesque: Literature, Landscape and Aesthetics since 1770*. Eds Stephen Copley and Peter Garside. Cambridge: Cambridge UP, 1994, 145–74.

Gatrell, V. A. C. *The Hanging Tree: Execution and the English People, 1770–1868*. New York: Oxford UP, 1994.

Gill, Stephen. "'Adventures on Salisbury Plain' and Wordsworth's Poetry of Protest 1795–97." *Studies in Romanticism* 11 (1972): 48–65.

—— *William Wordsworth: A Life*. Oxford: Clarendon, 1989.

Gilmour, Ian. *Riots, Risings, and Revolutions: Government and Violence in Eighteenth-Century England*. London: Pimlico, 1993.

Girard, René. *Violence and the Sacred*. Baltimore, MD: Johns Hopkins UP, 1979.

Girouard, Mark. *Life in the English Country House: A Social and Architectural History*. New Haven, CT: Yale UP, 1978.

Glen, Heather. *Vision and Disenchantment: Blake's Songs and Wordsworth's Lyrical Ballads*. Cambridge: Cambridge UP, 1983.

Glover, Richard. *Peninsular Preparation: The Reform of the British Army*. Cambridge: Cambridge UP, 1963.

Godwin, William. *Enquiry Concerning Political Justice and Its Influence on Morals and Happiness*. Ed. F. E. L. Priestley. 3 vols. Toronto: U of Toronto P, 1946.

—— *Things As They Are or The Adventures of Caleb Williams*, 1794. Harmondsworth: Penguin, 1988.

Goldberg, Brian. "'Ministry More Palpable': William Wordsworth and the Making of Romantic Professionalism." *Studies in Romanticism* 36 (1997): 327–47.

Goodwin, Albert. *The Friends of Liberty: The English Democratic Movement in the Age of the French Revolution*. London: Hutchinson, 1979.

Goodwin, Sarah Webster. "Romanticism and the Ghost of Prostitution: Freud, *Maria*, and 'Alice Fell.'" *Death and Representation*. Eds Sarah Webster Goodwin and Elisabeth Bronfen. Baltimore, MD: Johns Hopkins UP, 1993. 152–73.

Grunes, Dennis. "Wordsworth's Wandering in 'Resolution and Independence.'" *CLA Journal* 35 (1992): 339–53.

Hamilton, Paul. *Wordsworth*. Brighton: Harvester, 1986.

Harrison, Gary. *Wordsworth's Vagrant Muse: Poetry, Poverty and Power*. Detroit, MI: Wayne State UP, 1994.

Hartman, Geoffrey. *Wordsworth's Poetry 1787–1814*, 1964. Cambridge: Harvard UP, 1987.

Hay, Douglas, "Poaching and the Game Laws on Cannock Chase." *Albion's Fatal Tree: Crime and Society in Eighteenth-Century England*. Eds Douglas Hay et al. New York: Pantheon, 1975, 189–253.

—— "Property, Authority and the Criminal Law." *Albion's Fatal Tree: Crime and Society in Eighteenth-Century England*. Eds Douglas Hay et al. New York: Pantheon, 1975, 17–63.

Hazlitt, William. *The Spirit of the Age, or Contemporary Portraits*, 1825. London: Oxford UP, 1960.

Heffernan, James A. W. "History and Autobiography: The French Revolution in Wordsworth's *Prelude*." *Representing the French Revolution: Literature, Historiography Art*. Ed. J. A. W. Heffernan. Hanover, NH: U Press of New England, 1992, 41–62.

Heidegger, Martin. "... Poetically Man Dwells ..." *Poetry, Language, Thought*. Trans. Albert Hofstader. New York: Harper, 1971, 213–29.

Heinzelman, Kurt. "The Cult of Domesticity: Dorothy and William Wordsworth at Grasmere." *Romanticism and Feminism*. Ed. Anne K. Mellor. Bloomington: Indiana UP, 1988, 52–78.

—— *The Economics of the Imagination*. Amherst: U of Massachusetts P, 1980.

Henderson, Andrea K. *Romantic Identities: Varieties of Subjectivity, 1774–1830*. Cambridge: Cambridge UP, 1996.

Hewitt, Regina. *The Possibilities of Society: Wordsworth, Coleridge and the Sociological Viewpoint of English Romanticism*. Albany: State U of New York P, 1997.

Himmelfarb, Gertrude. *The Idea of Poverty: England in the Early Industrial Age*. New York: Vintage, 1985.

Hobsbawm, E. J. "Social Criminality." *Society for the Study of Labour History: Bulletin* 25 (Autumn 1972): 5–6.

Hodgson, John. "Tidings: Revolution in *The Prelude*." *Studies in Romanticism* 31 (1992): 45–70.

Hoffer, Peter C. and N. E. H. Hull. *Murdering Mothers: Infanticide in England and New England 1558–1803*. New York: New York UP, 1984.

Homans, Margaret. *Bearing the Word: Language and Female Experience in Nineteenth-Century Women's Writing*. Chicago: U of Chicago P, 1989.

Hone, J. Ann. *For the Cause of Truth: Radicalism in London 1796–1821*. Oxford: Clarendon, 1982.

Howard, William, "'Obstinate Questionings': The Reciprocity of Speaker and Auditor in Wordsworth's Poetry." *Philological Quarterly* 67.2 (Spring 1988): 219–39.

Hufton, Olwen H. *The Poor of Eighteenth-Century France 1750–1789*. Oxford: Clarendon, 1974.

Ingram, M. J. "Communities and Courts: Law and Disorder in Early Seventeenth-Century Wiltshire." *Crime in England 1550–1800*. Ed. J. S. Cockburn. Princeton, NJ: Princeton UP, 1977, 110–34.

Ingrao, Charles W. *The Hessian Mercenary State: Ideas, Institutions, and Reform under Frederick II, 1760–1785*. Cambridge: Cambridge UP, 1987.

Innes, Joanna and John Styles. "The crime wave: recent writing on crime and criminal justice in eighteenth-century England." *Rethinking social history: English society 1570–1920 and its interpretation*. Ed. Adrian Wilson. New York: Manchester UP, 1993, 201–65.

Izenberg, Gerald N. *Impossible Individuality: Romanticism, Revolution, and the Origins of Modern Selfhood, 1787–1802.* Princeton, NJ: Princeton UP, 1992.

Jackson, Geoffrey. "Moral Dimensions of 'The Thorn.'" *The Wordsworth Circle* 10 (1979): 91–6.

Jacobus, Mary. *Romanticism, Writing and Sexual Difference: Essays on the Prelude.* Oxford: Clarendon, 1989.

—— *Tradition and Experiment in Wordsworth's Lyrical Ballads (1798).* Oxford: Clarendon, 1976.

Jameson, Fredric. *The Political Unconscious: Narrative as a Socially Symbolic Act.* Ithaca, NY: Cornell UP, 1981.

Jarvis, Robin. *Romantic Writing and Pedestrian Travel.* New York: St. Martin's, 1997.

Jencks, Christopher. *The Homeless.* Cambridge, MA: Harvard UP, 1994.

Jervis, Robin. "Wordsworth and the Use of Charity." *Beyond Romanticism: New Approaches to Texts and Contexts 1780–1832.* Eds Stephen Copley and John Whale. London: Routledge, 1992, 200–17.

Johnston, Kenneth R. *The Hidden Wordsworth: Poet, Lover, Rebel, Spy.* New York: Norton, 1998.

—— "The Politics of 'Tintern Abbey.'" *The Wordsworth Circle* 14 (1983): 6–14.

—— *Wordsworth and the Recluse.* New Haven, CT: Yale UP, 1984.

Jordanova, L. J. "The History of the Family." *Women in Society: Interdisciplinary Essays.* Ed. Cambridge Women's Studies Group. London: Virago, 1981, 41–54.

Kelley, Paul. "Rousseau's 'Discourse on the Origins of Inequality' and Wordsworth's 'Salisbury Plain.'" *Notes and Queries* ns 24 (July–August 1977): 323.

Kelley, Theresa. *Wordsworth's Revisionary Aesthetics.* Cambridge: Cambridge UP, 1988.

Kidd, Alan. "Historians or polemicists? How the Webbs Wrote Their History of the English Poor Laws." *Economic History Review* 40 (1987): 400–17.

Kneale, J. Douglas. *Monumental Writing: Aspects of Rhetoric in Wordsworth's Poetry.* Lincoln: U of Nebraska P, 1988.

Koch, Mark. "Utilitarian and Reactionary Arguments for Almsgiving in Wordsworth's 'The Old Cumberland Beggar.'" *Eighteenth-Century Life* 13.3 (November 1989): 18–33.

Kroeber, Karl. "The Presence of Absences: Were the Other Two Wedding Guests William Wordsworth and Fletcher Christian?" *The Wordsworth Circle* 29 (1998): 3–9.

—— *Romantic Landscape Vision: Constable and Wordsworth.* Madison: U of Wisconsin P, 1975.

Lambert, Sheila, ed. *House of Commons Sessional Papers of the Eighteenth Century.* Vol. 103; George III, Bills 1796–7. Wilmington, DE: Scholarly Resources, 1975.

Langan, Celeste. *Romantic Vagrancy: Wordsworth and the Simulation of Freedom.* Cambridge: Cambridge UP, 1995.

Lefebvre, Georges. *The Great Fear of 1789: Rural Panic in Revolutionary France,* 1932. Trans. Joan White. New York: Schocken, 1989.

Legouis, Émile. *William Wordsworth and Annette Vallon*, 1922. Rev. edn New York: Archon, 1967.

Levinson, Marjorie. *Wordsworth's Great Period Poems: Four Essays*. Cambridge: Cambridge UP, 1986.

Liebow, Elliot. *Tell Them Who I Am: The Lives of Homeless Women*. New York: Free Press, 1993.

Linebaugh, Peter, "The Tyburn Riot Against the Surgeons." *Albion's Fatal Tree: Crime and Society in Eighteenth-Century England*. Eds Douglas Hay et al. New York: Pantheon, 1975, 65–117.

Lipking, Lawrence. *Abandoned Women and Poetic Tradition*. Chicago: U of Chicago P, 1988.

Liu, Alan. "Wordsworth and Subversion, 1793–1804: Trying Cultural Criticism." *Yale Journal of Criticism* 2.2 (1989): 55–100.

—— *Wordsworth: The Sense of History*. Stanford, CA: Stanford UP, 1989.

Lonsdale, Roger, ed. *The New Oxford Book of Eighteenth-Century Verse*. Oxford: Oxford UP, 1984.

Luck, James Murray. *A History of Switzerland*. Palo Alto, CA: Society for the Promotion of Science and Scholarship, 1985.

McFarland, Thomas. *Romanticism and the Forms of Ruin: Wordsworth, Coleridge and Modalities of Fragmentation*. Princeton, NJ: Princeton UP, 1981.

—— *William Wordsworth: Intensity and Achievement*. Oxford: Clarendon, 1992.

McGann, Jerome J. *The Romantic Ideology: A Critical Investigation*. Chicago: U of Chicago P, 1983.

MacLean, Kenneth. *Agrarian Age: A Background for Wordsworth*, 1950. New Haven, CT: Archon, 1970.

McLynn, Frank. *Crime and Punishment in Eighteenth-Century England*. New York: Oxford UP, 1991.

Magnuson, Paul. *Wordsworth and Coleridge: A Lyrical Dialogue*. Princeton, NJ: Princeton UP, 1988.

Malcolmson, R. W. "Infanticide in the Eighteenth Century." *Crime in England 1550–1800*. Ed. J. S. Cockburn. Princeton, NJ: Princeton UP, 1977, 187–209.

Matthews, T. S., ed. *The Selected Letters of Charles Lamb*. New York: Farrar, 1956.

Mayo, Robert. "The Contemporaneity of the *Lyrical Ballads*." *PMLA* 69 (1954): 486–522.

Mellor, Anne K. *Romanticism and Gender*. New York: Routledge, 1993.

Mockler, Anthony. *The Mercenaries*. New York: Macmillan, 1969.

Moorman, Mary. *William Wordsworth: A Biography*. Vol 1. Oxford: Clarendon, 1957.

Morton, Margaret. *The Tunnel: The Underground Homeless of New York City*. New Haven, CT: Yale UP, 1995.

Moss, Thomas. *Poems on Several Occasions*. Wolverhampton, 1769.

Mulroy, David. *Horace's Odes and Epodes*. Ann Arbor: U of Michigan P, 1994.

Munsche, P. B. *Gentlemen and Poachers: The English Game Laws 1671–1831*. New York: Cambridge UP, 1981.

Newlyn, Lucy. "'In City Pent': Echo and Allusion in Wordsworth, Coleridge, and Lamb, 1797–1801." *Review of English Studies* ns 32 (1981): 408–28.

Newton, Judith Lowder. *Women, Power and Subversion: Social Strategies in British Fiction, 1778–1860.* Athens: U of Georgia P, 1981.

O'Flaherty, Brendan. *Making Room: The Economics of Homelessness.* Cambridge, MA: Harvard UP, 1996.

Olejniczak, William. "Change, Continuity, and the French Revolution: Elite Discourse on Mendicity, 1750–1815." *The French Revolution in Culture and Society.* Eds David Troyansky, Alfred Cismaru, and Norwood Andrews, Jr. New York: Greenwood, 1991, 135–50.

—— "English Rituals of Subordination: Vagrancy in Late Eighteenth-Century East Anglia." *Consortium on Revolutionary Europe, 1750–1850* (1994): 628–37.

Onorato, Richard. *The Character of the Poet: Wordsworth in The Prelude.* Princeton, NJ: Princeton UP, 1971.

Owen, John B. *The Eighteenth Century 1714–1815.* New York: Norton, 1974.

Page, Judith W. *Wordsworth and the Cultivation of Women.* Berkeley: U of California P, 1994.

Paine, Thomas. *The Rights of Man,* 1791–2. New York: Penguin, 1984.

Parrish, Stephen. *The Art of the Lyrical Ballads.* Cambridge, MA: Harvard UP, 1973.

Pfau, Thomas. *Wordsworth's Profession: Form, Class, and the Logic of Early Romantic Cultural Production.* Stanford, CA: Stanford UP, 1997.

Philips, David. "'A New Engine of Power and Authority': The Institutionalization of Law-Enforcement in England 1780–1830." *Crime and the Law: The Social History of Crime in Western Europe since 1500.* Eds V. A. C. Gatrell, Bruce Lenman, and Geoffrey Parker. London: Europa, 1980, 155–89.

Philp, Mark, ed. *The French Revolution and British Popular Politics.* New York: Cambridge UP, 1991.

Porter, Roy. *English Society in the Eighteenth Century.* Rev. edn Harmondsworth: Penguin, 1990.

Poynter, J. R. *Society and Pauperism: English Ideas on Poor Relief, 1795–1834.* London: Routledge, 1969.

Quinney, Laura. "'Tintern Abbey,' Sensibility, and the Self-Disenchanted Self." *ELH* 64 (1997): 131–56.

Randel, Fred V. "The Betrayals of 'Tintern Abbey.'" *Studies in Romanticism* 32 (1993): 379–97.

Reed, Mark L. *Wordsworth: The Chronology of the Early Years, 1770–1799.* Cambridge, MA: Harvard UP, 1967.

—— *Wordsworth: The Chronology of the Middle Years, 1800–1815.* Cambridge, MA: Cambridge UP, 1975.

Reiman, Donald. "Of Beggars." *The Wordsworth Circle* 19 (1988): 71–6.

—— ed. *The Romantics Reviewed: Contemporary Reviews of British Romantic Writers.* Part A. Vol. 2. New York: Garland, 1972.

Ribton-Turner, C. J. *A History of Vagrants and Vagrancy and Beggars and Begging.* 1887. Montclair, NJ: Patterson, 1972.

Rieder, John. "Civic Virtue and Social Class at the Scene of Execution in Wordsworth's Salisbury Plain Poems." *Studies in Romanticism* 30 (1991): 325–43.

Roe, Nicholas. "Citizen Wordsworth." *The Wordsworth Circle* 14 (1983): 21–30.

—— *The Politics of Nature: Wordsworth and Some Contemporaries.* London: Macmillan, 1992.

—— "Revising the Revolution: History and Imagination in *The Prelude*, 1799, 1805, 1850." *Romantic Revisions.* Eds Robert Brinkley and Keith Hanley. Cambridge: Cambridge UP, 1992, 87–102.

—— *Wordsworth and Coleridge: The Radical Years.* Oxford: Clarendon, 1988.

Rogers, Nicholas. "Policing the Poor in Eighteenth-Century London: The Vagrancy Laws and Their Administration." *Histoire Sociale – Social History* 24.47 (May 1991): 127–47.

Ross, Marlon B. *The Contours of Masculine Desire: Romanticism and the Rise of Women's Poetry.* New York: Oxford UP, 1989.

Rossi, Peter. *Down and Out in America: The Origins of Homelessness.* Chicago: U of Chicago P, 1989.

Rousseau, Jean-Jacques. *Rousseau's Political Writings.* Trans. Julia Conaway Bondanella. New York: Norton, 1988.

Rudé, George. Introduction. Lefebvre, ix–xvi.

Ruggles, Thomas. *The History of the Poor.* London, 1793–4.

Ruoff, Gene. *Wordsworth and Coleridge: The Making of the Major Lyrics, 1802–1804.* New Brunswick, NJ: Rutgers UP, 1989.

Rybczynski, Witold. *Home: A Short History of an Idea.* New York: Viking, 1987.

Rylestone, Anne. "Violence and the Abandoned Woman in Wordsworth's Poetry." *Massachusetts Studies in English* 7.3 (1980): 40–56.

Rzepka, Charles J. "A Gift that Complicates Employ: Poetry and Poverty in 'Resolution and Independence.'" *Studies in Romanticism* 28 (1989): 225–47.

Sabin, Margery. *English Romanticism and French Tradition.* Cambridge, MA: Harvard UP, 1976.

Sampson, David. "Wordsworth and the Poor: The Poetry of Survival." *Studies in Romanticism* 23 (1984): 31–59.

Schama, Simon. *Citizens: A Chronicle of the French Revolution.* New York: Vintage, 1989.

Schoenfield, Mark. *The Professional Wordsworth: Law, Labor and the Poet's Contract.* Athens: U of Georgia P, 1996.

Schwartz, Robert. *Policing the Poor in Eighteenth-Century France.* Chapel Hill: U of North Carolina P, 1988.

Sheats, Paul D. *The Making of Wordsworth's Poetry, 1785–1798.* Cambridge, MA: Harvard UP, 1973.

—— "'Tis Three Feet Long, and Two Feet Wide': Wordsworth's 'Thorn' and the Politics of Bathos." *The Wordsworth Circle* 22 (1991): 92–100.

Simpson, David. *The Academic Postmodern and the Rule of Literature: A Report on Half-Knowledge.* Chicago: U of Chicago P, 1995.

—— *Irony and Authority in Romantic Poetry.* Totowa, NJ: Rowman, 1979.

—— *Wordsworth's Historical Imagination: The Poetry of Displacement.* New York: Methuen, 1987.

Siskin, Clifford. *The Work of Writing: Literature and Social Change in Britain, 1700–1830.* Baltimore, MD: Johns Hopkins UP, 1998.

Smart, Christopher. *The Collected Poems.* Ed. Norman Callan. Vol. 2. London: Routledge, 1949.

Smith, Adam. *An Inquiry into the Nature and Causes of the Wealth of Nations.* Ed. Edwin Cannan. New York: Modern Library, 1937.

Snow, David A. and Leon Anderson. *Down on Their Luck: A Study of Homeless Street People.* Berkeley: U of California P, 1993.

Southey, Robert. *Poems,* 1797. Oxford: Woodstock, 1989.

Spivak, Gayatri Chakravorty. *In Other Worlds: Essays in Cultural Politics.* New York: Methuen, 1987.

Sparrow, Elizabeth. "The Alien Office, 1792–1806." *Historical Journal* 33 (1990): 361–84.

Stephens, W. B. *Sources for English Local History.* The Sources of History: Studies in the Use of Historical Evidence. New York: Cambridge UP, 1981.

Stevenson, J. "The London 'Crimp' Riots of 1794." *International Review of History* 16.1 (1971): 40–58.

Stone, Lawrence. *The Family, Sex and Marriage in England 1500–1800.* Abr. edn New York: Harper, 1979.

Styles, John. "Criminal Records." *The Historical Journal* 20 (1977): 977–81.

Tate, W. E. *The Parish Chest: A Study of the Records of Parochial Administration in England.* Cambridge: Cambridge UP, 1946.

Taylor, James S. *Poverty, Migration and Settlement in the Industrial Revolution: Sojourners' Narratives.* Palo Alto, CA: Society for the Promotion of Science and Scholarship, 1989.

Thompson, E. P. "Disenchantment or Default? A Lay Sermon." *Power and Consciousness.* Eds Conor Cruise O'Brien and William Dean Vanech. New York: New York UP, 1969. 149–81.

—— *The Making of the English Working Class.* New York: Vintage, 1966.

—— *Whigs and Hunters: The Origin of the Black Act.* New York: Pantheon, 1975.

Thomson, Janice E. *Mercenaries, Pirates, and Sovereigns: State-Building and Extraterritorial Violence in Early Modern Europe.* Princeton, NJ: Princeton UP, 1994.

Thürer, George. *Free and Swiss: The Story of Switzerland.* Adapted and trans. R. P. Heller and E. Long. London: Oswald Wolff, 1970.

Tomlins, Thomas Edlyne, ed. *Statutes of the United Kingdom of Great Britain and Ireland.* Vol. 1. London, 1804.

Toth, Jennifer. *The Mole People: Life in the Tunnels beneath New York City.* Chicago: Chicago Review, 1993.

Turner, Victor. *Dramas, Fields and Metaphors: Symbolic Action in Human Society.* Ithaca, NY: Cornell UP, 1974.

Vanderstaay, Steven. *Street Lives: an oral history of homeless Americans.* Philadelphia: New Society, 1992.

Vander Weele, Michael. "The Contest of Memory in 'Tintern Abbey.'" *Nineteenth-Century Literature* 50 (1995): 6–26.

Vendler, Helen. "'Tintern Abbey': Two Assaults." *Bucknell Review* 36.1 (1992): 173–90.

Wallace, Anne D. *Walking, Literature and English Culture: The Origins and Uses of Peripatetic in the Nineteenth Century.* Oxford: Clarendon, 1993.

Wanko, Cheryl. "Leechcraft: Wordsworth's 'Resolution and Independence.'" *English Language Notes* 26.4 (1989): 58–62.

Webb, Sidney and Beatrice. *English Poor Law History.* Part I: The Old Poor Law. 1927. Hamden, CT: Archon, 1963.

Wells, Roger. "English Society and Revolutionary Politics in the 1790s: The Case for Insurrection." Philp, 188–226.

—— *Insurrection: The British Experience 1795–1803.* Gloucester: Alan Sutton, 1983.

—— *Wretched Faces: Famine in Wartime England 1793–1803.* New York: St. Martin's Press, 1988.

Welsford, Enid. *Salisbury Plain: A Study in the Development of Wordsworth's Mind and Art.* New York: Barnes & Noble, 1966.

Williams, John. *Wordsworth: Romantic Poetry and Revolution Politics.* New York: Manchester UP, 1989.

Williams, Raymond. *The Country and the City.* New York: Oxford UP, 1973.

—— *Marxism and Literature.* New York: Oxford UP, 1977.

Wlecke, Albert O. *Wordsworth and the Sublime.* Berkeley: U of California P, 1973.

Wolfson, Susan J. "The Language of Interpretation in Romantic Poetry: 'A Strong Working of the Mind.'" *Romanticism and Language.* Ed. Arden Reed. Ithaca, NY: Cornell UP, 1984, 22–49.

—— *The Questioning Presence: Wordsworth, Keats and the Interrogative Mode in Romantic Poetry.* Ithaca, NY: Cornell UP, 1986.

Wollstonecraft, Mary. *A Vindication of the Rights of Woman*, 1792. Ed. Miriam Brody. Harmondsworth: Penguin, 1985.

Woof, Pamela. "The Alfoxden Journal and its Mysteries." *The Wordsworth Circle* 26 (1995): 125–33.

Woolsey, Linda Mills. "Houseless Woman and Travelling Lass: Mobility in Dorothy Wordsworth's *Grasmere Journals.*" *Tennessee Philological Bulletin* 27 (1990): 31–7.

Wordsworth, Dorothy. *Journals of Dorothy Wordsworth.* Ed. Ernest De Selincourt. Vol. I. London: Macmillan, 1959.

Wordsworth, Jonathan. "The Five-Book *Prelude* of Early Spring 1804." *Journal of English and Germanic Philology* 76.1 (January 1977): 1–25.

—— *William Wordsworth: The Borders of Vision.* Oxford: Clarendon, 1982.

Wordsworth, William. *Descriptive Sketches.* Eds Eric Birdsall with Paul Zall. Ithaca, NY: Cornell UP, 1984.

—— *An Evening Walk.* Ed. James Averill. Ithaca, NY: Cornell UP, 1984.

—— *Home at Grasmere, Part First, Book First of the Recluse.* Ed. Beth Darlington. Ithaca, NY: Cornell UP, 1977.

—— *Lyrical Ballads, and Other Poems, 1797–1800.* Eds. James Butler and Karen Green. Ithaca, NY: Cornell UP, 1992.

—— *The Pedlar, Tintern Abbey, The Two-Part Prelude.* Ed. Jonathan Wordsworth. Cambridge: Cambridge UP, 1985.

—— *Poems, in Two Volumes, and Other Poems, 1800–1807*. Ed. Jared Curtis. Ithaca, NY: Cornell UP, 1983.

—— *The Prelude, 1798–1799*. Ed. Stephen Parrish. Ithaca, NY: Cornell UP, 1977.

—— *The Prelude 1799, 1805, 1850*. Eds Jonathan Wordsworth, M. H. Abrams, and Stephen Gill. New York: Norton, 1979.

—— *The Prose Works of William Wordsworth*, 3 vols. Eds. W. J. B. Owen and Jane Worthington Smyser. Oxford: Clarendon, 1974.

—— *The Salisbury Plain Poems*. Ed. Stephen Gill. Ithaca, NY: Cornell UP, 1975.

—— *The Thirteen-Book Prelude by William Wordsworth*. Ed. Mark L. Reed. Vol. 1. Ithaca, NY: Cornell UP, 1991.

Wordsworth, William and Samuel Taylor Coleridge. *Lyrical Ballads: The text of the 1798 edition with the additional 1800 poems and the Prefaces*. Eds R. L. Brett and A. R. Jones. 2nd edn. New York: Routledge, 1991.

Young, Arthur. *Travels in France during the years 1787, 1788, and 1789*, 1792. Ed. Jeffry Kaplow. Garden City: Anchor, 1969.

HISTORICAL MANUSCRIPTS/LEGAL DOCUMENTS

Cockermouth Workhouse Charter, 1740: PR/136/200, Carlisle PRO, Cumbria.

Nullification of Christopher Wallas' Vagrancy Pass: WQ/O/9: Kendal PRO, Cumbria.

Presentiment against Parish Constable: WQ/SR/376b/5: Kendal PRO, Cumbria.

Vagrancy Pass and Examination, Thomas Alkin: PR/3/78, Carlisle PRO, Cumbria.

Vagrancy Pass and Examination, Christopher Wallas: WQ/SR/376b/12–13, Kendal PRO, Cumbria.

Index

Abrams, M. H., 247n, 248n
Adams, Thomas, 38, 40, 230n
Addington ministry, 142–3, 193, 199–20
Althusser, Louis, 229n
Anderson, Leon, 12, 13–14, 223n, 224n
Anti-Jacobin Review, 242n
Antoinette, Marie, 149–50
Ariès, Philippe, 229n
Averill, James, 98

Beattie, James, 85, 223n, 238n
Beaumont, George, 188
Beaupuy, Michel, 212, 260n
Beier, A. L., 222n, 224n, 235n, 240n
Bentham, Jeremy, 17, 82–3, 116, 245n
Bewell, Alan, 240n
Bialostosky, Donald, 150–1
Blackstone, William, 120–1, 173
Blake, William, 64
Blau, Joel, 11–12, 16, 223n
Bloom, Harold, 245n
Bostetter, Edward, 246n
Brissot, Jacques-Pierre, 75
Brooks, Cleanth, 245n
Burdett, Francis, 249n
Burke, Edmund, 57, 59, 236n, 245n
    Letters on a Regicide Peace, 3, 187
    Reflections on the Revolution in France,
        4, 69–70, 73, 149–51, 184, 259n,
        260n
Burn, Richard, 7
Burns, Robert, 159
Burt, Martha, 226n
Byron, George Gordon, Lord, 22, 23

Calvert, Raisley, 221
Carroll, William, 223n
Chandler, James, 122, 231n, 233n, 235n
Chatterton, Thomas, 159
Christian, Edward, 7, 172–3, 175–6
Christie, Ian, 79, 237–8n, 242n
Cobban, Alfred, 230n
Coleridge, Samuel Taylor, 20, 22, 77,
    105–7, 112–13, 159, 186, 189–90, 201,
    220–1, 261n
Collings, David, 234n, 255n
Colquhoun, Patrick, 145–6, 234n
Combination Acts, 181
Cookson, J. E., 104, 200

Cowper, William, 28, 33, 46
Curwen, John Christian, 175

Darbishire, Helen, 43, 247n
de Man, Paul, 253n
De Quincey, Thomas, 22
Domestic ideology, 31–2, 37–44, 47–8,
    68–72, 138
Doyle, William, 230n
Duffy, Michael, 198
Dyer, George, 76

Eagleton, Terry, 229n
Eastwood, David, 79, 238n, 242n
Elliott, Marianne, 104
Emsley, Clive, 59, 79, 116, 181, 193, 199,
    200, 242n
England, social and economic
    conditions, 58, 117
English Murder Act, 81

Foster, Mark, 248n
Foucault, Michel
    and examination, 234–5n
    and execution, 237n
    and delinquency, 19, 140, 144–5, 152,
        249n
    and madness, 240n
    and the panopticon, 17, 82–3, 89
Fox, Charles James, 59, 144, 147
French Revolution
    and sacrifice, 54–5
    and vagrancy, 39–40
    see also Pitt ministry
Frend, William, 75–6, 122, 174, 193
Friedman, Geraldine, 259n
Friedman, Michael, 245n, 259n
Frosch, Thomas, 155, 157

Galperin, William, 258n
Garside, Peter, 49
Gatrell, V. A. C., 92, 237n, 239n
Gill, Stephen, 27, 45, 79, 106, 112, 133,
    163, 222
Girard, René, 33
Girouard, Mark, 228n
Glover, Richard, 200
Godwin, William, 67, 72–6 passim, 82,
    87, 122, 188, 212, 219, 225n, 237n

274